Governors and Legislatures:
Contending Powers

Governors and Legislatures: Contending Powers

Alan Rosenthal
Eagleton Institute of Politics
Rutgers University

A Division of Congressional Quarterly Inc.
Washington, D.C.

Printed in the United States of America

Second Printing

Library of Congress Cataloging-in-Publication Data

Rosenthal, Alan, 1932-
    Governors and legislatures: contending powers/Alan Rosenthal.
        p. cm.
    Includes bibliographical references.
    ISBN 0-87187-545-4
    1. Legislative power—United States—States.   2. Legislative bodies—United States—States.   3. Executive power—United States—States.   4. Governors—United States.   I. Title.
JK2494.R67   1990
320.4'04' 0973—dc20   90-1356
                                                                              CIP

To JKLTV

Contents

Preface

This book is based upon my observations, over the last twenty years, of the relationships between governors and legislatures in numerous states. I have studied them as they contest power, come into conflict, and explore the possibilities of cooperation. My purpose is simple and straightforward: to bring together coherently the fragments of what is known and what new things I have learned.

In writing about the states, one has to deal with different governors, different legislatures, different circumstances. In view of the variation in politics, personality, and practice across the states, generalizing is risky. But it is necessary even if the generalizations must be based on examples and not on complete and systematic data.

I trust that my observations—always offered with qualifications—will prove useful. I want to arouse the interest of college students and encourage their involvement in state government and politics. I hope to stimulate political scientists to do further research on governors and legislatures and the interaction between them. I hope that political practitioners—governors, legislators, and their staffs—who are so knowledgeable about their own states will benefit from a larger and comparative context.

The political significance of governors and legislatures is by no means new. Even before the resurgence of the states, governors and legislatures were important institutions, deserving of serious study, but now the justification for such study is even greater. The fact is, however, that the states have been neglected by political scientists, who have been absorbed elsewhere. State government has not been a fashionable field of study within the discipline for quite some time.

In this overlooked field, governors and legislatures have received some attention, but not very much. Relatively recent writing on governors includes both general studies of the office, and those on individual governors.[1] Much of the current literature on the office of governor stems from the efforts of the National Governors' Association (NGA) and its Center for Policy Research.[2]

Legislatures have received more detailed scrutiny, especially in the scholarly journal, *Legislative Studies Quarterly*. The National Conference of State Legislatures (NCSL) has produced useful materials, including its monthly magazine, *State Legislatures*. But few political scientists have attempted a general and comparative treatment of the subject. My earlier book, *Legislative Life*, may be the only one that covers the legislative beast in most states and from several angles, although a number of valuable works focus on the legislature in a single state.[3]

Some of these studies consider the governor's relations with the legislature or the legislature's relations with the governor, but they do so only in passing. The most thoughtful work, from a gubernatorial perspective, is an essay by Malcolm Jewell written almost twenty years ago.[4] Since then very little of a general nature has appeared, although single-state studies focusing on individual governors or legislatures, or both, are extremely informative about executive-legislative relationships. For example, one can hardly expect a more penetrating analysis than that of Rockefeller and the legislature in New York by Robert Connery and Gerald Benjamin.[5]

Despite the good work, there remains an unfilled space in contemporary literature. No one, to my knowledge, has examined how governors and legislatures relate to one another, as they go about fulfilling their respective roles, sharing power and governing the states. This book explores this largely uncharted terrain.

In writing, I have relied on varying sources for information. Materials published by NGA and NCSL, journalistic accounts, memoirs, and scholarly studies all have provided grist for this mill. These sources of information and ideas are cited throughout the text. I also have conducted interviews with a few governors, a number of governors' chiefs of staff, and many legislators, most of whom I ensured anonymity and few of whom are specifically cited. Some of what I discuss is based on projects and symposiums that I have conducted or in which I have participated. Much draws on my observations and experiences in the states over a period of many years. Because of the nature of the literature and because of my own experience, some states are mentioned for illustrative purposes more often than others.

I have been encouraged in this enterprise by people who know the subject well. Barry Van Lare, deputy director of the National Governors' Association, and all of the staff at the National Conference of State Legislatures—especially Bill Pound, executive director, Karl Kurtz, director of state services, and Carl Tubbesing, director of state-federal relations—have been extremely helpful. They, of course, bear no responsibility for my inaccuracies, misinterpretations, or criticisms of their employers. Nor does the fact that Pound, Kurtz, and Tubbesing work for legislatures and only Van Lare works for governors necessarily indicate a bias on my part. Despite a legislative past, I have tried to see executive-legislative relationships from both points of view.

Several academic colleagues, who have done exemplary research and writing in the general field, also merit thanks. Thad Beyle of the University of North Carolina, Malcolm Jewell of the University of Kentucky, Larry Sabato of the University of Virginia, Richard Nathan of the State University of New York at Albany, and Carl Van Horn of Rutgers University all provided critical advice.

At the Eagleton Institute of Politics, I am indebted to Joanne Pfeiffer, who maintained her wonderful sense of humor while putting the manuscript together and suffering my moods. Chris Lenart managed to avoid dealing directly with this enterprise, but she relieved me of many other chores so that I could work on this book.

At CQ Press, Joanne Daniels behaved like a good editor should— she held me to a tight schedule and kept me from droning on at even greater length. Nancy Lammers and Lys Ann Shore edited out much of the redundancy, but maybe not all of it, and Jamie Holland steered the manuscript through the production process with deliberate speed.

I always receive support—diffuse as it may be—from my children, whom I regard also as friends. John, Kai, Tony, and Lisa do not specifically encourage me to write, but simply having them around affords me this luxury. Also important for her presence in my life is Vivian. While others may get off the hook, I do expect her to read this book carefully and lovingly, absolving me of any errors that I have made.

I enjoyed writing this book, and I hope that practitioners in both the executive and legislative branches as well as students of state politics will enjoy reading it.

NOTES

1. Coleman Ranson, Jr., *The American Governorship* (Westport, Conn.: Green-wood Press, 1982); Larry Sabato, *Goodbye to Good-time Charlie*, 2d ed. (Washington, D.C.: CQ Press, 1983); Sarah McCally Morehouse, *State Politics, Parties and Policy* (New York: Holt, Rinehart and Winston, 1981); Robert H. Connery and Gerald Benjamin, *Rockefeller of New York: Executive Power in the State House* (Ithaca, N.Y.: Cornell University Press, 1979); and Jon Bowermaster, *Governor: An Oral Biography of Robert D. Ray* (Ames: Iowa State University

Press, 1987).

2. Drawing largely on NGA materials, Thad L. Beyle has made a number of valuable contributions. See, among other publications, *Being Governor: The View from the Office*, ed. Thad L. Beyle and Lynn R. Muchmore (Durham, N.C.: Duke Press Policy Studies, 1983).

3. Alan Rosenthal, *Legislative Life* (New York: Harper and Row, 1981); William K. Muir, Jr., *Legislature: California's School for Politics* (Chicago: University of Chicago Press, 1982; and Malcolm E. Jewell and Penny M. Miller, *The Kentucky Legislature: Two Decades of Change* (Lexington: University Press of Kentucky, 1988).

4. Malcolm E. Jewell, "The Governor as a Legislative Leader," in *The American Governor in Behavioral Perspective*, ed. Thad Beyle and J. Oliver Williams (New York: Harper and Row, 1972), 127-141.

5. Connery and Benjamin, *Rockefeller of New York*, 77-108.

1

Introduction

Albany, St. Paul, Tallahassee, and Jefferson City are where the action is today, with American federalism currently at a stage in which the states are resurgent and Washington reluctant. The New Federalism of the Nixon, Carter, and Reagan administrations—characterized by the three Ds of devolution, deregulation, and defunding—has placed a heavy burden on the states. The states have assumed the burden, if not happily at least vigorously.

The states, and not the federal government, are the present locus of initiatives in education, public welfare, the environment, growth management, and other areas. The contemporary role of the states with regard to Washington was signaled at the 1989 annual meeting of the National Governors' Association. President George Bush addressed the governors on the nation's need for educational reform, but at the same time emphasized that education was a state and local responsibility. Secretary of Transportation Samuel K. Skinner addressed them on the nation's need for improved highways and airports, but pledged only support—and not federal funds—for state efforts to raise taxes for such purposes.[1] Responsibility for deciding on and paying for many domestic programs has shifted from the federal government to the states. In addition, the states have responsibility for funding a number of programs that are mandated by the federal government. They must pay, even though they cannot decide.

Whatever the particular policy domain, the states appear to be playing a more active role than in earlier years. The amount of law and regulation enacted by states has been on the rise. More individuals and more areas of life are affected by this legislation. A larger number of interest groups is now represented at state capitals. More lobbyists are registered and are promoting the interests of a multiplicity of clients.

The struggle over outcomes is continuing and intense; the stakes for the contestants are high.

In the midst of all this activity are governors and legislatures, who have authority to formulate, enact, and implement policy in the states. Other actors—the courts, bureaucracies, interest groups, and the press—also take part in governance, but governors and legislatures are at the center of the system and share primary responsibility and predominant power. Just how they share the responsibility and how they exercise the power are questions I address in this book.

The two dimensions of relationships that are of principal concern here are that of power, and how it is distributed and exercised, and that of conflict versus cooperation, and how governors and legislatures try to settle their differences. No study of this subject could help but focus on governmental power and the contest between contenders in a system in which powers are separated into executive, legislative, and judicial and each of the three branches is supposed to check and balance the others. It is an ingenious system, designed to prevent tyranny, engender conflict, and give no set of actors or interests overwhelming or permanent advantage. Generally, it has accomplished these purposes at both the federal and state levels.

Early in the history of the states, legislatures had the upper hand. The new nation's experience with colonial governors, who were agents of England, became reflected in a constitutional distrust of the executive. Typically, under the original state constitutions, governors were selected by the legislature, limited to one term, and denied veto power. Soon after the period of national independence, the executive role increased and began to operate as a check on legislative power. Relationships were being worked out, the balance was shifting. By the early nineteenth century, governors were clearly becoming stronger. Authority to elect them was transferred from the legislatures to the people; their terms were extended to two or four years; and they acquired veto authority. Although the power of the executive continued to be somewhat diffuse through the 1800s, institutionally it gained on its rival. Instances of corruption and incompetence were undermining the power of the legislative branch, and the balance shifted further.

In the twentieth century, and particularly in the 1950s and 1960s, the executive succeeded in carving out a distinct advantage over the legislature. That advantage continues today, at least in the professional judgment of most political scientists, journalists, and other observers. Their view tends to be that the executive's role is initiation and leadership, while the legislative role is to respond by approving, rejecting, or amending. That model, the "independence model," is one of two that Charles O. Jones suggests characterize the relationship between the executive and legislative branches at the national level. The other is the "exchange model." Extending these models to the states, the former would emphasize the separateness of the two branches, with the governor as the principal overseer of the public interest. The latter would emphasize the interdependence of the two branches, with considerable bargaining going on between the two.[2] I, of course, see relationships between governors and legislatures in terms of the exchange model.

My contention, however, is that each has a leadership role and that the balance of power has not been stable in recent years but has changed considerably and in favor of the legislative branch. The result is that governors and legislatures today are relatively equal contenders, with neither side in the ascendant. Conflict between them, as they contest power and dispute policy, is an important aspect of their political and institutional lives. Cooperation, as they share in the exercise of power and jointly make policy, is also important. Their clashes and their collaboration are the heart of the executive-legislative relationship.

How one views the governor and the legislature is partly a matter of perspective. My normal perspective is legislative, deriving as it does from twenty years spent observing, consulting with, and writing about state legislatures. I have become, by this time, a legislative person, with a commitment to representative government and to the legislature as an institution. I do not believe myself to be so unusual. Scholars often become partisans of the institutions they study; they just have trouble acknowledging their bias.

Whatever my institutional partisanship, however, it is impossible to deny the central role of the governor in the relationship. When the two partners in state governance stand up to dance, it is the governor who appears to lead and the legislature to follow—that is, when they dance together.

Thus, we begin our exploration in Chapter 2 with the governor, and specifically with the governor's impressive array of powers. If one looks at the balance of power through gubernatorial lenses, as we do in that chapter, the executive presents a most imposing figure. When we alter our perspective in Chapter 3, we see the enhanced capacity and independence of the legislature, and the importance of legislative resources in a contest with the executive. But the legislature still does not match the governor. The pattern of executive-legislative relationships, as described next in Chapter 4, depends more on the governor than on legislators. It is the governor's orientation toward the legislature and his style and techniques of dealing with legislators that make the largest difference.

From the perspective of each of the institutions involved in the relationship, the governor would seem to come out on top, if not absolutely dominant. But when we abandon an institutional point of view to focus on the process itself, as in Chapters 5, 6, and 7, a different picture emerges. While the role of the governor in making policy, determining the budget, and running government does not diminish much, the role of the legislature is seen as substantially larger. The legislature, we find, is extremely influential with respect to the governor's agenda, in control of its own agenda, and involved far more extensively in major and minor matters than is the executive. As it has never done before, the legislature today also is exercising control over the budget and intervening in the administration of government itself.

In Chapter 8, I specifically address the dimension of conflict and cooperation, which indeed emerges throughout the book. First, the causes and consequences of conflict, and then the bases for cooperation are summed up. In concluding, I suggest that while conflict is inevitable and cooperation essential in the relationships between governors and legislatures, their prospective mix is uncertain. It will depend in large part on the strength and quality of leadership from the governor and from within the legislature.

NOTES

1. E. J. Dionne, Jr., "States Afraid of Being Outshone by Bush," *New York Times,* August 2, 1989.
2. Charles O. Jones, "Presidential Negotiation with Congress," in *Both Ends of the Avenue,* ed. Anthony King (Washington, D.C.: American Enterprise Institute, 1983), 96-130.

2

The Governor
as Chief Legislator

Legislating is by no means the governor's only role, but it is certainly a principal role. Governors initiate legislation, which legislators introduce on their behalf. They shape legislation as it is undergoing the political massaging of the legislative process. And they review legislation after its enactment, but before they sign it into law. Governors are believed to be the single most important figures in the process—truly the chief legislators in their states.

The textbook stereotype of gubernatorial preeminence in the legislative process, while overdrawn, is based largely upon the governor's substantial power base. Anyone with such a base must indeed exercise power in relations with the legislature. Intrigued by the concept of power, political scientists for some time have been cataloging elements of the governor's strength, usually comparing the fifty state governorships on several dimensions. The National Governors' Association has developed its own index for comparing the institutional powers of governors.[1]

Gubernatorial strength can be conceived of in terms of tenure potential, appointive powers, budget authority, and veto powers—the formal stuff of constitutions and statutes—as in most indexes. It can also be considered in terms of patronage, publicity, the promise or threat of campaign support or opposition, the possibility of advancement within the governor's party or faction in the legislature, and the calling of special sessions, as in some textbooks. Or it can be thought of as involving both formal and informal powers. Formal powers consist of messages, vetoes, the formulation and execution of the budget, control over state agencies, the administration of state programs, and appointments; informal powers include skills of bargaining and persuading, prestige of office, popular support, political party, and mass media.

Whatever the specific approach, the powers of the governorship appear impressive. And the governor's strength seems formidable, whatever the particular state—Maryland, Massachusetts, New York, and West Virginia, where the institutionalized powers of the governorship are greatest, or New Hampshire, Rhode Island, Vermont, South Carolina, Texas, and North Carolina, where the institutionalized powers are least.[2] Given their constitutional, political, and other resource bases, it is not surprising that governors are believed to have a commanding position in the states. And indeed they do. The powers at their disposal, as we shall explore below, translate into significant influence in the legislative process. The governor cannot avoid playing a role. The political system requires it; the public expects it; the legislature counts on it. But how dominant is that gubernatorial role? We shall explore that question throughout this book. First, let us look at the different kinds of power that governors exercise.

THE POWER OF INITIATION

Like legislators themselves, the governor has the power to initiate policy for the state. That is to say, he or she can propose ideas for legislation and propose expenditures in the budget. The governor's proposals may derive from various sources, such as interest groups, executive departments and agencies, and even legislators themselves, but whatever the seeds of parentage, the first major thrust in the process can be the governor's.

State constitutions provide for the initiation of policy by governors. Article V, Section I of the New Jersey Constitution is illustrative. It states that "the Governor shall ... recommend [to the Legislature] such measures as he may deem desirable." Constitutional provision and political custom allow, if they do not actually dictate, that governors will fashion and present a program for the legislature to enact. Therefore, through special addresses and messages and various other initiatives, the nation's governors announce their ideas and take subsequent steps to have them drafted into bills, which are introduced by key legislators and scheduled for consideration. From then on, it is up to the governor and staff to manage the initiatives through the process.

The first opportunity for the governor comes immediately upon taking office, in the inaugural address. The inaugural is not likely to detail a legislative agenda or focus on specific policies. It will probably lay out themes and a vision of the future, well removed from gubernatorial legislative priorities. Or it may outline a four-year agenda, as in the 1986 inaugural of Virginia governor Gerald Baliles. This address offers the governor an opportunity to communicate through the media to the people and, even more important, to the legislators who are always a governor's most attentive audience. The legislative agenda, whether relatively clear or blurred, thus begins to take shape.

The agenda becomes clarified further with the "state of the state" message, by means of which the governor details the substance of his or her legislative proposals, in terms of priorities for the legislative session. This is the vehicle that announces to all what policies and programs the governor will pursue and gives the legislature its first strong indication of what the governor has in mind. A skillful governor can use the "state of the state" message as a platform for his or her agenda and as a means of capturing the state's attention. The most skillful schedule the address for prime-time television.

In addition to these messages on special occasions, governors may deliver special messages on more ordinary occasions. During the course of a legislative session, a new issue may arise, and the governor may wish to bring a proposal for dealing with it to the attention of the legislature. Or he or she may take the opportunity to reiterate concern about a proposal advanced earlier. In either case, the message is likely to capture the spotlight, at least for a time.[3]

Governors may also initiate policy without resort to legislation, by exercising their authority to issue executive orders. Nine state constitutions and statutes in most other places specifically authorize governors to issue executive orders. Governors who invoke this power do not have to go to the legislature for decision. The chief executive often uses this device for plans to reorganize agencies and to create advisory or study commissions. In recent years the number of executive orders has increased. Wisconsin governor Lee Dreyfus (1979-1983), for instance, issued more executive orders in 1979 than his predecessors had issued during the previous eighteen years. Dreyfus's successor, Anthony Earl (1983-1987), issued even more.[4]

An occasional purpose of executive orders is to bypass a legislature that would not be sympathetic to the governor's proposal or a legislature that has already rejected his or her proposal. In Pennsylvania, for example, Governor Richard Thornburgh (1979-1987) was unable to privatize state-run liquor stores because of legislative opposition. He issued an executive order during the last days of his administration to accomplish his purpose.[5] Governor Richard Lamm (1975-1987) of Colorado in 1979 instituted a statewide growth policy by executive order when the legislature failed to act. But in this case the legislature's objections were so strong that Lamm rescinded the order.[6]

Not only do governors initiate, but in some respects they can also determine the timing for consideration of their measures. During the regular session, they may call for extraordinary procedures in the legislative process. In New York, for instance, a governor can use a "message of special necessity." The constitutional requirement that a bill be on a legislator's desk for three days before it can be passed into law can be circumvented by the governor's issuing a "message of special necessity." Such a process permits the governor to rush a measure through before legislators can figure out where they stand and before they can develop a counter-strategy.[7] New Jersey has a similar device in "emergency certification," which governors have used to expedite policies they favor.

Another illustration of the governor's influence over timing is the authority to call the legislature into special session and determine the subject of consideration. In twenty states only the governor, and not the legislature, can issue the call. In the rest either the governor or the legislature itself (by vote of a majority, three-fifths or two-thirds of the members of each house, or by the two presiding officers) can call the legislature into special session. In one-fifth of the states, the session is confined to the agenda specified by the governor's call; in the remaining states the legislature may add to the agenda. The governor's power in this regard is far from absolute. Even in Wisconsin, for example, where only the governor calls and states the purpose of a special session, "it is the legislature's power," according to Speaker Tom Loftus, "to act or not act, to convene and then adjourn to a more convenient time, and if it acts, to arrive at any solution to the problem it wishes."[8] As if to prove the point made by Loftus for Wisconsin, Governor Henry Bellmon (1963-1967, 1987-   ) of Oklahoma in 1989 called a special session of the legislature on tax reform, but not a single legislator was willing to introduce the governor's bill.

Probably the governor's greatest power of initiative is in the domain of budgeting. Ordinarily state constitutions require the governor to play a legislative role in this area. The governor has initial responsibility for preparing the budget and in most places is expected to submit an executive budget bill. In fact, it may be true that budget formulation is the most important of all the governor's powers, as was found some years ago in a survey of senators in eleven states.[9] The role of the budget, moreover, extends well beyond the appropriations process itself.[10] In an increasing number of states, policy issues are purposely raised in the budget and settled in the appropriations process.

The governor ordinarily delivers the highlights of the budget to the legislature in a special message. This budget message affords the governor a platform with legislators, the press, and the public for expressing his or her priorities for state spending and allocations among various governmental functions. The legislature is not compelled to follow the script prepared by the governor and budget director, but most take their cues from the executive proposal.

THE POWER OF REJECTION

The governor's second principal power, also directly tied into the legislative process, lies at its other end. If initiation allows governors the opening salvo, the power of rejection gives them the last, or almost the last, word. It really does more, for having the last word enables the governor to be party to discussions throughout the process.

Political scientists lavish considerable attention on the formal power to veto, which is possessed by all but one of the nation's governors. Only the chief executive of North Carolina lacks that power, and has tried to obtain it—albeit without success. Fifteen states give the governor even greater leverage by means of "executive amendment," or the like, whereby a governor can return a vetoed bill to the legislature with suggested amendments. Among these, Illinois, Massachusetts, Montana, and New Jersey provide the chief executive with an amendatory or conditional veto power. Illinois governors, for instance, can return a bill, to the legislature with specific recommendations for changes and language to amend the bill. If the legislature accepts the revisions by a majority vote in each house, the governor certifies the bill and it becomes law as amended. If the governor does not certify it, the bill is returned as a vetoed bill requiring a three-fifths vote in each house to override.[11]

The veto of legislation is a potent weapon, and one that is used with varying frequency by the nation's governors. Nelson Rockefeller (1959-1973) of New York used his authority liberally, vetoing anywhere from 20 percent to 35 percent of the bills passed by the legislature during 1965-1971.[12] Democrat Bruce Babbitt (1978-1987) of Arizona vetoed 21 bills his first year in office with a Republican legislature, 30 more in his next two years, and a total of 114 in nine years, thereby exhibiting considerable strength.[13] In the 1987 sessions, a number of governors made extensive use of their veto power. Republican James Thompson (1977-) of Illinois vetoed one out of every three bills sent to him by a Democratic legislature, and Republican George Deukmejian (1983-) vetoed almost one out of every ten passed by California's Democratic legislature. By contrast, in Connecticut, with Democrats controlling both branches, less than 3 percent of the public acts have been vetoed by the governor.

Once the governor casts a veto, it is normally the last effective word. Few vetoes are overridden, although the possibility to override always exists. In all but six states an override requires an extraordinary majority in each house. A three-fifths vote is needed in six states and a two-thirds majority in thirty-eight states. Such majorities are difficult to accomplish, especially in two-party states where members of the governor's party are inclined, out of a sense of loyalty and common interests, to uphold a veto. If the governor's partisans account for at least one-third of the members of a single house, an override on most issues is practically out of the question. Take Wisconsin as an example. The Republican governor in 1988 faced a senate with twenty Democrats and thirteen Republicans and an assembly with fifty-four Democrats and forty-five Republicans. As few as twelve members of the senate or, alternatively, thirty-four members of the assembly could sustain his veto. It is not at all surprising, therefore, that overrides are rare in Wisconsin and elsewhere. Although there has been some increase in their incidence nationally over the past thirty years,[14] only in unusual circumstances or in unusual relationships do legislatures override a governor's veto. One such relationship developed between Governor Michael Dukakis (1975-1979, 1983-) and the legislature in Massachusetts during his first term in office. He vetoed thirty-five bills and was overridden twenty-three times. In 1987 Governor Thompson of Illinois was overridden 29 times, but he vetoed 254 bills that the legislature had passed.

An effective weapon in the governor's arsenal of rejection devices is the line-item veto. Only in Indiana, Maine, Maryland, New Hampshire, Nevada, Rhode Island, and Vermont, in addition to North Carolina, does the governor lack the ability to veto a specific item in an appropriations bill. That means that a governor does not have to veto—or threaten to veto—an omnibus appropriations bill because he or she objects to a specific item within it. The item-veto power is exercised with telling effect by any governor who: (1) wants to maintain budgetary discipline; (2) refuses to acquiesce in legislative projects, whether "pork" or "turkeys" as the case may be; and (3) engages in bargaining and trading with legislative leaders and rank-and-file members.

It is generally as difficult for a legislature to override a line-item veto as a regular veto. In most states the requirement is two-thirds of those elected or those present, in others three-fifths of those elected, and in several others a majority of those elected. By way of illustration, in Wisconsin Governor Tommy Thompson (1987-) exercised 290 partial vetoes in the 1987-1989 bill, and the legislature was not able to override any of them.

Some governors use the veto, of whatever species, more often than do others. Frequency of use, however, is not necessarily an indication of gubernatorial power. As one study of the item veto notes: "Quantitative tests in this area are more likely to mislead than illuminate. "[15] Governors cast their veto for various reasons. They veto policies and budgetary provisions they oppose, and particularly those they oppose strongly. Or they attempt to make symbolic points or to convey messages to the legislature. Such vetoes are more likely to occur when the governor is of one party and the legislature is controlled by the opposition.[16] Especially as elections approach in states where government is divided and parties are competitive, the party in control of the legislature may advance a bill hoping to force a veto that will provide it with a political advantage at the expense of the governor's party.

The governor's veto is also employed for reasons other than principled opposition or partisan combat. The amendatory veto, in particular, lends itself to multiple uses. Often the sponsor discovers a flaw in an enacted bill and requests the governor to veto amendatorily so that a correction can be made. Sometimes the governor will use an amendatory veto to bring coherence to an area in which a number of bills have been enacted. An example is the crisis over Acquired Immune Deficiency Syndrome (AIDS), in which many bills have been introduced by legislators seeking to demonstrate concern and gain credit for action. The Illinois legislature in 1987 passed seventeen different AIDS bills, a number of which contradicted one another. Governor Thompson vetoed four, amendatorily vetoed three, and signed ten others, trying to fashion a coherent public program out of a potpourri of legislation. The legislature left it to Thompson to sort through the lot. He did so and responded that "the manner in which this package is crafted by my actions will provide Illinois with a reasonable public policy to deal with AIDS." [17]

As long as the governor stands by with the veto, legislators do not have to be overly scrupulous about everything they submit. They can respond to popular pressures, leaving it to the governor to be the statesman. Not infrequently legislators rely on the governor to veto bills that they enact, but which they really do not want to become law. They pass the buck to the governor, because they are reluctant to say no to influential statewide interests or powerful constituency groups. Normally, such bills die somewhere in the legislative process—buried in a standing committee, held up in the rules committee, or lost between the houses. Some, however, survive and reach the governor's desk, the last line of defense. Utah's governor Scott Matheson (1977-1985) explains, "A number of legislators often advised me ahead of time that they were going to vote for a particular bill because their constituents wanted it; however, they let me know informally that they would be happy with my veto." [18] New Jersey's governor Robert Meyner (1954-1962), reflecting on his years in office, expressed no tolerance for legislators' inability to resist the blandishments of special interests. He once branded legislators as "prostitutes" in passing bills with the expectation that he would bail them out by vetoing the bills.[19]

The actual exercise of the veto is important but probably less so than its threat in the context of executive-legislative dealings. Indeed, in many instances the use of the veto may signal the failure of gubernatorial persuasiveness rather than the success of gubernatorial power. That is because in many instances the very existence of the veto should enable a governor to persuade a legislator to withdraw a bill that the governor opposes. "If it's a terrible bill," comments the chief of staff of a southern governor, "it's best to deal with it ahead of time, so the governor does not have to veto it and embarrass the member." Governor Earl of Wisconsin operated in this way, working the legislature in advance, so that only the bills he wanted to sign would reach his desk.[20] Governor Robert Ray (1969-1983) of Iowa operated in a similar way. He would let legislators know at an early stage whether he would sign their bills, thus saving them the trouble of trying to push legislation through the two houses only to run into a veto.[21]

Often a governor will be able to signal his or her concern before a bill passes one house or the other, and it will be possible for the governor's staff and the sponsor to meet relatively early to work things out. Sometimes, however, a bill will not be identified as objectionable until it reaches the governor's desk for signature. Late as it may be, the opportunity for negotiation still exists, because in thirty-three states a legislator can recall a measure from the governor's desk. This allows a member to make changes called for by the governor and thus forestall a veto and embarrassment.[22]

The threat of a veto can be defensive, as in the cases already cited. "Make changes, or else I will veto the bill." "Recall the bill, or else I will embarrass you by vetoing it." Governors negotiate from a position of considerable strength throughout the process, for at its concluding step their views must be taken into account. They can defend on major issues as well as minor ones. Governor James Edwards (1975-1979) of South Carolina acknowledges using the threat of a veto many times. "We would have had two cents more taxes on gasoline right now if I hadn't had the veto. We would have had a nickel tax on beer. We would have had three cents tax on cigarettes if I hadn't used that veto, or the threat of a veto." [23]

But the veto threat also serves as an offensive weapon. By threatening to veto a member's pet bill or a member's item in the appropriations act, a governor can often secure the member's support for legislation near and dear to the administration. The veto power, in effect, allows the governor to take bills and appropriation items hostage. "Just think of the specter of individual legislators jumping down to the governor's office, pleading and begging and cajoling him not to veto something" is the picture Speaker Loftus paints.[24] But legislators can ransom their bill's release, offering votes in support of the governor's program. In order to receive the local projects they feel they need for reelection, legislators cooperate with the governor if they possibly can. "The mere threat of a governor's veto on the right project," writes one observer of Louisiana politics, "can bring almost any legislator to heel on another issue."[25] The veto thus gives the governor continuous leverage and the ability to discipline recalcitrant legislators. Trades need not be explicit; everyone knows that if a legislator resists the governor, he or she risks a pet project or even more.

The process can affect the legislature's major bills, as well as members' pet bills. The trade-offs lubricate the system. Democratic governor Babbitt in Arizona proved to be a master of such tactics, which was probably a necessity if he were to have any success with the Republican legislature. In the 1985 session he wanted legislation increasing teachers' salaries, but got nowhere. He began hinting that unless the legislature went along, he might veto its highway bill. At the end of the session, with no settlement in sight, he made it clear that he would veto the highway bill unless he received his education package and a few other items. "No kids, no concrete." Babbitt finally got what he wanted.[26]

THE POWER OF PROVISION

The other side of the power of rejection is the power of provision. The governor can fulfill members' needs, because he or she is the great provider. The governor can provide them with the appointments they desire, the projects their districts require, and the attention they demand. Or the governor may be able to bestow a three-digit license plate on a legislator's favored constituent. As one legislative participant, in accounting for the New Jersey governor's power, explained: "Sometime, over the course of their tenure, every legislator is going to need something."[27]

A few legislators may renounce the largesse that governors bestow, but not many. An observer of the political scene in Alabama stated that "any legislator who says he needs nothing from the Governor's office is either lying or stupid." And a member of the Alabama senate put it this way:

> Everybody wants something [from the administration]. You've got constituents who want appointments, jobs, grants, roads, etc. In politics,

it's you scratch my back and I'll scratch yours.... To a certain extent you do have to choose one or the other—getting things or opposing the Governor.[28]

Legislators are willing to play ball with the governor because otherwise they may not even be in the game.

While a few may want little or nothing, a typical member needs many things from the governor. Consider, for instance, a meeting between a two-term member of the Florida house and then-governor Bob Graham (1979-1987).[29] Although the legislator spent only a brief time in the governor's office, he had several items on his agenda. First, he asked the governor not to veto an appropriation item for a residence for the president of Florida A & M University or one for a multicultural educational laboratory. Second, he asked the governor to veto a bill favoring optometrists that had just passed the house. And third, he asked the governor to appoint a sixty-year-old black woman with twenty-one children to fill an unexpired term on the Franklin County school board.

The appointment powers of governors vary considerably across the states. As assessed by political scientists, only if governors name the top executives in their administrations are they considered to be powerful with respect to appointments. But from the perspective of dealing with the legislature, the higher positions count less than the smaller ones— the many posts on boards, commissions, and councils. These are the plums legislators want to secure for constituents in their districts and/or contributors to their campaigns. Most of the positions are unpaid, but they confer prestige and sometimes influence on the occupants. They are increasingly sought after. And they provide governors with the kind of patronage that helps keep legislators in line.

Traditional patronage appointments have lost much of their utility over the years, as civil service systems have been established and have grown. In dispensing patronage, governors also risk making enemies rather than friends, placating some legislators at the risk of annoying others, and having to deal with ingrates. Nonetheless, appointments do pay off. They enable governors to reward campaign contributors, build political backing, incur the indebtedness of interest groups, and—from our present perspective—trade for legislators' support.

Most governors, moreover, are reasonably well endowed when it comes to appointments. California's governor fills seats on over 300 boards and commissions, such as the Commission on Aging, Cancer Advisory Council, Commission on Fair Employment Practices, and Student Aid Commission. Illinois's governor has at his command 1,300 positions on 172 independent boards and commissions of an advisory or regulatory nature. Louisiana's governor appoints members of 135 boards and commissions regulating everything from mineral production on public lands to embalmers.[30]

Not all of such positions become vacant in a governor's term of office, but a good number do. Even in Florida, where the governor's power of appointment is perceived to be limited (since only ten of twenty-one major agencies are directly under his control), Bob Graham named thousands of individuals to governmental positions during his two terms in office. It should be noted that governors make use of appointments not only to build support in the legislature, but also to reward partisan followers. In reviewing some 350 of Florida governor Bob Martinez's (1987-   ) appointments in the first six months of his term, the *Miami Herald* found that more than half of those appointed were contributors to Martinez's 1986 campaign, the state Republican party, or Vice President George Bush's presidential campaign.[31]

Projects are also available for bestowal by governors. Highway contracts, which can be directed to a construction company within a particular legislator's district, traditionally have been important in the South. In Louisiana concrete has long been considered the "currency of power," and roads and bridges are traded liberally by governors for legislators' votes. The importance of highway projects for legislators is illustrated by the efforts of Kentucky governor Martha Layne Collins (1983-1987) to pass a gasoline tax increase in the 1986 session of the general assembly after its defeat in a special session the year before. She had her secretary of transportation negotiate the projects and achieved her objectives.[32] In Kansas, Republican Governor Mike Hayden (1987-   ) called a special session of the legislature in 1988 to fund a highway program. The Democratic senate minority leader supported it, since his district stood to benefit from a four-lane highway that would run through the area. To add to his support, Hayden expanded his proposal to include roads in more areas of the state. In Illinois, Governor Thompson put together a "Build Illinois" program that nicely melded economic development policy with pork. He adopted projects selected by legislators for his plan, and he agreed that about one-fifth of the funding for the program would be given to the legislature for allocation. The total was divided among the four party caucuses, strengthening the hand of legislative leaders who would have the most to say about who received what within the caucus.

Of great importance also for the power of provision is the support a governor can bring to a legislator's pet bills. With the governor's backing, one's bill is sure to receive a favorable report from the department or agency that is concerned. Furthermore, if a legislator is in favor with the governor, he or she is likely to receive greater and more immediate assistance from the executive branch on case work for constituents.

Beyond the material rewards are other benefits that governors also confer. These may not appear significant, but they add up to recognition and attention, which are prized by nearly everybody in politics. At times, governors merely have to do a simple favor. Milton Shapp (1971-1979), after two terms in Pennsylvania, indicated that the concessions he had to make to win over legislators could be quite minor—like making sure that the legislator was on the platform when a $26,000 check was delivered from the department of urban affairs to his district.[33]

The care and feeding of legislators by governors is almost inconceivable without social events—a reception at the mansion when the legislative session opens, breakfast meetings with the leadership, weekly luncheons, social gatherings near the end of the session. Members are flattered and impressed and, whatever their problems with gubernatorial policies, they warm toward the governor.

Especially when governors make an effort to regale legislators, they can build loyalty by so doing. Members enjoy the social recognition governors accord them, and they delight in the partying as well. Governor Edwin Edwards (1972-1980, 1984-1988) of Louisiana was a master of entertainment when he held office. He had a daily shuttle of legislators to the mansion for breakfast and for lunch. "Any legislator who wanted to play," writes a reporter, "had fun keeping up with it, being in on it." [34] Edwards even took legislators, along with campaign contributors, with him on a trip to Europe. The trip was billed as a fund-raising event, but it also served to soften up the legislators who went along. Governor Rockefeller operated in a different style but produced similar results with legislators. His wealth had substantial impact on politics in New York and on the legislature. He would invite legislative leaders and other legislators to his estate at Pocantico, to view the modern sculpture on the grounds, to tour the collection of paintings in the house and its galleries, and to dine and take in the exquisite scenery on the Rockefeller spread. Legislators could not help but be impressed. They naturally wanted to be invited back to Pocantico, but this depended upon staying on good terms with the governor. Thus, though Rockefeller's invitations may not have bought any votes per se, they surely had a subtle effect: they softened members up.

In the final analysis, a governor who plays his or her cards skillfully can also impress on legislators that he or she can help them down the road. As James D. Barber pointed out years ago in his study of members of the Connecticut General Assembly, for most legislators, and especially for the new ones, possibilities in the future are extremely ill defined.[35] Members will comply with a governor's wishes whenever they can, because of their hopes of what he or she may provide later on, possibly much later on. It might be an appointment for the legislator's constituent, a bill for the legislator's backer, an appropriation for the legislator's district, an appearance at the legislator's fund-raising event, recognition of the legislator's efforts, or an opportunity for the legislator to advance politically.

THE POWER OF PARTY

One of the governor's traditional roles has been that of leader of his or her party in the state. This role still exists, although it is not what it used to be.

Thirty years ago a number of governors had firm control of their statewide party apparatus. Nelson Rockefeller, for instance, consolidated control of the New York Republican party soon after his 1958 election. He could then rely upon his state chairman to exercise some discipline in the legislature. In Connecticut, state chairman John Bailey managed things for Governor John Dempsey (1961-1971), mainly through the senate party caucus. And in New Jersey Governor Richard Hughes (1962-1970) dealt with four or five county party leaders, who delivered their legislative delegations to the governor in return for patronage appointments. Whatever the particular mechanisms, governors in a number of states used to derive power from their connection to statewide and local parties. In an essay on executive-legislative relations during that period, Malcolm Jewell wrote: "The governor's leadership depends not only on the existence of a strong organization but also on his ability to control it." [36]

No longer is the political party the central political institution it used to be in many, but by no means all, states. Hence, governors are less likely to play a party leadership role. Robert Ray in Iowa, for instance, was not a party leader and was challenged from within the Republican party, despite the fact that he served as governor for a long period.[37] According to two students of the scene, governors no longer take themselves seriously as "titular head of the party." They spend less of their time on traditional party activities and forsake party as an instrument of governance and discipline in their dealings with the legislature.[38] It is revealing that none of fifteen former governors interviewed in 1978 and 1979 mentioned party leadership as one of their important duties.[39] Today's governors deviate from party; they tend to be less ideological, less partisan, and more pragmatic than their predecessors. This is probably essential if they want to accomplish anything.

But political parties still count, at least to some degree. And they continue to buttress gubernatorial power. Legislators are positively oriented toward governors of their own party, because they share an affiliation, associations, and policy preferences. As one staff member in New Jersey expressed the sentiment of the Republican assembly caucus toward Governor Thomas Kean (1982-1990): "He's popular and he's ours." Almost all legislators bring with them a set of party-favoring predispositions, which are learned through the years. They will go along with "their" governor, if they possibly can.

The organization of the legislature reinforces the influence of party. The legislative leaders of the governor's party—whether in the majority or minority—not only represent legislative party members to the governor, but also act as the governor's lieutenants in relating to legislative party members. One of these leaders' roles is trying to accomplish the governor's objectives by gaining passage for bills the administration favors and blocking bills the administration opposes.

Legislative leaders are expected to service the governor, albeit not as much as they once did. Republican Governor Richard Ogilvie (1969-1973) of Illinois remembered a breakfast meeting on taxes at the mansion in 1969. It was attended by Republican Senate President Russ Arrington and Republican house speaker Ralph Smith. When Ogilvie brought up income-tax legislation, "Arrington's face got red and his neck swelled. I remember his words exactly. He said, 'Who is the crazy son of a bitch who is going to sponsor this thing?' I looked at him and said, 'Russ, you are.' " Along with two other Republicans and a Democrat as cosponsors, Arrington introduced S.B.1150, the Illinois Income Tax Act.[40] Such demonstrations of party loyalty are few and far between, but they do occur even today. The Republican leaders in the Illinois General Assembly disagreed with Governor Thompson's tax packages in 1987 and 1988; however, like good soldiers they went along.

If one party dominates, as is the case in a number of states, partisan loyalty matters less. Without serious opposition as a threat, legislators have less incentive to rally around their governor. But party still counts. Take Utah, for example. Republican governor Norman Bangerter (1985-   ) had a difficult time with the Republican legislature, but not nearly so much so as Democratic governor Scott Matheson had had. Republican legislators would have been even tougher on Bangerter had he not been one of their own.

When governors head the ticket on which candidates for the legislature also appear, legislative party members have a stake in the governor's success. Legislators who used to be elected on a governor's coattails felt special loyalty, at least for a while. Even though legislators are much less likely to be elected on a governor's coattails nowadays, they do not want to run the risk that those coattails will drag them down. This may not create tight party cohesion in the legislature, but it does engender a fundamental attitude of party loyalty—especially in competitive states where governors will be on the ballot. That attitude leads to support for measures central to the governor's program and crucial to his or her standing with the public.[41]

Take the case of Pennsylvania, where after 1970 governors had the chance to succeed themselves for one additional term. That meant that most legislators of the governor's party who were running for reelection would run, to some extent, on the record of the administration. One political scientist observes that while the experiences of Governors Milton Shapp and Richard Thornburgh may not be conclusive, both were eligible to succeed themselves and did run successfully for reelection. Moreover, what press comments were made about intraparty tensions came mostly during their second terms in office.[42]

Governors also involve themselves more directly nowadays in legislative elections, thus creating at least a modicum of indebtedness on the parts of members whom they help. New members may feel a special debt. The governor is not usually the campaign manager for legislative races; the legislative parties and legislative leaders have taken on that function in recent years, replacing state and local party organizations. Nevertheless, a number of governors do believe that their intervention is entirely appropriate. A survey of thirty-seven states by the National Governors' Association (NGA) found that it was generally agreed that governors ought to take some role in general election campaigns. Half felt that they should campaign for their party's legislative candidates, as much and as hard as their schedules would permit. Another 40 percent thought some involvement, such as endorsements, was appropriate, but that a major campaign effort was not. The rest were of the opinion that governors should not participate to any great extent. It was also agreed that they should play a role in their party's primaries, as 15 percent called for active participation in the candidate-selection process, 64 percent advocated involvement in a few special cases, and 21 percent were of the opinion that under no circumstances should the governor or top staff ever be involved.[43] At the very least, governors are likely to raise funds that can be allocated to their party's legislative candidates.

Few governors eschew involvement altogether. The real choice each governor has, according to a handbook for governors published by NGA, is how deeply to become involved.[44] One governor may go all out, hoping to win control for his or her party in the legislature. Another may hold personal involvement to a minimum, so as not to risk alienating legislators of the opposition party who control the legislature.

Some try to walk a middle path when it comes to intervening in legislative elections.

In previous times, a few southern governors—in Louisiana and Kentucky, for example—actively intervened in their party's legislative primaries in order to help defeat incumbents who had opposed them. And when urban party organizations were much stronger, governors would sometimes ally with local party leaders to deny renomination to legislators who had voted against their programs. Governors nowadays, however, tend to stay out of their party's primaries, but they are far more likely to become involved in the general election.

Just how much of a return governors receive for their legislative party building cannot be known. It is likely that legislators who are newly elected, thanks in part to a governor's efforts, will maintain their loyalty, probably until their districts no longer are marginal and targeted and until they do not need to rely on the governor for assistance. Whatever the relationships, the environment is definitely changing, particularly in the more partisan states. The emerging system of permanent, continuous campaigning is beginning to affect the way governors interact with legislators.

THE POWER OF EXPERIENCE

In the role of chief legislator, the governor usually can draw on personal experience in executive office and in the legislature itself. Experience is not directly translatable into power; some conversion rate must be applied. But for a governor dealing with a legislature, the years spent in the house or senate, the time served in gubernatorial office, and future tenure prospects do make a difference.

Among the governors serving in the decade of the 1970s, three out of ten had been members of the legislature immediately before their elections as chief executive. Of the fifty governors holding office in 1988, thirty-one had served in the legislature and at least nine of them had been legislative leaders.[45] That experience could only be helpful to them.

Individuals like Governor Thomas Kean of New Jersey, who was speaker of the assembly, or Governor John McKernan, Jr. (1987-   ), who held a minority leadership position in the Maine house, had an understanding of the legislative process that proved invaluable to them. Madeleine Kunin (1985-) of Vermont could also put her years in the legislature to work in the governor's office; she had learned to appreciate the needs of legislators and the workings of the process. "Most importantly," she recalls, "the knowledge that all political action is to some degree a consensus process, a collegial process was gained in my years in the legislature."[46]

Hand in hand with this sensitivity go the relationships that governors developed in the legislature. Gerald Baliles served previously in the Virginia House of Delegates and was a member of the appropriations committee. His personal relationships with house members stood him in good stead when he became governor. He could deal effectively with rank and file in the house, although he had fewer ties with individual senators and instead worked through the leadership. Baliles's cooperative style toward the legislature, observers believe, was attributable in part to his legislative experience.

Individuals who have been in the legislature some years before their election to the office of governor maintain the relationships they established earlier. For example, John Waihee III (1986-) served one term in the Hawaii house and then four years as lieutenant governor before his election to governor in 1985. During his stint as lieutenant governor, he stayed in close touch with his former legislative colleagues, and particularly the leadership. When he became chief executive, he maintained his cordial relationships, even visiting legislators in their offices and attending Democratic party caucuses, something that his predecessors had not done.

Other things being equal, the period a governor has in executive office enhances his power. The passage of time facilitates the building of both personal and political relationships. Take Governor James Thompson of Illinois. He is a four-term governor, having held the office of chief executive longer than any other current governor in the nation. Over the period of his incumbency, Thompson developed strong ties to individual legislators, coming to know them personally and their districts intimately. The passage of time permitted Thompson, as it would any governor, to consolidate power.

Years ago the tenure potential and the actual tenure of governors were shorter than they are today. Almost half the states had two-year terms, and in one-third of the states governors could not succeed themselves for a second term. Today only New Hampshire, Rhode Island, and Vermont still have two-year terms for their governors. Only Kentucky, New Mexico, and Virginia preclude governors from immediately succeeding themselves, while twenty-two states have no constitutional limits on how long governors can serve. As a consequence of these changes, governors have the opportunity of serving for longer periods, and they appear to be doing so.[47] However, when governors are on their way out—in lame duck status, as it were—all of their previous experience loses salience. They are likely to suffer a decline in efficacy.

A few, such as Governor Michael Dukakis in Massachusetts after his unsuccessful presidential campaign, suffer a considerable loss of power when legislators know that their reign is coming to an end.

THE POWER OF UNITY

The principal advantage of the governor over the legislature stems from the fact that he or she is one, while they are many. In the opinion of Larry Sabato, a leading scholar on the office of governor, it is doubtful whether a legislature can ever gain the upper hand, because a body of several hundred cannot match a single executive. Being one, a governor is more capable of action, provides a better focus for people's expectations, and serves more as a favorite of the news media. In contrast, a legislature is composed of a variety of members representing different districts and competing interests, relatively independent of one another, who have to share policy-making power. As one member of the New Jersey legislature characterized the disparity: "The big difference between the governor and the legislature is that there is one of him and 120 of us." [48]

Compared with any legislature, governors are remarkably unitary, but some are more so than others who may be constrained by having to compete for the spotlight with other statewide elected officials. In New Jersey, for example, the governor is the only state official elected statewide. By contrast, forty-two states also have lieutenant governors who are elected statewide, twenty of whom are elected separately from their governors, thus setting up a potential for conflict between the two offices.

Even when they are of the same party, the two statewide officials can clash. None have clashed as vigorously as Governor Robert Ray and Lieutenant Governor Roger Jepsen in Iowa. During Ray's first term as governor, Jepsen, in presiding over the senate, publicly worked to advance Ray's program but privately complained about the governor's lack of legislative experience. A representative of the right wing of the Republican party, which did not expect Ray to serve more than a single term (he served five), Jepsen wanted to succeed the governor. He never did, but became "the number one enemy" of the governor. "There was nobody whose guts Robert Ray hated more than Roger Jepsen's," according to one of the governor's aides. [49] It should be noted, however, that a later lieutenant governor, Art Neu, was a loyal ally of Ray who helped him greatly in the Iowa senate where he presided.

When the governor and lieutenant governor are of opposite parties, there is more chance of mischief. In California, when Democratic governor Edmund Brown, Jr. (1975-1983) would leave the state, Republican lieutenant governor Mike Curb would try to overturn his decisions or policies. Brown would fly back immediately, and would be hesitant to leave the state again.

Although lieutenant governors may harass their governors, in few places does a lieutenant governor have an adequate base to contest power seriously with the governor. Texas is one such place. Here, the lieutenant governor, unlike the governor, is not limited to two terms. The Texas lieutenant governor traditionally has exerted strong and independent leadership over the senate, not only presiding but making committee assignments too. His senate base has made him one of the three dominant figures—along with the speaker of the house and the governor—in the state. And as chair of the legislative budget board, he plays a more important role in the development of the state budget than does the governor. Alabama, Georgia, and Mississippi have similarly powerful lieutenant governors who wield considerable influence by virtue of their leadership in the senate.

In most states, a number of officials are elected statewide, and they share an electorate with the governor. In fact, as of 1986 there were 509 separately elected officials other than the governor in the fifty states— fewer than the 709 of 1956, but still a large amount.[50] At one end of the continuum, more than ten officials are separately elected in Louisiana, Mississippi, North Carolina, and North Dakota, while at the other extreme only the governor is elected statewide in Maine, New Hampshire, and New Jersey.

The situation can be even more complicated. In Tennessee the governor and public utility commissioner are elected statewide, but the comptroller, treasurer, and secretary of state are elected by the legislature. The lieutenant governor is the speaker (not president or president pro tem) of the senate and is elected by that body. Surely the legislature is not without influence in the executive branch in Tennessee.

Difficulties between a governor and a separately elected official are not uncommon. In California, for example, the competition between Governor George Deukmejian and superintendent of public instruction Bill Honig has been heated. They disagreed on education reform and finance for years. In 1987 Honig wanted extra funds spent on education, but the governor refused. The Democratic-controlled legislature wanted more money for schools than the governor was willing to give. Deukmejian held firm, however, after having compromised with Honig and the legislature in prior years.[51]

Florida's cabinet system probably imposes as severe a constitutional limitation on gubernatorial power as exists in the states. Sharing executive power with the governor are six independently elected officials—the secretary of state, attorney general, comptroller, insurance commissioner and treasurer, commissioner of agriculture, and commissioner of education. They are known collectively as the cabinet because each not only administers a department of state government (the departments of state, legal affairs, banking and finance, insurance, agriculture and consumer services, and education), but each also serves equally with the governor on a number of boards that administer other departments. The governor is solely responsible for only half of the departments in Florida government.

Although reformers have attempted to amend the constitution and eliminate the cabinet, none has been successful. In 1978 Governor Reubin Askew (1971-1979) led a campaign to approve a constitutional amendment to abolish the cabinet, but the ballot proposition was defeated by almost three to one. There has also been talk of limiting to two the number of four-year terms for cabinet officers, but nothing has yet happened. They still have an unlimited number of terms, whereas governors may serve for only two successive four-year terms.

Florida's governor not only shares administrative authority, but has to consolidate cabinet support and stake his or her political prestige in dealing with cabinet colleagues. It is relatively easy for them to challenge the governor; they have little to lose, because in a confrontation between a cabinet official and the governor the governor is expected to win. Moreover, members of the cabinet have their own constituencies, independent of the governor's. Whatever the politics, the business of the cabinet, the collective decision making, and the weekly meetings take a substantial amount of time—time that could be used by the chief executive for other purposes.

Florida's governors have had to come to terms with the fact that cabinet members have their own allies in the legislature, as well as the constitutional authority to share certain decision-making power with the chief executive. Weak individuals tend to be overwhelmed, yet strong Florida governors have been able to overcome many of the limitations imposed on them by their constitution in general and the cabinet in particular.[52] Despite the obstacle of cabinet government, governors Askew and Graham have certainly been able to do so, exploiting their relative power of unity with regard to the legislature and making skillful use of their other powers.

THE POWER OF PUBLICITY

Because the governor is a single individual and the legislature is a collective institution, governors are far more likely than legislatures to command attention from the media and from the people. "The cacophony of legislator voices," writes a former member of the Washington legislature, "can rarely compete with a governor who can capitalize on his singular visibility in the media." [53] The power of publicity—that is, the ability to command broad attention—is surely one of the executive's principal strengths.

Until relatively recently publicity was not the resource for governors that it is today. The availability of television and other means of communication, however, now enables governors to speak to the public quickly and directly. Governors command the attention of both the print and electronic media by responding to crises, by staging events, or by making practically any movement at all. In some instances the effects are dramatic. As a new governor of Pennsylvania in 1979, Richard Thornburgh had to respond to the Three Mile Island nuclear accident. His calm demeanor and concern for the safety of the people in the area were projected over television. "Coming as it did early in a new administration, the focus on the Governor during those stressful days undoubtedly assisted him in his subsequent relations with the General Assembly," writes one political scientist.[54] The governor is usually good for a story, and the story can stand him or her in good stead.

The men and women who now occupy gubernatorial office have honed their communication skills and are often adept in using the media to reach the people of their states. Most governors today, and especially those in the larger states, recognize that the ability to mobilize broad public support through the media is supplanting the traditional small-group persuasive skills needed by their predecessors. Governor Mario Cuomo (1983-   ) of New York excels here. As a national figure he has extra sway with the Albany press corps. His skills at manipulating the media, assisted by a staff of "spin doctors," are superb. Dealing with narrow circles of elite decision makers no longer suffices for a governor, although going public cannot substitute for dealing more privately with the legislature.

Governors may be aided in communicating their views by the fact that their personalities are apt to engage the press. They work diligently to highlight their appealing qualities, drawing as needed on the talents of their press secretaries and other staff. Bob Graham of Florida, for example, was masterful in dealing with the Tallahassee press corps. His "work days," when he left the capitol to assume the job of a truck driver or teacher, would allow him to enunciate themes and build general approval. During his two administrations, he charmed the capital press corps by appearing in their annual skits in which reporters poked fun at Florida politicians. Graham sang and danced his way through his part in the show, and usually was the hit of the night. The press corps appreciated his talents as performer, and they also respected his performance as governor. "Graham cultivated the press like petunias," is the way one reporter characterized his approach. "He knew when to break out the sunshine and openness, when it was time for feeding, even the rarest knowledge of all, when not to lay on the fertilizer too thickly." [55]

Governors are also aided by their ability to stage events that the press will be sure to cover. Bill signings are such an event, and one the governor can invite legislators to attend and thereby single them out for special acknowledgment. The large majority of bills, of course, are signed privately by the governor in his office, with staff serving as counsel. But bills that appeal to an influential group, a large community, or the public at large receive spotlighted treatment.

Even though a governor may not have primary responsibility for a piece of legislation, he or she is the one who will receive media coverage upon signing it. Governor William Donald Schaefer (1987-   ) in 1988 signed into law a bill that made Maryland the first state to ban the sale of some cheap handguns. Although Schaefer's role in the bill's initiation and passage was secondary, the ABC morning news program televised him signing it. As far as the television-watching public is concerned, the governor makes it happen—whether that is really the case or not.

The "state of the state," budget, and special messages that governors deliver are designed to reach as many people in the state as possible. But they can be delivered in a variety of ways. Governor Martinez of Florida released his 1988-1989 budget piece by piece in a series of almost daily speeches, while other Florida governors had announced their budget proposals at one time in a single news conference. By dividing up his package, Martinez could generate news stories and pictures about each of his programs—to protect the environment, fight pollution, provide for transportation needs, build affordable housing, and improve early education of the disadvantaged. Newspapers across the state ran front-page color pictures of the governor diving at a state park off Key Largo to show the U.S. Secretary of the Interior the threat to Florida's coral reefs from offshore oil exploration. Television news programs showed him canoeing on the Wekiwa River to demonstrate the need to protect it from development.[56]

The fact of the governor's involvement in an issue attaches importance to it. According to Madeleine Kunin, the office affords him or her a unique perch—the "bully pulpit," which itself is "an instrument of power." So, even though the formal powers of chief executives may be circumscribed, former governor of Utah Scott Matheson advises that "what governors can and must do, is go out and drum up public support for what they want to achieve." [57] Governors do not make use of this power on each and every issue; to do so would be self-defeating, for at some point they would no longer be taken seriously by the press or public.

The "bully pulpit," so simple conceptually, involves the governor and staff in a substantial amount of work. The schedule must be scanned continuously so that the governor can take advantage of opportunities to articulate major themes. Statewide radio and television appearances must be timed to coincide with key events in the development of issues, such as presenting the budget, calling a special legislative session, announcing a veto, and so forth.[58] With attention to such detail, the governor's power of publicity can be used quite effectively to advance his or her priorities.

The legislature is no match. Individual members cannot attract similar attention. The press also views legislators very differently than the governor, who is perceived to be an authoritative and reliable source of information, while legislators are viewed skeptically. Or the governor is viewed as a leader, while the legislature is seen as obstructionist. Moreover, the press sees the governor as representing all the people, while legislators each represent only a few—mostly dominant—interests. Institutionally the legislature is an arena for conflict among competing interests and viewpoints. Thus, most legislative news coverage revolves around conflict, including charge and countercharge, maneuver and counter-maneuver, and sometimes stalemate. Such reporting has a much different effect on viewers than the positive coverage given the governor, who is seen attending events, dedicating roads, listening to people, and responding to emergencies. The legislature can never win in the press.

Legislators recognize the superior position of the governor when it comes to publicizing an issue or a position. If legislative leaders want to advance a controversial measure, they will probably have to rely on the governor to attract attention to it. Without the governor's support and publicizing capability, such a measure may lack the head of steam needed to chug through both houses. If individual members are seeking a spotlight for themselves, they can position themselves by the governor's side. A Minnesota senator, for example, indicated that although he and some of his colleagues were not completely sold on the details of one of the governor's proposals for education, they decided "to get on the train before it pulled out." They wanted to share in the positive publicity that only the governor would receive for such a proposal.

THE POWER OF POPULARITY

The governor's visibility in the state and ability to promote himself or herself and the administration through the media are tremendous assets.

They enable the governor to build a base of popularity with the citizens of the state that can be drawn on in relations with the legislature.

Governors begin their terms not with mandates for programs or policies, but with votes in the election. Receiving a large proportion of votes demonstrates an individual's appeal to the electorate as nothing else can. In the 1986 elections, for example, William Donald Schaefer's 82 percent in Maryland, James Blanchard's (1983-   ) 69 percent in Michigan, and Richard Bryan's (1983-1988) 73 percent in Nevada evidenced persuasive margins in the popularity of the winning candidates over the losers.

A newly elected governor, and particularly one who wins big, brings to office a repository of good will, rather than a mandate for specific programs. Legislators cannot fail to be impressed, for if there is one thing they are sensitive to it is the number of votes candidates receive. They respect politicians who receive many votes, and there is evidence that electoral support is reflected in the legislature itself.[59]

The election is the first step, but by no means the only one. The popularity game continues unabated after a candidate takes office. Thanks to the power of publicity and the role of the mass media, people in the state come to know their governor, no matter what his or her electoral margin. Scott Matheson recalls that when he had served as Utah's governor for only two years, his name identification was 99.5 percent, whereas the senior U.S. senator from Utah, who had been in office more than twelve years, was known by only about two-thirds of the people. And just before he announced his retirement, Matheson's approval rating with the public was still high, at 79 percent.[60] The fact is that the public relates to the chief executive. In many instances, the public develops a feel for the governor's personality and trust in his or her leadership. That was the case in Iowa, where Governor Robert Ray's ratings ranged from 71 percent to 82 percent during his successive terms in office.[61]

Some governors pay special attention to their standing with the public and prove remarkably effective in doing so. Rudy Perpich (1976-1979, 1983-   ) of Minnesota is one of them. He is constantly traveling the state, setting up a "capital for the day" and communicating effectively with the people locally. To take another example, Thomas Kean won election in 1981 by 1,700 votes, the smallest margin of any governor in New Jersey history. At the end of his first year in office, he was in trouble. Neither the political community in Trenton nor the statewide public gave very high marks to the new administration. Early in 1983, however, the governor added Greg Stevens to his staff as director of public information for the administration. Stevens's first task was to "communicate to the public what Tom Kean was doing." His strategy for doing so was to get the governor out of the statehouse and around the state. Recognizing that Kean's greatest political asset was his ability to deal with people, Stevens arranged to have him visit town meetings in community after community. The governor also had his own show on cable television, which helped him take his message directly to the public. Stevens commented:

> It's very hard in New Jersey for a governor to get his message across. It has to be done through constant repetition—getting out there and delivering your message over and over again. It takes a cumulative effect to make an impression in the public mind.

Despite a patrician background, Kean found that his personality sold in the Garden State. Greg Stevens knew how to market it. By April 1984 the governor's approval rating had risen to 57 percent from 33 percent the year before, and it continued to shoot up the following year. In 1985 he was reelected to office with 70 percent of the vote. And throughout his second term, two-thirds to three-quarters of the New Jersey public expressed approval of Governor Kean's job performance.[62]

Kean's public relations efforts were extensive and most effective. Whereas his predecessor in office had had one secretary handling the mail, Kean developed a sizable communication staff and a special office of constituent relations in the governor's office. Moreover, he was featured in a number of public service television advertisements—with actress Brooke Shields and other stars promoting tourism in New Jersey, with veterans and schoolchildren promoting the lottery, and not-so-incidentally promoting himself.

Statewide polling data, which are reported in Table 2-1 for twelve states, suggest a number of points. First, the popularity of governors can vary significantly from individual to individual, even more than from state to state. In Florida, Graham was much more popular than Martinez; in Maryland, Schaefer is more popular than Harry Hughes (1979-1987); and in Alabama, Guy Hunt (1987-) outpolls George Wallace (1963-1967, 1971-1979). Second, the popularity of individual governors can vary significantly from one year to the next. Third, a decline in the state's economy, a proposal to raise taxes, or some governmental scandal all can have a negative effect on a governor's rating in the polls.

Take the issue of taxes. In New Jersey, a tax package increasing the state sales tax from 5 percent to 6 percent and the state income tax on those earning over $50,000 caused Governor Kean's popularity to drop. In September 1982, before the legislation was enacted, his positive job performance rating was 39 percent. By February 1983, after the raised taxes had been signed into law, his rating was down to 33 percent.

TABLE 2-1   Popularity of Governor and Legislature (percentages giving positive rating)

State	Year	Governor	Legislature	Differences[a]
Alabama[1]	1988	61 (Hunt)	24	+37
	1987	52	30	+22
	1986	35 (Wallace)	30	+5
	1985	40	30	+10
California[2]	1988	46 (Deukmejian)	32	+14
	1987	53	—	
	1986	53	—	
	1985	51	—	
	1984	43	—	
	1983	36	23	+13
Florida[3]	1989	49 (Martinez)	38	+11
	1988	27	38	- 11
	1987	23	35	- 12
	1986	69 (Graham)	45	+24
	1985	67	47	+20
	1984	63	47	+16
	1983	67	47	+20
Kentucky[4]	1988	—	38	
	1987	35 (Collins)	—	
	1986	46	41	+5
	1985	47	—	
Maryland[5]	1989	61 (Schaefer)	51	+10
	1988	64	52	+12
	1987	67	50	+17
	1985	54 (Hughes)	44	+10
	1984	54	41	+13
	1982	38	38	
	1981	32	34	- 2
Minnesota[6]	1988	46 (Perpich)	—	
	1987	50	—	
	1986	70	—	
	1985	64	—	
	1984	68	—	
New Jersey[7]	1989	66 (Kean)	36	+30
	1988	74		
	1987	81	47	+34
	1986	80	47	+33
	1985	67	43	+24
	1984	57	31	+26
	1983	33	29	+4
	1982	39	32	+7

TABLE 2-1 Continued

State	Year	Governor	Legislature	Differences[a]
New Mexico[8]	1988	72 (Carruthers)	—	
	1986	12 (Anaya)	—	
	1985	16	34	- 18
North Carolina[9]	1987	66 (Martin)	41	+25
Ohio[10]	1988	54 (Celeste)	—	
	1987	62	—	
	1986	53	—	
	1985	48	—	
	1984	45	—	
	1983	32	—	
West Virginia[11]	1988	19 (Moore)	8	+11
	1987	29	26	+3
	1986	42	27	+5
	1985	53	—	
Wyoming[12]	1986	63 (Herschler)	43	+20

1. Capstone Poll, University of Alabama.
2. California Poll, The Field Institute; February 1988, January 1987, March 1986, February 1985, February 1987, March 1983 (for governor), and June 1983 (for legislature).
3. Survey Research Center, Policy Sciences Program, Florida State University.
4. Survey Research Center, University of Kentucky, April 1988, Spring 1986, and Spring 1985.
5. Survey Research Center (Institute for Governmental Service), College of Behavioral and Social Sciences, University of Maryland, Spring 1989, Spring 1988, Spring 1987, Spring 1985, Fall 1984, Spring 1982, and Spring 1981.
6. Minnesota Poll, *Star-Tribune* of Minneapolis and St. Paul, February 1988, April 1987, May 1986, August 1985, and March 1984.
7. *Star-Ledger*/Eagleton Poll, Eagleton Institute of Politics, Rutgers, The State University of New Jersey, March 1989, February 1988, February 1987, February 1986, April-May 1985, April 1984, February 1983, and September 1982.
8. KOAT-TV/Zin Poll, Zin Research Associates, Albuquerque, New Mexico; April 27-May 2, 1988, May 14-19, 1986, and March 29-31, 1985.
9. Carolina Poll, Institute for Research in Social Science, University of North Carolina.
10. The Ohio Poll, sponsored by *Cincinnati Post*, WCPO-TV, and University of Cincinnati; January 1988, January-February 1987, January 1986, May 1985, January-February 1984, and April 1983.
11. West Virginia Poll, Ryan/Sampler Research, Charleston, West Virginia.
12. Bureau of Government Research, University of Wyoming; October 1986.

TABLE 2-1 Continued

Note: A "positive rating" includes combined percentages of "excellent" or "good," in questions asking respondents to rate the job ____ is doing as governor or the job the ____ legislature is doing. The tabulated categories are "excellent," "good," "fair," "poor," and "don't know" in Alabama, Florida, Kentucky, Maryland, and Wyoming. In California the response categories are "excellent," "good," "fair," "poor," "very poor," and "don't know." In Minnesota, "strongly approve" and "approve" (which are combined in a positive rating) and "disapprove," "strongly disapprove," and "don't know." In New Jersey the categories are "excellent," "good," "only fair," "poor," and "don't know." In New Mexico, the 1988 governor's categories are "very good," "good," "not so good," "poor," and "undecided," while the 1986 and 1985 governor's categories are "excellent," "good," "fair," "poor," "very poor," and "undecided"; the 1985 New Mexico legislative categories are "excellent," "good," "fair," "poor," "extremely poor," and "undecided." In North Carolina the response categories are "excellent," "pretty good," "only fair," "poor," and "don't know"; in Ohio "approve," "disapprove," and "neutral" or "no opinion"; in West Virginia, the categories are "excellent," "good," "only fair," "poor," and "don't know."

a Positive (+) difference indicates governor more popular, while negative (-) difference indicates legislature more popular.

Kean's predecessor, Brendan Byrne, plummeted much more precipitously in 1974 when, after a debate on his proposals for a statewide income tax, his rating dropped from 56 percent to 33 percent positive.

In Florida, the low ratings of Governor Martinez can be explained by the battle over a sales tax on services. In February 1987 the governor announced his support for the tax; in its April session the legislature enacted the tax, and the governor signed the bill. By August public opinion polls were showing rising opposition to the tax and greatly diminished support for the governor. By the year's end and after bitter controversy, the sales tax on services was repealed (and replaced by a one-cent increase in the sales tax on goods). But ill feeling remained, and the governor's popularity did not revive until early 1989. He spent 1988 polishing his image: he traveled around the state more, getting out among the voters and the local media. But by the summer of 1989, he had already dipped again in the polls, gaining "excellent" or "good" ratings from only 43 percent of those polled.[63] A lagging economy and severe unemployment did damage to Arch Moore (1969-1977, 1985-1989) in West Virginia. The governor was blamed for the depressed state and, to add to his troubles, people seemed to have grown tired of him.

The low 1985-1986 ratings of Governor Toney Anaya (1983-1987) in New Mexico resulted from multiple factors. The state faced a deficit in 1983. Several officials in Anaya's administration had been brought to trial and convicted. His offer of the state as a sanctuary for refugees drew national criticism. And the *Albuquerque Journal* attacked him unceasingly. "It seemed," commented a pollster, "like he couldn't do anything right."

Most important, given our current concerns, the data in Table 2-1 indicate that legislatures ordinarily are not as popular as governors.[64] This should not come as a surprise. Institutions, which are basically abstractions, hold less appeal as far as the public is concerned than do individuals, who are flesh and blood. Individual legislators may rate high with their constituents in polls, but the institution is something else. Thus, in the ratings of gubernatorial and legislative popularity shown in the table, the governor comes out on top in twenty-nine comparisons, the legislature in four, and there is no difference in one comparison. Martinez in Florida and Anaya in New Mexico, for the reasons already mentioned, are seen to trail their legislatures in popularity; on the other hand, Kean in New Jersey has consistently led. Moore in West Virginia does not fare too well, but the legislature fares even more poorly.

It would seem that, to a large degree, the legislature's popularity depends on the governor's. In some states legislatures are traditionally more popular than in others. But the governor can pull the legislature up—or pull it down. That is because the governor is the one who tends to receive credit or blame for the economy, taxes, scandals, and assorted boons and banes. The governor frequently bears some responsibility for these, and the legislature frequently bears some as well. As the governor goes, so goes the legislature—benefiting or suffering in tandem, but seldom rising as high or sinking as low. Job performance data for the governor and the legislature in New Jersey, shown in Figure 2-1, portray the relationship. The popularity of New Jersey's governors (Cahill in 1972-1973, Byrne in 1974-1980, and Kean in 1982-1989) rises and falls more sharply than does that of the legislature. The legislature's popularity tends to range in the 20s and low 30s, but it manages to ride Kean's coattails when he surges in 1985-1989.

Not only do circumstances tend to eat into a governor's popularity, but the passage of time may be erosive as well. It may be part of the natural cycle of political life, as the office becomes diminished in the eyes of the public by their familiarity with the incumbent. Moreover, the governor may trade in some popularity in order to achieve objectives. This seems to have happened to Mario Cuomo in New York, whose favorable rating dropped from 77 percent in January 1988 to 58 percent in May 1989.[65] Michael Dukakis in Massachusetts ran unsuccessfully for president, announced that he would not run for governor again, and proposed a $600 million tax increase; he saw his approval rating plummet to 19 percent.[66]

Even if a governor is fortunate or skillful enough to build and maintain personal popularity, there is no guarantee that it will be converted into power in the legislature. The issue of conversion is no

FIGURE 2-1   New Jersey Governor and Legislature
            (Positive Job Performance Rating)

Percentage

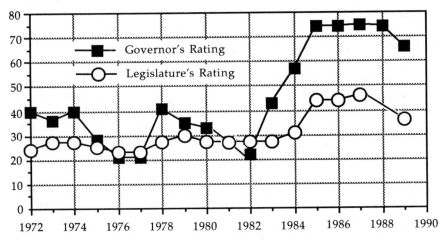

Source: Eagleton Institute of Politics, Rutgers University.

Note: If more than one poll is taken during a year, ratings are averaged for the year. No gubernatorial job performance questions were asked in 1981, so no gubernatorial ratings are reported for that year. No legislative job performance questions were asked in 1988, so no legislative ratings are reported for that year.

simple one. Political scientist Bert Rockman, in his summary of the literature on legislative-executive relations, points out with regard to the federal level: "The role of popular standing is very complex in accounting for legislative support of presidential proposals."[67] Yet there is a predisposition on the part of Congress to go along with a popular president whenever it can. Similarly, gubernatorial popularity probably predisposes a legislature to be friendly, if other factors are relatively equal. Making a favorable impression on the public, a governor is in a position to make a positive impression on the legislature. It is easier for a popular governor to deal with the legislature; he or she is better able to lead, for legislators are more inclined to follow.

In Iowa Robert Ray could persuade legislators to do what he wanted because of his popularity. During the last eight or nine years of his administration, when his standing with the public was highest, he was able to accomplish more. In 1969 and 1970, when his standing was lower, legislators were more inclined to oppose the governor. By 1974, when Ray's approval rating ranged between 70 and 85 percent, legislators stood on line to give him support.[68] But Matheson of Utah and Lamm of Colorado, despite their popularity with the public, had a difficult time with legislatures controlled by the opposite party.

In order to exploit their popularity, governors must act on behalf of their legislative program or for legislative purposes. Most governors do, to one degree or another. Graham, for instance, provided effective leadership in Florida because of his popularity and adroit use of the press to appeal to the people. Legislators had to take his proposals seriously, even though they did not like it when their "smiling Governor" received the credit for programs that never would have been enacted without the work of the house and the senate.[69]

In New Jersey, Kean acknowledged popularity as one of the factors contributing to his success. "Popularity is important in getting things done," he stated. "With a 75 percent rating, legislators have to be sensitive to your programmatic appeals." By contrast, he continued, legislators find it easy to attack the governor if he is not popular. Kean had to rely on his popularity in dealing with a divided legislature and, although the governor did not get everything he wanted, his popularity surely paid off.

THE POWER OF PERSUASION

A popular governor is not necessarily an effective one, as far as relations with the legislature are concerned. Popularity helps governors achieve the high ground, but it is not sufficient. Other powers of the governor also help. The power of initiation permits governors to set the agenda, at least to some extent. The power of rejection enables them to negotiate with legislators from a position of considerable strength. With the veto, in its various forms, governors wield a big stick, to go along with the carrots of appointments, projects, and preferment they use liberally in the care and feeding of legislators. The power of party affords governors a role that directly affects the careers and fortunes of legislators of their own political faith. The power of experience gives governors the know-how and the know-whom that come in so handy in political life. The power of unity conveys upon governors the inestimable advantage of being one in comparison to the many. This enables them to exploit the power of publicity, reaching out to people directly and through the media and developing a positive image and public support throughout the state.

Each of these powers alone is not sufficient to make a governor "chief legislator." But taken in combination, they are impressive. Together they allow the governor to persuade legislators—directly and personally and indirectly through the media—that what he or she wants by way of policy, expenditures, and operations is what they ought to grant, in their own interests. The governor clearly is in the catbird seat when working persuasive wiles on the legislature. The governor can address a legislator, as no one else can, with an appeal—backed by power—that is difficult to turn down: "I want this." "I need this." "The people of the state need this." "You are a vital part of that." "Without you, the whole thing goes down." Given their advantages, it is a wonder that governors ever lose. But the fact is that legislatures have significant power of their own and the will to use their power.

NOTES

1. See Thad L. Beyle, "The Institutionalized Powers of the Governorship: 1965-1985," *Comparative State Politics Newsletter* 9 (February 1988): 23-29.
2. Office of State Services, National Governors' Association, *State Management Notes: The Institutional Powers of the Governorship: 1965-1985* (Washington, D.C.: NGA, June 1987, rev. 1989).
3. National Governors' Association, Office of State Services, *Transition and the New Governor* (Washington, D.C.: NGA, November 1982), 95.
4. William T. Gormley, *Taming the Bureaucracy*, (Princeton, N.J.: Princeton University Press, 1989), 136.
5. Ibid., 140.
6. Thomas H. Simmons, "Colorado," in *The Political Life of the American States*, ed. Alan Rosenthal and Maureen Moakley (New York: Praeger, 1984), 77.
7. Robert H. Connery and Gerald Benjamin, *Rockefeller of New York: Executive Power in the State House* (Ithaca, N.Y.: Cornell University Press, 1979), 81.
8. Alan Rosenthal, ed., *The Governor and the Legislature* (New Brunswick, N.J.: Eagleton Institute of Politics, Rutgers University, 1988), 66.
9. E. Lee Bernick, "Gubernatorial Tools: Formal vs. Informal," *Journal of Politics* 41 (May 1979): 656-664.
10. National Governors' Association, *Transition and the New Governor*, 81.
11. Jack R. Van Der Slik and Kent D. Redfield, *Lawmaking in Illinois* (Springfield, Ill.: Sangamon State University, 1986), 165-166.
12. Connery and Benjamin, *Rockefeller of New York*, 98.
13. David Osborne, *Laboratories of Democracy* (Boston: Harvard Business School Press, 1988), 116.
14. Charles W. Wiggins, "Executive Vetoes and Legislative Overrides in the American States," *Journal of Politics* 42 (November 1980): 115.
15. U.S. House of Representatives, Committee on Rules, 99th Congress, 2d Session, "Item Veto: State Experience and Its Application to the Federal Situation" (Washington: General Printing Office, December 1986), 197.
16. See, for example, James J. Gosling, "Wisconsin Item-Veto Lessons," *Public Administration Review* 46 (July-August 1986), 297-298. This analysis of Wisconsin budgets shows that item vetoes were used more frequently when a Republican governor faced Democratic majorities in both houses.
17. "N E W S from the Office of the Governor," Springfield, Illinois, September 21, 1987.
18. Rosenthal, *The Governor and the Legislature*, 39.
19. Donald Linky, "The Governor," in *The Political State of New Jersey*, ed. Gerald

M. Pomper (New Brunswick, N.J.: Rutgers University Press, 1986), 108.

20. Sharon Randall, "From Big Shot to Boss," *State Legislatures*, July 1988, 36.
21. As noted by Dennis Nagel, in Jon Bowermaster, *Governor: An Oral Biography of Robert D. Ray* (Ames: Iowa State University Press, 1987), 280.
22. Gerald Benjamin, "The Diffusion of the Governor's Veto Power," *State Government* 55 (1982): 103-104.
23. National Governors' Association, *Reflections on Being Governor* (Washington, D.C.: Center for Policy Research, NGA, February 1981), 103.
24. Quoted in *Milwaukee Sentinel*, August 31, 1987.
25. John Maginnis, *The Last Hayride* (Baton Rouge, La.: Gris Gris Press, 1984), 8.
26. Osborne, *Laboratories of Democracy*, 138-139.
27. Alan Rosenthal, "The Governor and the Legislature," in Politics in *New Jersey*, ed. John Blydenburgh and Alan Rosenthal (New Brunswick, N.J.: Eagleton Institute of Politics, Rutgers University, 1979), 164.
28. Harold W. Stanley, *Senate v. Governor, Alabama 1971* (University, Alabama: University of Alabama Press, 1975), 49.
29. The meeting, attended by the author, took place on June 20, 1986.
30. Charles G. Bell and Charles M. Price, *California Government Today*, 2d ed. (Homewood, Ill.: Dorsey Press, 1984), 226; Richard J. Carlson, "The Office of the Governor," in *Inside State Government: A Primer for Illinois Managers*, ed. James D. Nowlan (Urbana, Ill.: Institute of Government and Public Affairs, University of Illinois, 1982), 28; and Maginnis, *The Last Hayride*, 7.
31. Cited in *St. Petersburg Times*, September 7, 1987.
32. Malcolm E. Jewell, "The Governor as a Legislative Leader," in The *Governor in Behavioral Perspective*, ed. Thad Beyle and J. Oliver Williams (New York: Harper & Row, 1972), 139; Maginnis, *The Last Hayride*, 22; and Malcolm E. Jewell and Penny M. Miller, *The Kentucky Legislature: Two Decades of Change* (Lexington: University Press of Kentucky, 1988), 234.
33. National Governors' Association, *Reflections on Being Governor*, 210.
34. Maginnis, *The Last Hayride*, 96.
35. James David Barber, "Leadership Strategies for Legislative Party Cohesion," *Journal of Politics* 28 (May 1966): 350-355.
36. Jewell, "The Governor as a Legislative Leader," 129.
37. Bowermaster, *Governor*, 116.
38. Thad L. Beyle and Lynn R. Muchmore, "Governors in the Federal System," in *Being Governor: The View from the Office*, ed. Thad L. Beyle and Lynn R. Muchmore (Durham, N.C.: Duke Press Policy Studies, 1983), 17.
39. Lynn R. Muchmore and Thad L. Beyle, "The Governor as Party Leader," in *Being Governor*, 50.
40. Joan A. Parker, *Summit and Resolution: The Illinois Tax Increase of 1983* (Springfield, Ill.: Sangamon State University, 1984), 2.
41. Jewell, "The Governor as a Legislative Leader," 131.
42. Sidney Wise, *The Legislative Process in Pennsylvania*, 2d ed. (Harrisburg, Pa.: Bipartisan Management Committee, House of Representatives, 1984), 88.
43. Thad L. Beyle, "The Governor as Chief Legislator," in *Being Governor*, 142.
44. National Governors' Association, *Governing the American States: A Handbook for New Governors* (Washington, D.C.: Center for Policy Research, NGA, November 1978), 187.
45. Larry Sabato, *Goodbye to Good-Time Charlie*, 2d ed. (Washington, D.C.: CQ Press, 1983), 33-40; Randall, "From Big Shot to Boss," 34.
46. Madeleine Kunin, Address to the Center for the American Woman and

Politics Forum for Women State Legislators, San Diego, Calif., November 19-22, 1987.
47. Sabato, *Goodbye to Good-Time Charlie*, 102-105.
48. Ibid., 81; Rosenthal, *The Governor and the Legislature*, 68, and Rosenthal, "The Governor and the Legislature," 155.
49. Bowermaster, *Governor*, 83, 114.
50. Data furnished by Thad Beyle.
51. Richard Zeiger, "Will Deukmejian Freeze Out Bill Honig?" *California Journal*, September 1987, 443.
52. David R. Colburn and Richard K. Scher, *Florida's Gubernatorial Politics in the Twentieth Century* (Tallahassee: University Presses of Florida, 1980), 114.
53. Unpublished manuscript, "Legislator," by George W. Scott.
54. Wise, *The Legislative Process in Pennsylvania*, 89.
55. Howard Troxler, in *Tampa Tribune*, August 9, 1987.
56. Randolph Pendleton, in *Florida Times Union*, January 31, 1988.
57. Rosenthal, *The Governor and the Legislature*, 23.
58. National Governors' Association, *Transition and the New Governor*, 31.
59. Sarah P. McCally, "The Governor and His Legislative Party," *American Political Science Review* 60 (December 1966): 923-942.
60. Rosenthal, *The Governor and the Legislature*, 47; *Salt Lake Tribune* Poll, as reported in *New York Times*, February 28, 1987.
61. Samuel C. Patterson, "Iowa," in *The Political Life of the American States*, 87.
62. Rick Sinding, "The New Tom Kean: A Greg Stevens Production," *New Jersey Reporter*, October 1983, 12-17. Data on the New Jersey governor's job performance ratings are from *Star Ledger*/Eagleton Poll, Eagleton Institute of Politics, Rutgers University. Not every governor's personality would sell as well. A former member of the staff of New Jersey governor William Cahill (1970-1974) remarked, "If I sent Cahill out [around the state] every day he'd be in a fight every day."
63. *St. Petersburg Times*, January 1, 1989; Mason-Dixon Poll of July 22-24, 1989, as reported in *Miami Herald*, July 28, 1989.
64. National surveys, sponsored by the Council of State Governments and the Martin School of Public Administration of the University of Kentucky, in 1987 and 1988 asked citizens how they would rate the job their governor was doing and how they would rate the job their legislature was doing. The positive ("excellent" and "good") ratings of the governor were 76.5 percent in 1987 and 71.8 percent in 1988. The positive ratings of the legislature were 65.4 percent and 63.8 percent in the two years. A national poll may underestimate the disparity in the popularity of many governors and legislatures, in their own states.
65. According to a poll by the Marist Institute of Public Opinion, *New York Times*, May 25, 1989.
66. Boston-Globe/WBZ Poll, March 1989, as reported in *Boston Globe*, April 3, 1989.
67. Bert A. Rockman, "Legislative-Executive Relations and Legislative Oversight," in *Handbook of Legislative Research*, ed. Gerhard Lowenberg, Samuel C. Patterson, and Malcolm E. Jewell (Cambridge, Mass.: Harvard University Press, 1985), 536.
68. Bowermaster, *Governor*, 137, 277.
69. *Orlando Sentinel Star*, January 30, 1986.

3

The Resurgent Legislature

The power of the governor is impressive, raising the question of how the legislature can possibly compete. The fact is that the legislature can and does compete, because it has a firm base for exercising power. Moreover, as an institution the legislature has changed dramatically in the past twenty years. It has new capacity and a revived sense of independence, which make it willing to come into contest with the executive. And the widening gap between the perspective of the legislature and that of the governor makes conflict even more likely. In the not-so-special case of divided government, in which the governor is saddled with the additional burden of dealing with one or both houses of the legislature under control of the opposite party, additional conflict is unavoidable. Finally, increasing fragmentation within the legislature compounds the problems that a governor faces in trying to exert leadership.

COUNTERVAILING POWER

On April 4, 1988, the Arizona senate rendered its decision in the trial of Governor Evan Mecham on three articles of impeachment. It convicted him on two of them—trying to block an investigation into an alleged death threat made by a state official, and misusing proceeds from his inaugural ball to pay off campaign debts. The action of impeachment by the house and conviction by the senate would appear to demonstrate the ultimate power of the legislature. Yet the case of Mecham is practically unique: Only three other governors have suffered a similar fate in the twentieth century. Impeached, convicted, and removed from office were Democrats William Sulzer of New York in 1913, John Walton of

Oklahoma in 1923, and Henry S. Johnston of Oklahoma in 1929. Impeachment is a rare occurrence; it is seldom even threatened by a legislature, and it is certainly not the way legislatures keep governors in line.

Legislative power vis-à-vis governors must stem from sources other than this ultimate recourse. The legislature's ability to prevail in a battle of wills, by means of overriding a gubernatorial veto, may be one such source of legislative power. In Utah, for example, most of Democratic governor Scott Matheson's vetoes during his years in office were overridden by a Republican legislature. That showed substantial power. The override certainly is used more frequently than impeachment, but it too is relatively rare. It is of marginal utility only, in the power relationship between the legislature and the governor.

The principal source of the legislature's power with regard to the governor stems from the legislature's ability to block the executive. That is its real check. Legislatures can modify, delay, reject, badger, and frustrate governors, and can stop them from doing what they want to do. Any governor who has policy proposals to enact into law or spending priorities to put into effect has to reach agreement with the legislature. Bills must be enacted and a budget must be passed by the legislature. Whatever else governors have, they need the cooperation of their legislatures too. Thomas Kean of New Jersey learned that lesson before he took office. "If my ten years in the state assembly had taught me anything," he recalled in his second term as chief executive, "it was that a legislature can hamstring a governor." [1] The legislature has the power to block the governor if enough members agree on that as a goal and if they have sufficient determination to pursue it.

As long as the governor wants something, the legislature will be in a position to bargain. The more he or she wants, the stronger the legislative position. The less the governor wants, the weaker the legislative position. The legislature cannot threaten with opposition or hold proposals hostage in return for gubernatorial largesse, if the governor has no proposals to bargain against. Any governor who wants anything at all, however, must come to terms with the legislature.

Most governors, even conservative ones who do not believe in activist government, have agendas to accomplish. This is because governors are viewed by the press, the political community, the public, and posterity in terms of the success in the legislature of their legislative programs. "The judgment," according to Brendan Byrne of New Jersey, "will be on the major things you've accomplished." Often accomplishment can be measured, particularly by the press, in terms of the number of a governor's proposals that are enacted. That implies that how effectively governors deal with the legislature often will determine the success of their entire administration. And the legislative effectiveness of governors normally will be based on the number or percentage of their proposals enacted. The governor's scoreboard or "batting average" standard is a deceptive one, however. It does not distinguish qualitative aspects of the measures proposed. The governor may have won the little ones, but lost the big ones. Moreover, the measures presented by governors may be tailored to fit whatever they think the legislature will accept. After all, governors decide what to take on. They and their staff list the successes after each legislative session; they talk about what they achieved, not what they failed to achieve; they put spin on the record. Nonetheless, people judge by the numbers. As deficient as it may be, students of the subject believe that the "batting average" is still the best index of the governor's ability to deal with the legislature.[2] For better or worse, it is the one that is most commonly used.

Besides seeking the positive judgment of their contemporaries, governors are interested in monuments. They want to leave behind something visible when they depart from office. Usually, that means some initiative has to be enacted into law. Construction projects, as a visible reminder to future generations of the chief executive responsible for them, are ideal, but something less tangible may also serve. In New Jersey, for example, Brendan Byrne wanted to be remembered for the Pinelands Preservation Act, which he steered through the legislature, rather than for the sports complex at the Meadowlands or for the casinos at Atlantic City. His successor, Thomas Kean, wanted to be remembered for educational reform. If Byrne, Kean, and other governors are to have the place they wish in the history of their states, they have to come to terms with their legislatures. Their need to achieve furnishes the legislature with its principal power, the ability to keep them from doing so.

A STRONGER INSTITUTION

Because of their strategic positions, legislatures have the potential to share power with the chief executive. Yet until recently legislatures have had difficulty making use of their potential. In most places they were weak, playing second fiddle to the governor—if they played in the orchestra at all. When the Eagleton Institute surveyed legislators in Maryland (1968), Connecticut (1970), and Arkansas (1972) about the respective strength of the executive and legislative branches, it found that 60, 73, and 72 percent respectively perceived the governor to be stronger, while the rest were divided between those who thought the two branches were equal and the few who thought the legislature was stronger.

Not only were they dominated by the executive, but also legislatures were deficient in the capacity required of twentieth-century political institutions. With few exceptions, they met in antiquated facilities, had insufficient time to do the job, lacked professional assistance, and were in dire need of structural and procedural overhaul. According to a leading political scientist at the time, "state legislatures may be our most extreme example of institutional lag." [3] Without sufficient capacity, legislatures could not share equally in governance with chief executives and state bureaucracies. Consequently, they rarely initiated major policies of their own; rather, they responded as best they could to those initiated by the executive. They engaged in only cursory review of budgets, leaving it to the executive to determine how much would be expended and on what. They had little idea of how programs were being conducted and how well they were really working; instead, legislatures trusted the running of government to the tender mercies of administrators in the various state departments and agencies.

LEGISLATIVE REFORM

It is possible that state legislatures would have remained largely unchanged had it not been for the reapportionment revolution of the 1960s. Starting with *Baker v. Carr* (1962), the entire basis of legislative representation changed. The effects were dramatic, as redistricting proved catalytic in states across the nation. Although political scientists have been unable to establish a firm connection between reapportionment and policy outcomes in particular places, they have shown resulting changes in the group and partisan balance in legislatures and changes in districts and members. A new type of legislator came upon the scene—lawyers and other professionals, activists who were interested in the reform of government. The composition of legislatures changed dramatically, and for the better.

Take the case of Florida, which underwent a major transformation in membership in 1966-1967. Although the legislature had managed to reapportion itself, the U.S. Supreme Court in *Swann v. Adams* (1967) decided that it was still malapportioned. The Court declared the previous year's elections invalid and ordered another election based on a new formula. In this election Republicans gained, and more important, the legislature shifted away from rural control and domination by the so-called "porkchoppers." When the legislature convened in April 1967, many of the members were new, with about one-third of the senate and over half the house first elected in the special elections two or five months before.[4] As described by a legislative member of that period:

These were new faces thrust into an old institution, without ties—no ties to the leadership, no ties to the lobbyists, no ties to the old Cabinet officers who had been there from time immemorial. They were brand new on the scene and they felt they were taking a fresh look at the institutions [of government].[5]

These newcomers soon acquired power and learned how to use it, working successfully to modernize the legislature, the executive branch, and the judiciary. In its 1968 session, the Florida legislature adopted a new constitution, which was ratified by the voters later that year. No sooner had the constitution been adopted than the legislature moved to strengthen itself vis-à-vis the governor.[6]

The legislative reform movement began in the late 1960s, although in a few cases—notably that of the California assembly led by Speaker Jesse Unruh—reform started earlier. The principal impetus for reform was reapportionment and the new crop of legislators and dynamic young leaders who insisted on providing themselves with the tools needed to exercise power responsibly. Other factors also contributed to the reform movement that swept the states in the late 1960s and 1970s (and which continues in some states, such as Nevada, even today).

A number of organizations and groups turned their energies to state legislatures, and their efforts made a difference. Important in this respect was the support of private foundations, principally the Ford Foundation and the Carnegie Corporation, which funded seminars, conferences, and studies. The American Assembly held regional and national conferences and published a volume of essays sounding the clarion call for reform.[7] The National Municipal League put the subject on its agenda. The American Political Science Association embarked on a state legislative service project, preparing manuals for legislators in about one-fourth of the states. The National Legislative Conference, which included legislators and legislative staff as members (and later merged with two other groups into the National Conference of State Legislatures), used its councils to promote reform from within.

The Eagleton Institute of Politics at Rutgers University was an academic group that expressed concern with the state of state legislatures in the mid 1960s. As the research and development arm of the National Conference of State Legislative Leaders, it was commissioned by the legislatures to conduct studies of the organization and procedures in Rhode Island, Maryland, Florida, Connecticut, Mississippi, Wisconsin, and Arkansas and to make recommendations for reform. The institute also held annual conferences, from 1966 to 1975, for specially selected legislators from the fifty states. Many of the 431 legislators who attended these conferences over the decade, upon their return to their states, played key roles in achieving legislative reform.

As much as any other national organization in the late 1960s, the Citizens Conference on State Legislatures (CCSL) was influential in promoting reform. It helped organize and then collaborated with citizen commissions in states around the country, participated in running seminars for legislative leaders, and conducted a program to increase the public's awareness of the need for legislative improvement. The endeavor for which CCSL will long be remembered, however, was its study evaluating and ranking state legislatures from 1 to 50 on the basis of their functionality, accountability, information-handling capacity, independence, representativeness, and overall.[8] The legislatures that ranked highest—those of California, New York, and Illinois were 1, 2, and 3—made no complaints. But those that ranked low were critical of CCSL's study, and with good reason, since the basis for the specific items rated, the positive and negative directions, the weights applied, and the scores awarded were all highly questionable.

Whatever the methodology, the evaluation had a profound political impact. In response, many legislatures took steps to modernize, and thereby to raise their rankings. More than a decade after the CCSL report was issued, the Advisory Commission on Intergovernmental Relations (ACIR) assessed the changes made in the years following the evaluation study. Much had happened. Of the seventy-three recommendations proposed by CCSL, legislatures changed significantly in regard to thirty-eight and made little or no change on five, while thirty others could not be assessed by ACIR because of a lack of information.[9]

LEGISLATIVE CAPACITY

As a result of the coordination of legislator-insiders and citizen-outsiders, the reform movement succeeded in producing major change in many legislatures and at least modest change in others. Undoubtedly, the most observable and lasting effect of reform has been the rise in legislative capacity, which is based mainly on increased time, better organization, and more staff assistance.[10]

Legislatures spend considerably more time at the job than they did earlier, and they make more effective use of it. First of all, the amount of time they spend in session has increased. In 1960 the legislatures of only eighteen states met annually, while those in thirty-two states met every two years. Today, in contrast, forty-three legislatures—by formal or informal arrangement—meet every year, while only seven are still on biennial schedules. Special sessions provide additional time for members to work at their trade.

Just how many days they meet is another important question. Constitutions in thirty-two states limit the length of legislative sessions, in one way or another, but in the rest the number of days spent in session has risen steadily into the 1980s. Increasing work loads and pressures, moreover, have spurred legislatures to use time more efficiently. Consequently, they have begun to set deadlines for bill-drafting requests, introductions, committee action, and so forth. One of the greatest advances has been the use of the interim—the period between one legislative session and the next—for work by standing and special committees. Taking into account regular and special sessions and interims, legislatures spend considerably more time on the job than they used to.

Furthermore, legislatures now are organized more effectively than before, especially in terms of their committee systems. Twenty years ago, although standing committees could be found in every legislative chamber, with few exceptions they were primarily paper committees. They did little to review and revise bills referred to them and were far from being the focal point of the legislative process that they are today. Since legislative reform, committee systems virtually everywhere have been overhauled. In some places the overhaul has been accompanied by a reduction in the number of committees. In some it has meant a reduction in the number of assignments for legislators. Both changes seem to have made a positive difference.

The example of Maryland's consolidation of committees is instructive. Before the general assembly reduced the number of committees, only half the members of the legislature had meaningful assignments. With consolidation, committees became more representative of groups in the state, and they achieved a broader jurisdiction and balance. Members no longer felt themselves relegated to the sidelines but considered that by means of their committee assignments they had a piece of the action. Meetings of the committees were fairly well attended, and the public seemed satisfied. All of this led to the development of a system whereby members were expected to support committee-reported bills on second reading (although they could defect on third reading), permitting decisions to be made in committees and helping legislative leaders exercise managerial control.

Today, committees nearly everywhere are truly the workhorses of the legislature, allowing a division of labor, opportunities for members, a degree of specialization, more intensive scrutiny of substantive matters, and a broader distribution of influence within the legislature. The contemporary significance of committees is shown in a recent survey of two thousand legislators, who were asked to rank, from the eight alternatives offered to them, the three most important decision-making arenas in the legislature. Almost two-thirds of the respondents ranked regular committee meetings first, second, or third, just below the presiding officers and majority leaders.[11]

Probably more than any other single factor, the expansion of professional staffing is responsible for the increase in legislative capacity. Although the professional staffing of legislatures began half a century ago, with legislative reference bureaus and legislative councils, it was not until the 1960s that substantial growth began to take place. The modern system of professional staffing developed first in California, and within a decade it was being adopted across the nation. By the outset of the 1980s, there were sixteen thousand full-time, year-round staff members—professional, administrative, clerical—working for legislatures throughout the country. California and New York each had seven hundred full-time professionals, Florida and Michigan five hundred each, and Pennsylvania and Texas four hundred apiece. Currently, there are twenty thousand full-time, year-round staff members. California has 1,773 full-time professionals, New York 2,140, Florida 1,013, and Texas 912, after substantial increases in recent years.[12]

Staff members today perform an assortment of tasks, including bill drafting, policy research, fiscal analysis, and postaudit or program evaluation. Because of the assistance they render, the legislative process works better than before, with greater attention and continuity of concern being devoted to both major and minor issues. Although staff is the major currency with which a legislature buys independence from the executive, no single reform taken alone accounts for the contemporary spirit of legislative independence. Nothing happens in isolation, and a combination of factors usually makes the difference. In Connecticut the Legislative Management Act of 1969, creating the Joint Legislative Management Committee and several staff agencies, was a critical event. In Maryland the consolidation of committees, accompanied by the assignment of staff support, made a difference. (Maryland's new office building for delegates, it should be noted, was designed with only six committee meeting rooms. Thus, any expansion of the standing committee system would not be feasible, and the consolidation of committees could not easily be reversed.)

THE SPIRIT OF INDEPENDENCE

Reform's effects, and particularly those on public policy, are not easily measurable. Yet the question is frequently asked, Has legislative reform led to better public policy? The answer is probably yes, but the case is impossible to prove.

Whatever the effects of legislative modernization, they have been qualitative in their nature and indirect in their route. Samuel Patterson is one political scientist who speculates that legislative reforms, or at least some of them, have had as their principal result making legislators feel better.[13] Their impact, according to this view, has been primarily therapeutic. Even if this were the case, such an effect should not be underestimated.

Without doubt, a sense of efficacy accompanied the strengthening of legislative institutions. As legislatures developed professionally, increasing their capacity, legislators began to feel that their institutions should be independent of the governor and the executive branch. They began to take their state constitutions and checks-and-balances theory more seriously than before. "If the legislature is to perform its constitutional mandate," declared Speaker John Martin of Maine, one of the legislative leaders in the reform movement, "it must continually assert its status as a coequal branch of government with the executive." [14] Legislators had become jealous of their rightful prerogatives, believing that they, and not the governor, had primary responsibility for setting public policy. They had become concerned, moreover, that the executive had encroached on the legislature; and they began thinking that they had to challenge the governor, lest the constitutional balance shift further against them.

GUBERNATORIAL IMPETUS

In some places the emergence of the spirit of legislative independence was facilitated by governors themselves, especially governors of the opposite party. In those states dominated by the Democratic party, the election of Republican governors galvanized the legislature. The election of Linwood Holton (1970-1974) had much to do with the development of a stronger legislature in Virginia. "I think the legislature was much too submissive to governors in the past," commented the majority leader of the Virginia house. "We won't ever go back to that," he insisted. "It doesn't matter whether the governor is Democratic or Republican, we won't go back." [15]

The situation was similar in Kentucky, where the advent of a Republican chief executive—Louie Nunn (1967-1971)—marked the beginning of a movement toward an independent legislature. Shortly after Nunn took office the general assembly created an interim committee system and a consolidation of standing committees in the house from about seventy to fifteen. In 1970 the appropriations and revenue committees undertook their first review of the budget, with one staff person. Until then, the governor's budget had gone right to the floor. When Nunn was succeeded by strong Democratic governors, Wendell Ford (1971-1974) and Julian Carroll (1974-1979), the balance swung back to the executive. But the Kentucky general assembly had had a taste of independence and persevered. A permanent legislative budget staff was established in 1978. A new timetable for legislative elections and sessions, established by constitutional amendment and adopted in 1979, helped diminish gubernatorial influence by taking legislative elections out of the gubernatorial election year. Legislative leaders had formerly been chosen at a prelegislative conference at the beginning of the governor's term, and the governor had selected the legislative leaders. Under the new calendar, the legislative leaders were elected at an organizational session in January of odd-numbered years, with biennial sessions held in even-numbered years. Thus, when a new governor took office, the legislative leaders would already have been chosen and in office for a full year. As a consequence of this and "because the legislature has grown more professional and more powerful, whereas there has been less change in the governorship," in Kentucky there is now "a more even balance of legislative-gubernatorial power." [16]

In Florida, too, legislative independence was spurred by the election in 1966 of the first Republican governor in about one hundred years. Claude Kirk's (1967-1971) relationship with the Democratic legislature, and even with members of his own party, was a stormy one. According to a former legislator, Governor Kirk deserves some of the credit for what happened to the Florida legislature:

> It was Claude Kirk, really, that forced the Florida Legislature to finally decide we had to be an equal party in the process in Tallahassee. And basically what he did was he scared the hell out of the Democrats who had had it up there for over a hundred years. . . . Claude Kirk . . . didn't mean to do it now, but nevertheless, he was the catalyst that pushed us over the top.[17]

One incident, perhaps more than any other, aroused the legislature and stimulated its independent spirit. It involved an increase in legislative salaries. The legislature had decided to raise its pay from $1,200 a year to $12,000. The step had been agreed to by senate and house and by the majority and minority. The pay raise passed, but then Kirk vetoed the bill. In doing so, he breached an agreement with his own minority leader in the house, recalled a former senator. "At that point, House, Senate, minority, and majority all got together and as an institution we asserted our independence." The Republican leader even took the floor to apologize to his colleagues, "who took my word for the word of the man downstairs that what just happened would not occur." [18] The legislature easily overrode the veto; the Republicans remained estranged from their governor; and the Florida legislature went on to develop into one of the strongest such bodies in the nation.

Governors from time to time promoted legislative independence by trying to block legislative reforms. This happened in Connecticut, where Democratic governor John Dempsey had had little difficulty dominating the Democratic-controlled general assembly. In late 1967 the legislature commissioned the Eagleton Institute to conduct a study of its organization and procedures. On the basis of recommendations made in that study, the legislature in 1969 passed a reform package that was recognized as its declaration of independence. Governor Dempsey objected, and he vetoed the act. His veto, however, was overridden by unanimous votes in both the house and senate, an unprecedented occurrence. The veto and its override served to unite both parties in support of the legislative institution—a rare display of bipartisanship in what otherwise was, and continues to be, a very partisan state.

The New York legislature also has come a long way since the time when it lacked the will and resources to go up against the executive. Governors Alfred Smith (1923-1929), Thomas E. Dewey (1943-1955), and Averell Harriman (1955-1959) had the upper hand, and Nelson Rockefeller predominated through his several administrations. But even during the Rockefeller era, as two political scientists pointed out, absolute gubernatorial control was not the case. The legislature had acquired the capacity to stand up to the governor, and legislative leaders, even those of the governor's party, took an independent public stance. During Rockefeller's ascendancy, the legislature kept strengthening itself, "perhaps as a defense against his strong leadership style." A stronger legislature was, ironically, one of the legacies that New York's most powerful governor left to his successors.[19]

LEGISLATIVE INSECURITY

The legislature's sense of independence is also fed by the egos of legislators who compare themselves to governors. They see governors as imperious. A legislative leader in New York spoke for many of his colleagues when he remarked: "Relating to governors is like relating to the Pope, except that the only thing you have to kiss on the Pope is his ring." Legislators see themselves in the trenches with bayonets fixed, while governors shout orders from far behind the lines. The late Jesse Unruh, who served as speaker of the assembly and then treasurer of California, tells an amusing story to illustrate legislative resentment:

> [This is] the story that I think best describes the difference between the executive branch and the legislative branch: There were three sailors who shipwrecked on this Aleutian Island and they were out ashore with nothing except the little kit of carpenter tools and a lot of driftwood. So they built a little "lean-to" to shelter themselves from the

inclement weather, but pretty soon they were starving. The only animal life on the entire island were these huge, ferocious kodiak bears and they decided they had to kill one of them . . . and thought the only chance they had to kill one was to slip up on one of these animals when he was asleep. So they drew lots and one fella took the knife and went out across the frozen tundra and came across this bear in an ice wallow, slipped up on him and made a lunge at him with a knife. The bear woke up and rolled over. . . . So this fella, turns and runs for the hut as fast as he can go. The bear is about three jumps behind, but by the time he gets to the front door the bear closed this down to one jump. This guy runs in the front door right on through the back door and says to his colleagues, "Get him fellas! I'm going back for another one."

And, I couldn't help but think that's the way the governor brings in his message to the legislature. He says, "Here is this year's budget. Get him fellas! I'm going back and prepare next year's." [20]

Governors sometimes feed legislative insecurities, although they may do so unwittingly. They claim credit for what legislators believe they themselves have achieved. Rudy Perpich, for example, travels around Minnesota after a legislative session talking about his administration's accomplishments (which the legislature sees as its own). When he visited New Prague, the hometown of house speaker Robert Vanasek, the governor announced a Main Street improvement project funded in the transportation bill passed by the legislature. Not only did the governor thus slight Vanasek, who had helped shepherd the bill through the legislature, but he also mispronounced Vanasek's name repeatedly in his speech to the local luminaries.[21]

Whether legislators acknowledge it or not, there is more than a dash of jealousy in their attitude toward governors. Few legislators do not aspire to gubernatorial office, and few do not believe that they could do as good a job as the incumbent. The problem, as they see it, is that they have not been as fortunate—lucky, well endowed, or strategically connected—and the opportunity has not come their way. Furthermore, with the professionalization of political careers, more and more legislators scan the horizons for higher office. As ambitious politicians, legislators would like to be where the governor is. New Jersey's legislative leaders are particularly susceptible to the lure of gubernatorial office. Some of them even get a taste of it while serving in the legislature. Because the state has no lieutenant governor, the line of succession is, first, the president of the senate and second, the speaker of the assembly. When the governor is out of the state, the senate president assumes office as acting governor, with the power to sign bills, command executive staff, and use the governor's state trooper, car, and helicopter. If the governor is one who travels frequently, as both governors Byrne and Kean did, legislative leaders soon grow accustomed to the position. The question, "Why shouldn't I be governor?" comes easily.

No matter how much stronger legislatures have become, legislators still suffer from an inferiority complex. That is because they see themselves as individuals rather than as an institution. Individually, they are no match for the governor. The tension between legislators and the executive in Illinois, as explained by a former legislative staff member and agency director, illustrates the point:

> A lot of it, I think, comes from the fact that most legislators are dependent on the governor and the executive branch for issues and information, and they resent it. Despite all the legislative staff and all the various committees and commissions, in the end the agencies run the government, and all legislators—and legislative staff—can do is try to keep up.[22]

Legislatures, according to this view, are still subordinate to governors, and that makes them even more assertive than otherwise. Subordinate or not, today's legislatures "do not want it to appear they are being pushed around by the Governor."[23] They used to be happy to serve their governor, but no longer. Instead of saying, "What cliff does the governor want me to jump off today?" they now say, "What cliff are we going to push the governor off today?"

Legislative leaders understand that power is a finite commodity. "The power pie," according to a former majority leader in the Wisconsin senate, "never gets larger"—but it can be divided differently. Thus, an increase of power to the governor can only come about by decreasing the power of the legislature.[24] From leadership's perspective, it may be necessary to assert and reassert independence. This entails the exercise of power in an actual contest with the executive. Wisconsin's Democratic speaker, Tom Loftus, has had a tumultuous relationship with Republican governor Tommy Thompson. Although aspiring to gubernatorial office himself, Loftus has become a firm believer in the assertion of legislative authority. He asks how one can induce the legislature to exercise its powers in order to demonstrate to the executive and to legislators themselves that they are coequal. His concern is that legislative muscle will atrophy if it is not used from time to time. "If you see *a justifiable* opportunity to slap the governor around," Loftus maintains, "do it." That way the leader can show members that they have power. "The governor will rant and rave, and criticize. He or she will use the bully pulpit to vilify the leaders. Your mother will call you and ask why you didn't do what the governor wanted." But the point will have been made, Loftus insists, and the spirit of independence will have been reinvigorated.[25]

THE CLASH OF PERSPECTIVES

The increasing tug and pull between the legislative and executive branches of government is exacerbated by the widening gap between their perspectives. If one wants to understand why governors and legislatures compete and come into conflict, the differences in perspectives have to be taken into account. As people move from one job to the other, from legislator to governor, they see the world very differently than they did before. As a result, they quickly change their stripes. Madeleine Kunin, a former legislator, reflects that on being elected governor of Vermont, "I had truly walked out of one branch of government through an open door, shut it behind me and opened a new door to another chamber." She no doubt benefited from her experience in the legislature, but "a different perspective, a different responsibility does take over."[26]

The most significant differences to be kept in mind are the following.

1. *The district/state difference.* The governor's electorate and constituency comprise the entire state. Each legislator's electorate and constituency lie within his or her district. Wisconsin's Thompson describes the contrast: "Now instead of representing 47,000 people as I did in my assembly district, I represent 4,750,000 people with divergent views and I have to widen my scope." Governors must concern themselves with the needs and preferences of people throughout the state, while legislators are required to attend only to public opinion within their own districts. This difference in representation leads to differences in policy positions, since constituency opinion may be out of line with state opinion and district interests may not be identical with statewide interests. For example, when he was in the Wisconsin legislature, Thompson opposed seatbelt legislation; as governor, he has threatened to veto any repeal of it.[27] Governors and legislators also represent different interests, as shown by the 1971 budget battle in New York. Rockefeller gave first priority to the avoidance of business and income tax increases that might affect the state's ability to attract and retain industry. Legislative leaders and legislators, by contrast, gave priority to eliminating new automobile registration fees, the burden of which would fall on individual car owners in their districts.[28]

2. *The special interest/general interest difference.* The question is whether legislators from narrow constituencies can behave other than parochially, particularly if they want to be reelected. Chief executives can and do: They try to define a public interest that is separate and distinguishable from the sum of parochial interests. A legislator's stock in trade, by contrast, is parochial and special interests. An illustration of

this difference is the so-called "beer bill" (AB1500) in California, where the governor was better able than the legislature to withstand special-interest pressure. In the legislature, an intense, organized special interest—the beer wholesalers who wanted exclusive-territory contracts—could triumph over a relatively apathetic and poorly organized public interest. Not so in the executive branch—the governor vetoed the bill.[29]

3. *The piecemeal/comprehensive difference.* Legislators are less likely to consider policy comprehensively, while governors are somewhat more apt to do so. A policy or program for the governor is frequently broad-gauged and thematic. A policy or program for legislators is whatever bills on a general subject receive majority support in both houses and are enacted. Often, policy is contained in an amendment to a bill or in a conference committee compromise. Legislators are very much involved at the operational level of policy making, while governors are further removed and can better see the bigger picture. A former legislator from Washington makes the distinction in the domain of revenues. Legislators, he points out, prefer the "chicken plucking method of taxation"—a little here, a little there. Governors, by contrast, prefer income and sales taxes, the more general revenue producers.[30]

4. *The compromise/coherence difference.* Carl Van Horn and his colleagues draw a contrast between the legislative decision-making process of "cloak-room politics" and "chief-executive politics," the process dominated by governors.[31] The former, of course, consists of negotiations designed to overcome opposition, since the legislative task is to hack out a compromise. Governors also must compromise. Yet they give the appearance of offering the public coherent policies—and to some extent they do—while the legislature struggles to devise patchwork settlements. A legislative fiscal officer in Ohio distinguished between the two processes:

> A collective body also tends to waver and seek the solution of least resistance, whereas single-mindedness and steadfastness such as the executive possesses tend to surround an issue with an aura of rightness.[32]

5. *The short-range/long-range difference.* The legislative point of view is immediate, since the legislature is preoccupied with ensuring that bills are enacted before the session ends. Nearly everything revolves around processing legislation, and members are greatly concerned with promoting their own bills *now*. Little consideration can be given to what comes later or to whether the legislation will accomplish its objectives. The legislature is a problem-solving body, but the problem to be solved often becomes that of ensuring that a bill is enacted rather than the

original problem that gave rise to the bill's introduction. The executive also has to consider expediency, since persuading the legislature to adopt executive proposals is critical. Thus, Governor William Winter (1980-1984) of Mississippi, encouraged by people rallying around his thoughtful program for higher education, still had to keep his eye on concrete educational goals. "Proposals that are viewed as too esoteric or visionary," he cautioned, "cause legislative eyes to glaze over." [33] Despite practical constraints, the executive can, and often does, take a longer point of view. As the chief of staff to a governor in a New England state commented, "The legislature lives in the here and now, while the governor has to look to tomorrow."

6. *The collective responsibility/individual responsibility difference.* Legislators share responsibility; no individual member bears it fully. Moreover, the complicated nature of the process is such that legislators can pass the buck—from committee to committee, from party to party, from rank and file to leadership, from house to senate or from senate to house. And buck passing is not at all uncommon, since few legislators want to make enemies or take blame. Legislators, moreover, can adopt ideological positions and, as long as their constituents are like-minded, not worry about the practical implications. They can also spend freely, seeking appropriations for their districts and their pet programs, since individually they do not have to shoulder responsibility for the overall budget. Reciprocity is implicit in the legislative process: "If you vote for my money bill, I'll vote for yours." Governors question the will of legislators to hold the fiscal line. Thomas Kean is very critical of the New Jersey legislature, which he believes by its very nature overspends. Because they are accountable only to their districts and have to face frequent elections, Kean points out that "members tend to talk economy but vote for every spending measure that might conceivably benefit a constituent" If the governor won't say no, according to him, no one else will.[34]

Unlike legislators, governors cannot easily evade responsibility. The buck normally stops at their desks. The electorate holds them accountable; so do the media that empowers the executive in its relationship with the legislature. Madeleine Kunin, a former legislator who has served as governor of Vermont since 1985, describes her role:

> No longer can I run for cover or take comfort in the will of the majority, or blame the recalcitrant behavior of the other party for things that go awry.... Nor can I blame the leadership, the other house, the mean-spirited chairman of a specific committee, nor alas, can I blame the arrogant, uncaring, politically motivated executive branch.

A legislator, Kunin points out, can advocate further funding for child care, for social workers, for special education, as she did when she was in the House. But as governor, she must make choices, constrained by the need to balance expenditures with revenues. Legislators, furthermore, have the luxury of an outside perspective even though they are consummate insiders. They do not have to run the government or administer programs, and they can take pot shots at the executive for whatever goes wrong. As a legislator, Kunin points out, one has the freedom to say: "Why don't they fix that? Why don't they change that? Why don't you just throw them out?" But as governor, "it is your administration and everything that happens within it is yours and you are responsible for it." [35] Legislators may have to make policy, but governors must make policy work.

DIVIDED GOVERNMENT

The governor derives some advantage from the role of leader of the party, as was discussed in Chapter 2. But the executive must also deal with members of the opposition party, and, depending upon their numbers, their disposition, and their skill, the governor may run into trouble. Milton Shapp, who ran a large business before he became governor of Pennsylvania, thought being a corporate chairman was much easier than being chief executive of a state. Members of his board may have had different ideas than he did, but at least nobody on his board was working for a competitor. In Harrisburg, by contrast, Shapp explained, "I feel like I have 253 members on my board and almost half of them work for a competitor." [36] Suppose further that more than half work for a competitor—that is to say, that the opposition party controls the legislature or controls one house of the legislature.

If partisanship works to governors' advantage when their party has a majority in the legislature, it works to their disadvantage when their party is in the minority. Partisanship cuts both ways. When the same party controls both the executive and legislative branches, the principals have some incentive to reach agreement despite the institutional differences we have been discussing. But when government is divided, not only are there rivalries between separate institutions, but also there is likely to be greater conflict between opposing parties.

The trend since the 1960s has been toward divided party control of state government. This is attributable in part to candidate-centered campaigns for state legislatures and the increasing incidence of split-ticket voting. It is also attributable to the growth of the Republican party in the South and the victories of its gubernatorial candidates in a number of southern states and to gains made by Democrats in formerly Republican states, like Vermont and Indiana, in the North. Thus, by the beginning of 1990 power was divided in twenty-nine states, where the governor faced one or both houses of the legislature controlled by the opposition party. Partisan control of the states is shown in Table 3-1. In fifteen states Republican governors face a Democratic legislative majority (in thirteen of them the Democrats have a majority in each house); in fourteen states Democratic governors face a Republican legislative majority (in four of them the Republicans have a majority in each house).

The governor and the legislature are both affected by party control, but the former probably more so than the latter. Legislatures are more likely to make life difficult for opposition-party governors than the reverse. Over the years some governors have had a particularly difficult time in their dealings with partisan legislatures. For example, Cal Rampton (1965-1977) and Scott Matheson served back to back for twenty years (until 1985) as Democratic governors in the strongly Republican state of Utah. The Republican legislative majority was so large that it was practically veto-proof. Almost every time Matheson vetoed a bill, the legislature would call itself into session and override the veto. "There is absolutely nothing a governor can do about that," Matheson recalled. The only hope is that the public will grow tired of the practice and make changes through the election process. Democrat Richard Lamm, in Colorado, also suffered at the hands of a partisan, confrontational Republican legislature through most of his years in office. "If I want A, all of a sudden you find an amazing amount of support for Z. . . . The problem is that cooperation is looked upon by some Republicans as consorting with the enemy." For Lamm the tension between the two branches of government was systemic, but divided government had added the dimension of divisive competitiveness.[37] Some governors found it easier, possibly because of their personalities and their approaches. James Thompson of Illinois, for example, has had to deal with a Democratic legislature since 1977. But he and the legislature overall have had a good and productive working relationship.

Where the legislative majority party decides on a policy of confrontation—whether for policy or for electoral purposes—conflicting relationships will result, as in Utah and Colorado. When Thomas Kean was elected governor of New Jersey, the assembly speaker, Alan Karcher, pursued an oppositionist strategy. The Democrats opposed virtually every one of the governor's initial policy initiatives and fought him for an entire year on the budget. "I came to feel that if I came up with a cure for the common cold," Kean wrote, "Karcher and the Democrats would say, maybe that's okay, but let's hold two months of hearings on it."[38] After a while, however, the Democrats relented. They were losing their battle with Kean in the press and would probably lose

TABLE 3-1   Partisan Control of Legislatures and Governors, 1990

	Partisan Control of		
State	*Senate*	*House*	*Governor*
Alabama	D	D	R
Alaska	R	D	D
Arizona	R	R	D
Arkansas	D	D	D
California	D	D	R
Colorado	R	R	D
Connecticut	D	D	D
Delaware	D	R	R
Florida	D	D	R
Georgia	D	D	D
Hawaii	D	D	D
Idaho	R	R	D
Illinois	D	D	R
Indiana	R	D/R[a]	D
Iowa	D	D	R
Kansas	R	R	R
Kentucky	D	D	D
Louisiana	D	D	D
Maine	D	D	R
Maryland	D	D	D
Massachusetts	D	D	D
Michigan	R	D	D
Minnesota	D	D	D
Mississippi	D	D	D
Missouri	D	D	R
Montana	R	D	R
Nebraska	(Nonpartisan, unicameral)		R
Nevada	R	D	D
New Hampshire	R	R	R
New Jersey	D	D	D
New Mexico	D	D	R
New York	R	D	D
North Carolina	D	D	R
North Dakota	D	R	D
Ohio	R	D	D
Oregon	D	D	D
Pennsylvania	R	D	D
Rhode Island	D	D	R
South Carolina	D	D	R
South Dakota	R	R	R
Tennessee	D	D	D
Texas	D	D	R
Utah	R	R	R
Vermont	D	R	D
Virginia	D	D	D

TABLE 3-1   Continued

| State | Partisan Control of | | |
	Senate	*House*	*Governor*
Washington	R	D	D
West Virginia	D	D	D
Wisconsin	D	D	R
Wyoming	R	R	D

[a] Democrats and Republicans are tied 50-50, with parties sharing control.

in public opinion as well. They adopted a new strategy of compromise, and the pattern of executive-legislative relationships in New Jersey shifted substantially.

Conflict between an executive office controlled by one party and a legislative chamber controlled by the other may be grounded in philosophical and policy differences, but it is based immediately on partisan competition at the polls. Opposing parties have as a prime objective defeating each other in elections. To do this, each tries to discredit the other, not only during an election campaign but also during the conduct of government. Governor Shapp described how he fared at the hands of Republicans in the Pennsylvania general assembly:

> On many bills—not just budget bills, but many other bills of substance—they would rather see that bill go down to defeat, because it could hurt the current administration if it wasn't passed, than to have a bill passed that might redound to their own political disadvantage.

In state after state, politics prevailed, according to Shapp. "As long as you have a two-party system, and as long as you have states where legislatures are somewhat evenly divided, you are going to have this type of situation." [39]

As more states and more state legislatures have become competitive, partisan posturing and positioning and shifting blame back and forth have become part of the process. A minority party becomes extremely frustrated with its status and grows more partisan as a result. In California, where the Democrats have controlled the legislature—with little exception, for the past thirty years, partisanship has increased because of a militant group of Republicans (the "Proposition 13 babies" elected in 1978), the struggle over reapportionment, and the leadership style of Republican governor George Deukmejian. Conflict within the legislature and between the legislature and the governor, as reflected in members' positions on roll-call votes, has become fodder for the election campaigns. At times, too, the parties are so competitive that either can win a majority in the next election and thus the battle for control of the legislature is especially fierce.

The growth of the Republican party in the South has changed legislative politics substantially. In Virginia, house Republicans have learned to act as a bloc, and house Democrats in response are also acting more in concert. In Tennessee, too, house Republicans—who were content when they had Lamar Alexander (1979-1987) as governor—developed greater group identity and militancy when a Democrat won the governorship.

The rise of partisanship in Florida, associated with the Republican upsurge, is particularly striking. Currently, although the Democrats still lead the Republicans in voter registration, 35.9 percent to 30.0 percent, a larger number of Floridians identify as Republicans (41.0 percent) than as Democrats (32.5 percent).[40] The GOP has nearly 40 percent of the members of the house and threatens to take control of the senate within the near future. For some years Republicans organized as the minority party in the senate and the house, but only recently have the Democrats organized majority party offices in the two chambers.

Partisan opposition to the governor in the legislature revolves about the desires of both parties to gain electoral advantage. As leaders of their party statewide, governors and their programs are prime targets for the opposition. If the governor can be discredited, then the governor's legislative party will suffer as well and the possibility of the opposition gaining control or capturing seats will improve.

LEGISLATIVE FRAGMENTATION

At the 1988 annual meeting of the National Governors' Association, William Donald Schaefer spoke frankly of his troubles with the Maryland general assembly. "I got 188 governors," he complained.[41] The positive reaction of his colleagues indicated that they understood what he meant.

As was discussed in Chapter 2, one of the most striking contrasts between the two branches of state government is the unity of the governor on the one hand and the fragmentation of the legislature on the other. The legislature is composed of individuals, each of whom represents a different district and interests and has his or her own values and ambitions. Each responds uniquely to a particular governor. It is an oversimplification, therefore, to examine executive-legislative relations as such. The governor must deal not with a single institution but with the two parties, two houses, and a dizzying assortment of personalities that constitute the legislature.

Fragmentation is an endemic condition, for in any American legislature—and particularly the U.S. Congress[42]—power is highly decentralized. Some legislators have slightly more power and others slightly less, but essentially each elected representative has a vote and a say. Not only is the system fragmented, but also it may become more so, because centralizing tendencies are weakening.

FACTION AND RIVALRY

In addition to conflict between the parties, schisms within party ranks create particular difficulties for governors who want to exercise leadership. The disagreement may not be made public, but it can be sharp and even bitter on the inside. Iowa's Robert Ray, for example, found it easy to work with a legislature controlled by the opposition party. He preferred for disputes to become vocal and public rather than being kept under wraps. And he may indeed have had as difficult a time passing legislation through Republican legislatures as through Democratic ones.[43]

Factions exist within most legislative parties. In New York, for example, although the Democrats are dominated by members from urban areas and the Republicans by suburban interests, the former party has its reformers and regulars and the latter its conservatives and moderates, as well as geographical divisions. As governor, Michael Dukakis encountered the problem of legislative divisiveness in Massachusetts. "There are a lot of people who call themselves Democrats under the same umbrella," Dukakis observed. The Massachusetts General Court (as the legislature in the Bay State is officially termed) contains conservative Democrats, and urban, suburban, and rural Democrats, but few Republicans. "And when you've got majorities of four to one in the Legislature," Dukakis concludes, "I'm sure you recognize that that is by no means an unmitigated blessing." [44]

In a number of places governors have trouble establishing a firm base of support within the legislature. Dan Walker (1973-1977) of Illinois encountered not only the regional parochialism typical of many states, but also a permanently hostile coalition of Chicago mayor Richard Daley's loyalists. It was virtually impossible for the governor to put together a strong coalition of his own. Milton Shapp of Pennsylvania had similar problems trying to unite factions and to cultivate, with any consistency, a majority of Democrats. Consequently, the governor was confronted by a legislature that held a few supporters, a sizable bloc of opponents, a group of independents among his own partisans, and a united Republican contingent standing in opposition.[45]

Power is divided not only between the parties and within the parties but also between the house and the senate. The division may be reinforced by a split in partisan control, as in twelve states as of early 1990, or by a coalition of Democrats and Republicans in one or the other chamber. Even without partisan division, however, the house and senate are markedly different institutions and contestants for position and power. As a rule, the house is more partisan, the senate less so. Governors have to take the differences into account and be able to steer clear of the sometimes intense rivalry between the two bodies. Otherwise they can be caught in a perilous crossfire.

Just as legislators in general appear to be envious of governors, so members of the house (which is referred to by the uninitiated or insensitive as "the lower chamber") would appear to be envious of their senate colleagues. A member of the Washington house relates that when freshmen Democrats are oriented they are told that the Republicans are the opposition and the senate is the enemy. And a majority leader in the Evergreen State told a junior member, "The House considers the Senate a liquid waste landfill area." In Washington, at any rate, the two hundred feet across the rotunda from house to senate might just as well be two hundred miles.

Yet despite the derision that many representatives heap upon their senate colleagues, few pass up an opportunity to run for the senate. A seat in the senate, which in most places has a four-year term instead of two years and a larger constituency, is considered by practically any red-blooded American politician to be "higher office." That is attested to by the fact that never (or practically never) does a senator give up his or her seat to run for the house.

The house-senate rivalry in Florida serves as an example. With a legislative session beginning, it might seem that one of the house's main objectives is to embarrass the senate. Face-to-face discussions between the respective leaderships are few and far between, but considerations of what the senate is up to and how it can be thwarted form part of the house's continuing calculations. The objective is to pass more house bills through the senate than vice versa and to prevail in conference-committee negotiations on the budget. Since the late 1960s the split in Florida has been due partly to the progressivism of the house as compared with the conservatism of the senate, with both governors Askew and Graham aligned with the former against the latter.[46] Today the traditional rivalry between the two bodies is further complicated by the presence of a Republican governor, a coalition of conservative Democrats and Republicans in control of the senate, and a far stronger Republican contingent in the house.

CONGRESSIONALIZATION OF THE LEGISLATURE

Although the natural state of a representative assembly is fragmentation, in a number of respects legislatures are more fragmented today than twenty years ago when legislative reform was beginning.[47] Earlier, legislative leaders had more commanding positions and power was more tightly held. Partly as a consequence of modernization and reform, legislatures have been democratized, with resources more broadly distributed and the gap between leaders and rank and file narrower.

Committee systems have been strengthened. Now, standing committees are agencies of specialization, and the legislative workload is parceled out among them. Each committee rules over its own turf. Committee chairs have emerged as figures with whom lobbyists, department and agency heads, and even governors must reckon. Ten or twenty standing committees, each doing its own job, constitute a potent decentralizing force in a legislative body.

Legislative staff is more dispersed nowadays than formerly. Years ago, the dominant staff was the office of legislative council or an equivalent service agency. Staffing was nonpartisan and administratively centralized. The pattern has changed. First, partisan staffing for the Democrats and Republicans in each house has been established in a dozen or so states. Second, in a number of places, such as Louisiana and Oklahoma in the early 1980s, agencies that worked for both the senate and house split up, so that each chamber wound up with its own staff.[48] Third, standing committees in states like California, Florida, and New York acquired their own professionals. Fourth, in a growing number of places legislators have individual staffs at the capitol or in their districts. Whatever the particular pattern, practically everywhere staffs are larger and more accessible to members. If the knowledge furnished by staff constitutes power, then power within the legislature is shared among more members today. With such power, they can stand firmer in the face of gubernatorial argument.

Another fragmenting tendency results from the many groups and lobbyists who make use of the legislature as a playing field for particular interests. The overall influence of special interests may or may not be greater than formerly, but their numbers and activities have grown substantially. This growth has occurred because of the rise in the political awareness and mobilization of previously uninvolved segments of the population; the development of multistate business enterprises; the upsurge in ideological politics and single-issue groups; and the reduction of the federal government's role in various policy arenas and the consequent increase in action at the state level. Most states have also witnessed explosive growth in the number of lobbyists, and as they seek to satisfy their appetites, lobbyists and their clients pull legislators in different directions.

No doubt, the most powerful buttress for institutional fragmentation is the constituency basis of legislative representation. This is becoming more, rather than less, pronounced with the trend away from multimember districts and toward single-member ones. This form of representation encourages parochialism, tying members more closely to their districts. The more closely legislators are tied to their districts, the more difficult it is for them to consider statewide interests. The governor, however, must represent statewide interests.

These fragmenting tendencies are reinforced further by two other trends—the professionalization of the legislative career and the individualized and persistent nature of legislative campaigns. Twenty years ago, legislatures were dominated by attorneys, businessmen, insurance brokers, farmers, and ranchers, all of whom continued part time in their private occupations while serving part time as citizen legislators. Not anymore. Today the trend, particularly in the larger states, is toward more full-time professional legislators and fewer part-time citizen members. Legislators' salaries have risen—reaching as high as $57,000 in New York, $39,881 in Michigan, and $39,105 in California—and the legislative career has become far more attractive, not so much as an end in itself but mainly as a step on the ladder to higher office.

Even in those states where relatively few members serve full time, many are spending more time than before on their legislative duties. It is not at all unusual for most to spend half time or more. Moreover, another trend is under way: Average tenure is on the rise, as members seek to remain in legislative office until they can run for something else or as long as they can afford it financially.

One quality that distinguishes the new breed of full-time, professional politicians from the old breed of part-time, citizen legislators is ambition. The latter were content to spend a few years in legislative office and then return to private careers. The former, by contrast, would like to spend most of their careers in government and politics. They find public office appealing and the game of politics exhilarating.

Not many of the new breed voluntarily leave the legislature, other than to run for higher office. Consequently voluntary retirement rates are down from earlier years in most states. Legislatures in California, Florida, Illinois, Michigan, New Jersey, and Wisconsin lose only 5 to 10 percent of their members to voluntary retirement. Even in Kentucky and Tennessee, which still have essentially citizen legislatures, the numbers who choose to leave are lower than they used to be. There are, of course, exceptions, such as New Hampshire with its $200 a year salary, where one out of every three members voluntarily leaves the legislature when his or her term expires.

Because legislative office has come to hold such appeal, job security is now a principal goal for incumbents, who want to hang on until they can move up. This requires that they attend diligently to their next election, which takes place every two years in the case of house members in forty-six states (but four years in Alabama, Louisiana, Maryland, and Mississippi) and every four years in the case of senate members in thirty-eight states. No longer do incumbents entrust electoral matters to state, county, or local parties. Today, campaigns are candidate-centered, designed and operated by candidates and with the individual candidate's fate as the primary objective.

Politics and elections have always been a principal concern of legislators, but that concern looms even larger nowadays. The results for the legislature are significant. Legislators are more involved than ever before in raising money for their campaigns, and as a consequence some of their energies are diverted from the legislative process. Moreover, members behave differently when they are under electoral stress, and the effects on the legislative process are pervasive. Much of what members have to do, in order to ensure their reelection, consists of proving themselves outside of the legislature, back home in their districts.

The challenge to governors is to overcome the fragmentation and the individualism of the legislature on behalf of their own programmatic priorities. It is no small challenge, and whether governors succeed depends not only on the resources they command but also on how they exercise power.

NOTES

1. Gerald Benjamin, "The Albany Triad," *Comparative State Politics Newsletter* 9 (February 1988): 7; Thomas Kean, *The Politics of Inclusion* (New York: Free Press, 1988), 83.
2. Coleman B. Ransone, Jr., *The American Governorship* (Westport, Conn.: Greenwood Press, 1982), 138.
3. Alexander Heard, ed., *State Legislatures in American Politics* (Englewood Cliffs, N.J.: Prentice Hall, 1966), 3.
4. David R. Colburn and Richard K. Scher, *Florida's Gubernatorial Politics in the Twentieth Century* (Tallahassee: University Presses of Florida, 1980), 111.
5. Remarks of Richard A. Pettigrew (Florida Senate Seminar, "Legislative Reform in Historic Context," West Palm Beach, Fla., January 11, 1985).
6. Colburn and Scher, *Florida's Gubernatorial Politics in the Twentieth Century*, 180.
7. Heard, *State Legislatures in American Politics* is the volume.

8. John Burns, *The Sometime Governments* (New York: Bantam Books, 1971).
9. Advisory Commission on Intergovernmental Relations, *The Question of State Government Capability* (Washington, D.C.: ACIR, January 1985), 122-123.
10. This section is based on Alan Rosenthal, "The State of State Legislatures: An Overview," *Hofstra Law Review* 11 (Summer 1983): 1187-1192.
11. Wayne L. Francis and James W. Riddlesperger, "U.S. State Legislative Committees: Structure, Procedural Efficiency, and Party Control," *Legislative Studies Quarterly* 7 (November 1982): 454-455.
12. National Conference of State Legislatures, *A Legislator's Guide to Staffing Patterns* (Denver: NCSL, August 1979). Recent data were provided to the author by NCSL.
13. Samuel Patterson, "Conclusion: On the Study of Legislative Reform," in *Legislative Reform and Public Policy*, ed. Susan Welch and John G. Peters (New York: Praeger, 1977), 219.
14. Alan Rosenthal, ed., *The Governor and the Legislature* (New Brunswick, N.J.: Eagleton Institute of Politics, Rutgers University, 1988), 85.
15. *Washington Post*, February 25, 1979.
16. Malcolm E. Jewell and Penny M. Miller, *The Kentucky Legislature: Two Decades of Change* (Lexington: The University Press of Kentucky, 1988), 186-218.
17. Remarks of Kenneth "Buddy" McKay (Florida Senate Seminar, "Legislative Reform in Historic Context," West Palm Beach, Fla., January 11, 1985).
18. Remarks of Ken Plantt (Florida Senate Seminar, "Legislative Reform in Historic Context," West Palm Beach, Fla., January 11, 1985); Allen Morris, *Reconsiderations*, 3d ed. (Tallahassee: Florida House of Representatives, Office of the Clerk, October 1985), 94.
19. Robert H. Connery and Gerald Benjamin, *Rockefeller of New York: Executive Power in the State House* (Ithaca, N.Y.: Cornell University Press, 1979), 80, 108.
20. In an address to the Illinois General Assembly, March 3, 1983, quoted in Joan A. Parker, *Summit and Resolution: The Illinois Tax Increase of 1983* (Springfield, Ill.: Sangamon State University, 1984), 23.
21. Betty Wilson, "Perpich's Tax-Bill Veto Signals a Deepening Rift in the DFL Family," *Star-Tribune*, June 14, 1989.
22. Richard J. Carlson, "The Office of the Governor," in *Inside State Government: A Primer for Illinois Managers*, ed. James D. Nowlan (Urbana: The Institute of Government and Public Affairs, University of Illinois, 1982), 24.
23. National Governors' Association, *Governing the American States: A Handbook for New Governors* (Washington, D.C.: Center for Policy Research, NGA November 1978), 5.
24. William Bablitch, in Lawrence Baum and David Frohnmeyer, eds., *The Courts: Sharing and Separating Power* (New Brunswick, N.J.: Eagleton Institute of Politics, Rutgers University, 1989), 70.
25. Rosenthal, *The Governor and the Legislature*, 66.
26. Madeleine Kunin (Address to the Center for the American Woman and Politics Forum for Women State Legislators, San Diego, Calif., November 19-22, 1987).
27. Sharon Randall, "From Big Shot to Boss," *State Legislatures*, July 1988, 38.
28. Connery and Benjamin, *Rockefeller of New York*, 193.
29. Walter Zelman, "Beer: A Case Study in Special Interest Politics," *California Journal*, October 1987, 505-509.
30. Unpublished manuscript, titled "Legislator," by George Scott.
31. Carl E. Van Horn, Donald C. Baumer, and William T. Gormley, *Politics and*

Public Policy (Washington, D.C.: CQ Press, 1989).

32. Richard G. Sheridan, *State Budgeting in Ohio*, 2d ed. (Columbus: Legislative Budget Office, 1983), 27.
33. William Winter, "The Changed Role of the Governor in Higher Education," *State Government* 58 (Summer 1985): 57-58.
34. Thomas Kean, *The Politics of Inclusion* (New York: Free Press, 1988), 63.
35. Kunin Address, November 19-22, 1987.
36. Paul B. Beers, *Pennsylvania Politics Today and Yesterday* (University Park, Pa.: State University Press, 1980), 387; also National Governors' Association, *Reflections on Being Governor* (Washington, D.C.: Center for Policy Research, NGA, February 1981), 204.
37. Rosenthal, *The Governor and the Legislature*, 39; Thomas H. Simmons, "Colorado," in *The Political Life of the American States*, ed. Alan Rosenthal and Maureen Moakley (New York: Praeger, 1984), 78; and Sharon Sherman, "Powersplit: When Legislatures and Governors Are of Opposing Parties," *State Legislatures*, May-June 1984, 12.
38. Kean, *The Politics of Inclusion*, 84-85.
39. National Governors' Association, *Reflections on Being Governor*, 204-205.
40. Suzanne L. Parker, *The Florida Annual Policy Survey 1989* (Survey Research Center, Florida State University, n.d.), Appendix C. The survey was conducted in January and February 1989.
41. R. H. Melton, "Schaefer Goes on a Roll," *Washington Post*, August 9, 1988.
42. The contemporary Congress is the epitome of the fragmented legislature. A new political culture—characterized by a new breed of politicians, new channels of mass communication, and new ways of financing campaigns—shook the old power structure of Congress in the early 1970s. See Hedrick Smith, *The Power Game: How Washington Works* (New York: Random House, 1985), 651-652.
43. Jon Bowermaster, *Governor: An Oral Biography of Robert D. Ray* (Ames: Iowa State University Press, 1987), 160.
44. National Governors' Association, *Reflections on Being Governor*, 65.
45. Beers, *Pennsylvania Politics Today and Yesterday*, 396.
46. Douglas St. Angelo, "Florida," in *The Political Life of the American States*, 165.
47. This section is based on Alan Rosenthal, "The Legislative Institution: Transformed and at Risk," in *The State of the States*, ed. Carl Van Horn (Washington, D.C.: CQ Press, 1989), 69-101.
48. This decentralizing trend may have run its course, according to Brian Weberg, "The Coming of Age of Legislative Staffs," *State Legislatures*, August 1988, 24.

4

Executive-Legislative Relations

Although the composition, capacity, coherence and motivation of a legislature are important, the executive's approach to the exercise of power is probably the critical factor in relations between the branches. James Sundquist, who served on the staff of a U.S. senator and then in a subcabinet position in the federal executive, has examined interactions in Washington. His conclusion is that the balance between executive and legislative power depends more on the attributes of the president than on the character of Congress.[1] It is likely, too, that the orientations, styles, and techniques of governors count more than the characteristics of legislatures. Any inquiry into relationships should begin with the governors—who they are, how they operate, and what they want. This chapter, therefore, will examine executive-legislative relations from the gubernatorial perspective.

The institutional powers of the governorship, which are grounded in the constitution and political culture of the state, shape the office. They provide the basic framework in which governors and legislators interact. Yet they are by no means binding on governors whose power depends in part on their political personality.

Some governors manage to be strong leaders, despite institutional impediments. Richard Riley (1979-1987), for instance, possessed minimal formal powers as governor of South Carolina. Nevertheless, he provided effective leadership, among other achievements winning approval of a sweeping educational reform package in the 1984 legislative session. Florida's governors also have been constitutionally restrained, primarily by a cabinet system, but both Reubin Askew and Bob Graham proved to be strong governors in a weak-governor state with a powerful legislature. Iowa, too, had a relatively weak-governor system, but Robert Ray's tenure and skill made it significantly stronger. Even in North Carolina, the one state where the governor is alleged to suffer mightily from lack of the veto power, individuals do reasonably well shepherding their programs through the legislature.

Some governors turn out to be weak even though their offices are endowed with substantial authority. David Treen (1980-1984) of Louisiana is an example. His office had considerable authority, which his predecessors had exercised vigorously. Yet as governor, Treen was uncomfortable with legislators and lobbyists, resistant to take charge of patronage, and generally not disposed to wield power.[2] He was also a Republican dealing with a Democratic legislature, and that did not help at all.

In Louisiana, as in New Jersey and New York, most governors turn out to be strong, and weak governors like Treen are exceptions. But such exceptions mean that the differences from one governor to another within a particular state are more striking than the differences in the powers of governors across states. Maryland's recent governors demonstrate the point. Marvin Mandel (1969-1977) dominated the legislature by dint of his insider's skill in bargaining, persuading, and using patronage.[3] By contrast, Harry Hughes believed that it was the responsibility of the legislature to take the lead in policy making. Hughes was a relaxed, retiring governor, by virtue of his political personality and philosophy. His successor, William Donald Schaefer, who took office in 1987, offered the sharpest contrast. He jolted the legislature by demanding that it give him exactly what he wanted, and he enjoyed confronting leaders and rank and file alike.

As further examples of striking differences in the political personalities between governors in the same state, consider how different in approach and relationships with the legislature the following pairs of governors have been: Gerry Brown and George Deukmejian in California; Ella Grasso (1975-1980) and William O'Neill (1980-) in Connecticut; Meldrim Thomson (1973-1979) and John Sununu (1983-1989) in New Hampshire; James Rhodes and Richard Celeste in Ohio; Richard Riley and Carroll Campbell, Jr. (1987-) in South Carolina; Richard Snelling and Madeleine Kunin in Vermont; and Anthony Earl and Tommy Thompson in Wisconsin.

ORIENTATION TOWARD THE LEGISLATURE

In considering executive-legislative relations, one of the most important elements of governors' political styles is their orientation toward the legislature. What do they know about that body and how do they feel about it? "I've learned [by being in the legislature] what I think many a governor learns," Madeleine Kunin advised a group of women legislators, "and that is a successful governor means one who works well with a legislature." [4] Working well with a legislature is prerequisite, if only because a substantial part of a governor's time is spent at the job. According to sixteen governors and a number of appointment secretaries and schedulers, who were surveyed in 1976, an average of one-sixth of governors' time is devoted to the legislature. For a number of them, dealing with the legislature is considered the most difficult and demanding part of their job. [5] Practically all governors regard their legislature as a problem and are happy when the legislature adjourns and the legislators leave town. Former member of Congress Ab Mikva, who is now a federal judge, recalls that when he was serving in the Illinois general assembly he was carrying an administration bill for Governor Otto Kerner (1961-1968). He helped it through the house, but the bill died in a senate committee. In apologizing to the governor for losing the bill, Mikva said that the behavior of the senate was making a "unicameralist" out of him. Kerner replied, "That would solve half the problem." [6]

RESPECT AND ENJOYMENT

The governor's attitude toward the legislature, on coming into office, is a key determinant of the relationship the two branches will develop over time. Governors may intend to get along with the legislature or use legislators as whipping boys. They may want to work closely with legislators or keep them at arm's length. Their decision depends on whether their party controls the legislature, what the leadership is like, and the circumstances at the time. It also depends upon what they think of the legislative branch of government as a political institution.

At one extreme are a few governors who believe that the legislature is truly coequal, or even superior, and that it bears primary responsibility for making public policy. This was the orientation of Harry Hughes during his eight years as governor of Maryland. For him, the governor's role was a limited one. The same was true for John Y. Brown (1979-1983) of Kentucky, who conceived of government as running according to business principles with the legislature as the policy-making board.

At the other extreme are those governors who are disdainful of the legislature and generally believe in the supremacy of the executive. Not many articulate such feelings publicly, but a number share them. Robert Ray was one governor who expressed himself on the subject. "The legislature was one thing that really got to him," one of his aides said. It could not be controlled and it was hard to deal with. "He'd have been happy if the legislature never met. . . . His Christmas present was when we adjourned," said a legislative leader. At one point, during the last week in June, a delegation of Shriners wearing clown suits came into his office, and Ray said, "Oh, I thought the legislature adjourned already."[7] No admirer of the legislature in Des Moines, Ray also was critical of the species generally. If you lined the fifty legislatures up against the wall and blindfolded 50 governors, according to him, it would not matter which legislature they picked out. All were equally unattractive.

A number of Ray's colleagues go as far in vilifying the legislature. Milton Shapp, for instance, included the Pennsylvania legislature among such disasters as storms, floods, and infestations of the gypsy moth.[8] On occasion, a governor is especially provoked, as was Republican James Martin (1985-) who in 1985 faced a partisan Democratic legislature in North Carolina. Martin called the Tar Heel legislators "arrogantly repulsive" and owned up to his lack of success, explaining, "I had a difficult time draining the swamp with all the alligators in it."[9] Few governors are as critical of the legislative branch as is Schaefer of Maryland. After suffering some criticism, but nonetheless achieving most of his programmatic objectives during two legislative sessions, he told his gubernatorial colleagues at a National Governors' Association meeting that he was not worried about the federal government encroaching on his power. "I'm more worried," he said, "about the state legislature taking my power away." The more circumspect governors in attendance were sympathetic; they reportedly roared their agreements.[10]

The orientations of most governors lie somewhere between the extremes of docility and arrogance. They have a basic respect for the legislature and the legislative process, although from time to time they may be critical and use strong-arm tactics, which causes them to be perceived as antagonistic by some members. A number of them like dealing with the legislature. In fact, it is a favorite part of the job for Governors John McKernan, Jr., of Maine and Gerald Baliles of Virginia, who take pleasure in this aspect of their work. Bill Clinton (1979-1981, 1983-) is another one who is happiest testifying before a standing committee or rounding up votes in the Arkansas general assembly. He cannot stay put at the desk in his office, but visits constantly with legislators. John Waihee III of Hawaii is another governor of this stripe. He thinks from the perspective of a legislator, relishing the give-and-take of the process. He is referred to as the "twenty-sixth senator" or the "fifty-second representative" because of his close involvement with the legislature. Waihee's staff frequently think they are listening to a legislator when the governor discusses process and strategy with them. Madeleine Kunin also likes rubbing elbows, politicking, and even fighting with the legislature. She enjoys spending time in the legislative arena, in what she feels is her element.

Legislative vs. Executive Experience

How governors see the legislature is partly a function of their experience in political life. The most significant experience in this respect is that of having served in the legislature. Individuals who have experience in the legislature prior to gubernatorial office have several advantages. First, they have a sense of what is legislatively possible. Blair Lee (1977-1979) says that neither he nor Marvin Mandel "had any great illusions about what could and could not be done" legislatively in Maryland and that their programmatic success derived from their "knowledge of what would or would not wash downstairs in the General Assembly." [11] Second, they have friends and acquaintances left over from their days in the legislature. These personal contacts stand them in good stead when they are rounding up support for their proposals. But familiarity may also be somewhat of a disadvantage. People with whom the governor served may still think of him or her as a legislator. Terry Branstad, a former legislator serving as governor of Iowa, points out that "it's been kind of tough to convince some of my former colleagues that I'm in a different role now as chief executive and I have to deal with them in a little different way." [12] Third, governors with prior service in the legislature usually develop a healthy respect for the legislative, process—one that allows them to understand legislators' viewpoints, empathize with their objectives, and appreciate their problems. The importance of legislative experience is well illustrated by the case of Marvin Mandel, who had been the speaker of the Maryland house before being voted by the general assembly to succeed Spiro Agnew (1967-1969), who left the governorship for the vice presidency of the United States. Maryland legislators, who were interviewed by a political scientist, attributed Mandel's success with the legislature to the following factors: 6.7 percent said that it derived from the strength of the executive institution; 21.7 percent said that it derived from the fact that he was a masterful politician; and 53.6 percent said that it derived from his legislative experience.[13]

Legislative experience usually proves to be helpful, but it is no guarantee of productive relationships. The tradition in Florida has been to recruit governors from the legislature. Of the twenty-one men elected governor since the turn of the century, only five came to Tallahassee without prior legislative service. But such service counted very differently depending on the individual involved. Bob Graham, for example, had been elected to the house in 1966 and the senate in 1970, where he spent eight years. One year he was even voted "most valuable senator" by his colleagues. Nevertheless, when he became governor in 1979, legislators believed that he lacked the temperament needed to manage the legislative process. His first chief of staff explained Graham's difficulties in terms of "the fact that he was to some degree independent" and "not part of the leadership team" when he was in the legislature.[14] He had been "in" the legislature, but not "of" the legislature. In Utah, Governor Bangerter's experience as House speaker may even have been counterproductive. He expected legislative leaders to go along with him because they were his old friends. They resented his taking them for granted. Had they not been his friends, however, it is possible that they would have treated him more harshly than they did.

If having been a legislator tends to orient a governor toward the legislature in a positive fashion, having been a mayor seems to work the other way, by engendering impatience and a lack of appreciation for the process. Martinez as mayor of Tampa could issue commands and make things happen overnight. But as governor, he could not act so decisively, and he did not know which levers to use in order to influence the legislature. Schaefer as mayor of Baltimore enjoyed a hands-on approach to governing. He was used to a strong-executive system, in which the mayor was not restrained by a weak city council (on which he had served earlier). Therefore, on becoming governor his frame of reference was entirely different from that of legislators, and it remained that way. Unlike most members of the Annapolis political community, Schaefer had neither sympathy for nor patience with the slow and convoluted legislative process.

STYLE AND TECHNIQUE

Governors' orientation toward the legislature—or how they regard the process and its participants—will affect their style, or how they behave in the process and with respect to its participants. A variety of possibilities present themselves, and all governors probably adopt the style that suits their personality and works best for them.

Two experts on the office of governor in Florida have examined gubernatorial styles on a continuum, ranging from the amiable to the heavy handed. Governors at one end of the continuum sought cooperation through friendliness. They were not always successful, because they exercised too little leadership. Governors at the other end preferred confrontation and were content with an impasse they could blame on the legislature. Overall, they had little success. The governors who occupied a middle ground believed in negotiation. They were willing to confront the legislature, but they would not allow confrontation to reach a point where there was no room for maneuver and neither side had a graceful way out. Leroy Collins and Reubin Askew were of the latter type. They were the most successful.[15]

LEGISLATIVE AND EXECUTIVE GUBERNATORIAL STYLES

Many contemporary governors can be characterized according to whether their style is essentially "legislative" or "executive" in nature. Governors of the former type speak the language of the legislature, emphasizing one-on-one dealings, personal relationships, and the building of consensus. Governors of the latter type speak a different language. They remain more aloof from the day-to-day workings of the legislature; personal relationships count less for them; and they are more inclined to stand up for principle and take a confrontational approach. Few governors fit perfectly into one type or the other, but executive-legislative relations can be better understood if these styles are kept in mind.

Among those governors who were legislators at heart, the epitome no doubt was Marvin Mandel, who before holding executive office dominated the general assembly as speaker of the house of delegates. As governor, Mandel would never criticize a legislator publicly. Nor would he ask members to vote against their constituencies unless absolutely necessary, and then he would structure the situation so that they continued to look good back home. He maintained friendly and personal relationships and frequently invited legislators into his office and made them privy to inside information. He was sensitive enough to try to avoid the appearance of executive domination, going so far as to lose some battles intentionally so that legislators would feel they were independent. Without doubt, Mandel sympathized with the legislature and the legislature cared for him; there was "a feeling of comfortableness that the legislature has with him."[16]

A few governors approach Mandel in style. Ned McWherter of Tennessee, Bill Clinton in Arkansas, and Gerald Baliles in Virginia are among them. They believe there is always room to negotiate. But most governors, however they may try, are not natural legislative animals. Ronald Reagan (1967-1975), who as president built a reputation for being personable, did not get along well with the California legislature for most of his eight years as governor. That is because, as the Republican speaker during his first term observed, Reagan "didn't operate on a personal basis," as had Pat Brown before him. Reagan's relationship with the legislature improved during his second term, and it was far better than that of his successor, Edmund "Pat" Brown's (1959-

1967) son, Edmund "Gerry" Brown, Jr. During his five terms as governor of Iowa, Robert Ray suffered frustration in his relationships with the legislature. He did not appreciate the importance of personal relationships in legislative politics and did not understand how members could disagree for reasons unrelated to policy. His attitude was, "If it's a good bill, they ought to be for it." [17]

Florida's Askew and Graham, despite their legislative experience and attempts to build consensus, did not have a "legislative" style when they were governors. Askew's populism and his penchant for preaching appealed to the electorate of the Sunshine State; however, it irritated the legislature's leaders. Graham's style was even more abrasive to legislators. They did not really like Graham, but they respected him and gave him substantial support nonetheless. They complained constantly about him, accusing him of wavering in his commitment to various programs he advocated and of vetoing their bills and appropriations for their districts after assuring them that he would approve. Even Graham's personal habits rubbed them the wrong way. "He always nods his head," observed an influential senator. "I think sometimes he's left people with the impression that he's agreed with them, when he hasn't." [18]

Some governors are "executive" by nature, and tend to be combative and confrontational. They stand on principle and are not reluctant to scrap with the legislature or go over the head of the legislature to the press and people. Governors James Longley (1975-1979) of Maine and Arch Moore of West Virginia are among this lot. John Sununu was confrontational in his first term as governor of New Hampshire, but he modified his style during his final term in 1987-1988. Brendan Byrne took on the New Jersey legislature repeatedly—over taxes, the pinelands, and other issues—in order to get his way. His attorney general, John Degnan, labels the style of the administration's politics as that of confrontation. "The Governor made the issue, he drew the line, he threw the gauntlet down." And Byrne agrees: "John Degnan says that I was a confrontational Governor, and probably I was." [19] By contrast, his successor, Thomas Kean, was very much the consensus builder who backed away from battles with the legislature.

William Donald Schaefer has probably displayed the most combative and confrontational style of any current governor. There is little room for compromise with him. "No session is successful," he claims, "unless we get 105 percent of what we have proposed." [20] Walking through the senate office building during the course of a legislative session, he declared it a "war zone." For a period of almost six months, he suspended communications with the speaker of the house, and for a while he tried to undermine the authority of the president of the senate with his colleagues.

WHAT WORKS WITH THE LEGISLATURE

Whatever the dominant style—amiable or confrontational in tone, "legislative" or "executive" in nature—governors have at their disposal a wide variety of techniques. Among the most noteworthy are the following.

Standing Tall. Not unlike John Wayne in the cowboy movies of the 1940s and 1950s, governors are expected to be tough. The exhibition of strength, and perhaps the twisting of an arm, normally pays off. Governors who are strong appear to have greater success in working matters out with the legislature than do more passive ones. Even chief executives who appeared mild mannered could demonstrate muscle when the occasion arose. Underneath Robert Ray's smile, according to his ally and lieutenant governor, Art Neu, "he was just as tough as nails when he had to be." A legislator agreed that although Ray was perceived generally as "a good guy" underneath he was a "very tough, mean political guy" as well. By contrast, his successor, also a "decent guy" was softer. "Politically I just don't sense he has his hands on the wheel all the time" was the characterization of Terry Branstad.[21]

Governors not only want to have that inner toughness but, even more important, they realize that their success in the legislature depends upon legislators perceiving them as strong. That means that governors must be willing to "talk tough" to legislators and "even kick them in the groin." Rockefeller was one who intuitively grasped this principle, and he operated accordingly, frequently playing the assembly against senate, Republicans against Democrats, faction against faction, and leader against leader to gain his ends.[22]

Florida's legislators, and the leadership in particular, respect gubernatorial strength. Although they disliked Askew's puritanical style, they were always hesitant to cross him. He played hardball, remembered who did not cooperate with him, and as often as not got even. In contrast, Graham's early performance was regarded as weak. The legislature saw him as indecisive and gave him the nickname, "Governor Jello." Even after he recovered stature and began to achieve success in the legislature, Graham avoided close contact with members and relied on his chief of staff instead. It took the governor a while to shake the nickname legislators had inflicted on him.

Standing tall entails not only the appearance of strength and decisiveness, but a willingness to punish one's enemies. There are governors, such as David Treen of Louisiana, who are not comfortable either handing out carrots or using a stick. Others, like Martha Layne Collins, are intimidated by confrontation and therefore will go to great lengths to avoid debating issues with legislators.[23]

The importance of strength is shown by the case of New Jersey. Here, members of the political community expect governors to provide leadership and even twist arms. Although the legislature is no longer dominated by the governor as it used to be, it continues to look to the executive for leadership, especially on difficult issues. The legislature expects the governor to have a position and to fight for it. Legislators are disappointed, even irritated, when the executive does not furnish leadership. A counsel to Governor Byrne explained: "When the governor has not been perceived as strong, he has come in for criticism not only from the press and the public, but also from the legislature itself." [24] It would appear that New Jersey legislators *want* to have their arms twisted. It makes them feel loved, or—better still—owed.

Garden State legislators did complain about Byrne's heavy hand, with discipline normally administered by his staff. But they were even more critical of Kean's gentle touch. Unlike his predecessors, Kean refused to promise, threaten, or cajole legislators to win support for his policies. He just would not talk tough or threaten legislators with political retribution or any loss of benefits. Kean's idea of exerting pressure was to make an hour-and-a-half telephone call from China or somewhere remote to try to persuade a legislator to support his position. By not using "hot oil and pokers," he disappointed his own cabinet members. One of them, a former legislator, remarking on the contrasting styles of Kean and Byrne, said: "There are times when I think he should have smacked some people around the room a little more often, if he even did it at all." On one occasion, Kean went further than was his custom, but with little success. When his school-takeover plan was in jeopardy, he threatened not to campaign for several Republican members unless they supported him. Given the close division in the legislature and the partisan nature of politics in New Jersey, Kean's threat was not really credible. He relented, and his demonstration of political muscle proved ineffectual.

Consulting Members. Informing legislators of executive plans and programs and listening to what they have to say are tactics that seem to pay off.

Today's governors tend to seek advice on both the substance and the political prospects of their proposals. They are more likely, however, to welcome comments on the latter than on the former. Some of the most skillful governors are open to advice on both questions. Governor Ray of Iowa, for example, would call the Republican senate majority leader, Cal Hultman, down to his office in advance of the session. He would give him a list of proposals and ask, "What can I get the votes for?" The leader, in turn, would tell Ray what had to be struck from the list. The governor would also ask leaders and rank and file what was on their agendas and what they needed in light of their districts. Then, the governor and leaders would sit down, negotiate, and agree on choices. As far as substance was concerned, however, Ray insisted that his proposals were right and that the legislature ought to cooperate. McWherter of Tennessee operates in similar fashion. He brings legislators in for consultation, but his substantive decisions are not necessarily affected as a consequence.[25]

Governor Martin Schreiber (1977-1979) of Wisconsin sees the advantages in consulting. He is of the opinion that members of the legislature furnish the most realistic sounding board a governor can hope to have. In reflecting on his tenure in office, he notes:

> As I look at some of the things I might have done differently, included would be regrets that I did not contact legislative leaders who I consider to be my friends earlier in the decision-making process. I think that early contact is helpful.

By the same token, Schreiber continues, it is risky to seat seven or eight legislators around a table and ask them to give their opinion on a particular subject.[26] But risky or not, consultation on balance seems to promote the interests of governors in their dealings with the legislature.

A governor may meet with legislators on a few occasions before the session, informing them of the plans, asking what is on their minds, and inquiring as to what they suggest be included in the governor's program. Later on the governor might run a finished proposal by the legislature to determine whether it had sufficient support and what could be done to strengthen its chance of passage. Governor Clinton of Arkansas has been particularly adept in his use of consultation as a technique. Every member of the Arkansas general assembly is invited to a small group meeting with the governor before the session begins and can tell the governor what is on his or her mind. While the session is under way, Clinton meets with one or a few legislators at breakfast or over sandwiches in his office and asks: "What will it take to make the proposal O.K., to get your support?"

Legislators take consultation most seriously. They do not want to be left out of the decision-making loop. Lack of consultation can cost the governor support or even engender opposition. Yet a governor can also succeed without consulting. Sununu made up his own mind and did not really listen to what legislators had to say. Still, he dominated the New Hampshire legislature.

Talking Turkey.   It is helpful to communicate in the legislator's language of patronage and deals, of give and take, with no one walking away empty-handed. The legislature is a web of relationships and transactions; everything is linked to something else, and reciprocity is a guiding principle. "If you help me on this, I'll help you on that." Legislators insist that governors appreciate this and act accordingly. Some governors do; they are willing to give up matters that they care less about in order to win support for their priorities. Other governors are not disposed to trade, but want each issue decided on its own merits. And some governors do not even remember who helped them in the past.

Michael Dukakis is one governor who failed to acknowledge political friends. In that regard, he took a principled stand against patronage during his first administration (but a more pragmatic one during his second and third terms). At the outset, he announced to Massachusetts Democrats who believed in and practiced patronage that there would be none during his tenure. Dukakis simply did not play by any political rules familiar to Massachusetts politicians. Thomas McGee, the speaker of the house, did not understand how the governor could hire someone unknown to him in preference to a friend. A "perfect ingrate" was how one legislator described Dukakis. A former member of his campaign staff, who was then elected to the legislature, commented on how the governor would not help his friends. "I couldn't get the time of day" from him, he said. Another legislator remembers Dukakis in the same way. "We all joked about it in the legislature," he commented. "If you wanted something, you had to oppose him." As a result of his aloofness, his pedantic lecturing, his spurning of patronage, and his neglect of friends, Dukakis's relations with the legislature were exceedingly poor.[27]

Dukakis reversed himself, however, when he returned to office in 1983. Patronage became the practice, with campaign workers given highest priority. The senate president went so far as to comment that "Dukakis has raised patronage to a fine art." Most significant in the governor's transformation was the appointment to a key position in the Department of Public Works of a former house member and close friend of the leadership. This appointment meant an enormous amount to the speaker and the majority leader, and it signaled that the governor wanted to go into partnership with the legislature.[28]

Generally, relationships with the legislature are facilitated if the governor is willing to make a deal, to trade so that a legislator gets what he or she wants in return for giving the governor support on an issue. Rockefeller of New York was a master of this technique, a genuine believer in quid pro quo. If he needed votes for his program, he was not averse to making "side payments"—an administrative job, a project for a member's district, a judicial appointment—in exchange. Today, barter is a high art form in New York, with members referring to the issues involved in deals as "arranged marriages." They are wedded to each other, not because they have a natural connection, but because they are being traded against each other, like brides for cattle.[29]

Trading can involve the priorities of governors on the one hand and those of the legislative leadership, reflecting members' desires, on the other. Each party to negotiations will have a "laundry list," and each will attempt to agree on items of mutual interest, trade off on others, and dispense with the rest. The governor's attitude here is, "You'll get a little and I'll get a little, after we meet and sort things out." Trading can also take place at a more mundane level, with legislators willing to give their votes to the governor in return for appointments and special projects. A conversation might proceed, with the legislator saying, "I'd like to be with you on this issue, Governor, and while I have a few minutes of your time. . . . " Governors themselves need not become involved, but instead can filter these exchanges through staff intermediaries. "You have a bill on our desk, and we'll certainly try to sign it," says the governor's legislative liaison, "and, by the way, how are you going to vote on this other issue?"

Trading can also be done on speculation. Governors may give in advance, recognizing that they can call upon legislators for payment later on. They build up credit that way. Edwin Edwards (1972-1980, 1984-1988) of Louisiana, for instance, would agree to just about any reasonable request from a legislator, letting the bureaucracy say no if necessary, but meanwhile accumulating credit.[30] In Illinois, Governor Thompson takes an approach similar to that of the late Mayor Richard Daley of Chicago. He would rather do a favor for a legislator than have a favor done for him. For Thompson, that is money in the bank.

Some governors, however, are not disposed to trade with legislators. Robert Ray was not one to barter, at least not until the last minute and out of desperation. If he did not have enough votes, he might be willing to make concessions, but otherwise he stood firm. Compromise was not in his blood, particularly since he usually was convinced that his answers were best for Iowa. He acknowledged that "he couldn't play the game they play in the legislature." That aggravated legislators, who wanted Ray to play the games they play upstairs." They thought Ray was bullheaded, unwilling to engage in the customary give-and-take required of governors.[31]

Thomas Kean of New Jersey also found it difficult to deal. In his autobiography, he relates that one senator agreed to vote for the governor's budget in return for a judgeship and another senator would have cooperated with the governor on an issue if his uncle received a state job. He said no to both, reporting that no deals were made throughout his two administrations. Nor did Kean use the line-item veto politically, to reward friends and punish enemies. He remembered whom he had helped and "would look him in the eye and say, 'I've helped you out, now I need you on this one.'" At times his appeals would work, but sometimes they fell on deaf ears.[32]

Rubbing Elbows. Many governors make personal contact with legislators on a relatively frequent basis. Nearly all former governors who were surveyed several years ago advocated an open-door policy for legislators. Nine out of ten would accede to a request by a senior legislator to see the governor with no subject specified; nine out of ten would accede to a request by a legislative leader of the opposition party to see the governor with no subject specified; and eight out of ten would accede to a request by a freshman legislator to see the governor with no subject specified.[33]

In addition to the open door, which allows legislators to walk into the governor's office and spend ten to fifteen minutes (either on several specified days each week or at any time), chief executives go out of their way to meet with members of the senate and house. James Thompson spends a great deal of time in the general assembly. Before key votes, the Illinois governor is sure to be on the floor, since the rules of both the senate and house permit it. "I sit next to my Republican leader," he says, "and I stare at the senators or the house members, as the case may be, and watch the votes go up on the tote board." [34] Thompson believes that his presence has "both a calming and a salutary effect," as his agents scurry about doing their legislative liaison duties.[35] Bill Clinton is another one who enjoys rubbing elbows with legislators whenever he can. As governor of Arkansas, he attends and testifies at committee meetings, stands outside the chamber calling members off the floor, and spends time on the floor as well. He is almost always on the spot and in the midst of deliberations, and is as directly involved with the legislature as any governor in the nation.

Massaging Egos. Governors often make an effort to take into account the psychological needs of the individual legislator and those of the legislature as an institution.

Relationships with members are advanced when governors invite them to receptions at the mansion or ask them to participate in a bill-signing ceremony. Legislators like to share center stage with the chief executive, because it brings them publicity they might not otherwise receive. When the governor signs a popular bill, so many legislators want to have their picture taken with him that the signing may have to be moved out of the governor's office and into the capitol rotunda.

Another effective technique is for the governor to call each legislator after the session, just to check on how they are doing, or to host a party the night before adjournment so that legislators will leave town in a good mood.

Little favors can mean a lot to legislators, as the use of free passes to the Oaklawn Park racetrack at Hot Springs, Ark., illustrates. The governor of Arkansas receives ten thousand free passes from the State Racing Commission. With each pass, the regular admission fee of one dollar is waived. The cost is inconsequential, but it is a question of "pride rather than pocketbook." Free passes confer "insider" status, and legislators want to distribute them to their constituents and thereby enhance their own standing. Although they receive some passes directly from the commission, legislators who are in the governor's good graces may receive many more of them.[36]

As important as anything else are the visits that governors make to the home districts of legislators, where in their opening remarks they praise the local representatives vociferously. This impresses constituents and warms the heart of even the most independent member. Governor Schaefer of Maryland, however, operated in exactly the opposite way. At a Chamber of Commerce breakfast in Prince Georges County, he criticized several members of the county's legislative delegation for having cut his budget.

Rockefeller was especially adept at stroking legislators—in his office, at the mansion, or at his Pocantico estate on the Hudson. He was most concerned about the egos of legislative leaders. For example, Democratic speaker Anthony Travia, whose ambition was to be governor, was often invited to sit in the governor's ornate chair during conferences at the statehouse.[37]

The legislature's collective ego also requires nurture. Leaders and members alike insist on institutional recognition and credit. They want to feel, and want it to appear, that the legislature is an equal partner with the executive in governing. Baliles of Virginia appreciates this requirement. A former legislator, he is scrupulous in giving the general assembly full recognition; indeed, he goes out of his way to give the legislature credit. And he believes that on many issues the legislature ought to work its will, while he works collaboratively to achieve legislative objectives.

It seems that the more credit governors give to the legislature, the further they can get with their priorities. North Dakota's George Sinner (1985-) abandoned credit almost entirely in order to achieve an economic development program. He delegated its formulation to the interim committee system of the legislature, having made the conscious decision to allow the legislature to come up with the ideas. Then, he allowed the speaker of the house to take credit for the legislative package. In abandoning control, Sinner succeeded in getting what he wanted—an economic development program.

If governors are willing to give credit away, or to share credit with the legislature, they may sacrifice slightly what they can claim as their personal achievement in a campaign for reelection. But the sacrifice will be minimal, and it will be more than balanced by what the governors achieve in their relationship with the legislature. Usually, though, there is enough credit for the executive and legislature to share; many contemporary governors realize this and exercise their power accordingly.

DEALING WITH LEGISLATIVE LEADERSHIP

Executive-legislative relations will vary depending upon the ability of the governor to get along with the legislature's leaders, and vice versa. Given the fragmentation, parochialism, and individualism that are endemic to the legislative process (and may currently be on the rise), legislative leadership plays a vital role in trying to keep things from flying apart. Just as governors bear responsibility for developing state-wide policies and budgets, so do the leaders of the house and senate. Leaders are the only ones who can represent the legislature—the senate or the house, the majority or the minority—to the press and public, and in negotiations with the governor.

The majority party's leaders—and principally the speaker in the house and the president, president pro tem, or majority leader in the senate—and the minority party's leaders as well, particularly if they are members of the governor's party, constitute the legislature's leadership.

As such, these individuals stand between legislative rank and file and the governor. To varying degrees, they speak for the membership in setting priorities. And if they are of the governor's political faith, they usually can be counted on to advocate his or her program to their partisan flock. The governor needs them to line up necessary votes.

Dealing with leadership by no means precludes governors from direct relationships with individual members, who may chair major committees, exercise influence on their own, or simply have a decisive vote. Indeed, the dispersion of power occurring in state legislatures has multiplied the number of influential legislators whose favor must be curried by a governor. But unlike a governor's contact with members, which normally is occasional and sporadic, a governor's contact with leaders is more likely to be ongoing and structured.

THE POWER OF LEADERS

Leaders vary in strength depending on the state. Few speakers of the house and presidents, presidents pro tem, or majority leaders of the senate can issue commands and expect members to obey. The day of the autocratic leader is past, for those who hold power too tightly risk revolt within the ranks. Leaders depend on the backing of their members. In recent years powerful leaders in Massachusetts, Mississippi, and Oklahoma have lost that backing and been forced by their caucuses to step down. And other leaders, in Connecticut and North Carolina, have been overthrown by bipartisan coalitions.

Leaders do have occasion to discipline members, but such occasions are relatively few. They may remove uncooperative members from their positions chairing a committee, from committee assignments, or from assistant leadership positions. For example, Speaker Jon Mills of Florida punished three house members who did not support the leadership position on the services tax during a special session in 1987. He removed two of the offending members from the appropriations committee and took away the majority whip position from another. In most places, but not everywhere, leaders may refuse to calendar a member's bills for floor action. The speaker in New Hampshire cannot use his calendaring power to kill a member's bill, for every bill reported by a house committee must be considered on the floor. Instead, the speaker can refuse to appoint the sponsor of a bill to a committee of conference, thereby barring him or her from a critical stage of the process. Leaders may exclude a member from the inner circle or withhold small benefits, such as a parking space nearer the capitol, a trip out of state, or additional secretarial assistance. The main disciplinary power of leaders is withholding, not taking away.

The leaders of state legislatures today use the carrot far more frequently than the stick. What weighs most heavily, as far as their power is concerned, is not whom they punish directly but rather to whom they distribute benefits and from whom they withhold them. The style of Michael O'Keefe, senate president in Louisiana, suggests how the small favors bestowed by leadership can add up to significant power. As described by John Maginnis:

> If you need a state trooper to give you a ride somewhere, he'll get it for you. If you need a bill killed in committee, he'll help you kill it. He'll do favor after favor and won't ask anything in return. But when he needs you to vote with him, and he doesn't ask often, he'll just say, 'I need you on this one.' And you may be voting against your mother when you vote with O'Keefe, but you'll go ahead and vote with him anyway.[38]

Contemporary leaders try to keep members happy, both to retain their leadership positions and to be able to build consensus on issues of public policy.

The strength of leadership varies. At one extreme, leadership is weak in Nebraska, where the speakership of the unicameral has been a rotating position and leadership has been in the hands of committee chairs or the particular sponsors of legislation, depending on the issue. Nebraska governor Kay Orr (1987-   ) must operate on her own with the forty-nine members of the nonpartisan legislature. At the other extreme, leadership is strong in states such as California, Colorado, Florida, Illinois, Massachusetts, New York, Ohio, Rhode Island, and Texas.

Strong leaders present an imposing front in dealing with the governor on behalf of their legislative parties and chambers. They have the authority to bargain, for they can deliver their members' support and carry out their part of any deal they make with the governor. If the leaders have the ability to provide needed support or effective opposition, the governor is inclined to work with them—to meet, confer, and negotiate as equals. They depend on one another. A legislative leader has the power to counteract the will of the governor. He or she can keep the governor from vetoing legislative bills by lining up votes for the governor's projects.[39]

A FEW-PERSON GAME

The relationship between the governor and legislative leaders in Illinois is an especially close one, with a "summit process" the mode for conducting business. Four individuals participate in summit meetings: Governor James Thompson, House Speaker Michael Madigan, Minority Leader Lee Daniels, and Senate President Philip Rock. If the governor and the leaders reach agreement, arrangements are made for the final vote, and then the scenario is followed. If a measure does not have the necessary backing, it is withdrawn, and no one has to go out on a limb. This arrangement proved effective until the 1988 session, when the process broke down.

The gubernatorial-leadership relationship in New York is also close. Twenty years ago legislative leaders here had tight control over members. Governor Rockefeller worked closely with the leaders, and once he had their agreement, there was normally little difficulty in shepherding his priorities through the legislature. But the situation began to change, and leaders found it harder to negotiate on their own. "What will the members accept?" became the key question. Increasingly, leaders had to win concessions from the governor to make policies and programs salable in their respective caucuses and chambers.[40]

The top leaders in New York—the speaker of the assembly and majority leader of the senate—still hold considerable power, but in contests with the governor, they are far less unilateral actors. They have to manage and be responsive to their legislative party caucuses. Their power depends on the willingness of the rank and file to go along. As one political scientist describes the situation:

> In each house the leader is limited in the exercise of his powers by his desire to retain his position, which depends upon the support of the members of his party. The effectiveness of his leadership is a function of his ability to serve the needs of the members, to anticipate their dissatisfaction, and to keep them relatively happy and comfortable.[41]

As speaker, Stanley Fink clearly understood the tasks of modern legislative leadership. To keep members of the Democratic caucus in the assembly together, he provided them with leadership titles, enlarged their staffs, expanded their political operation, sought the views of rank and file, and altered legislation to accommodate as many of them as possible. Fink could thus speak on behalf of a unified Democratic majority that felt involved in the process.[42]

Since Fink's retirement, the ante has been going up. Mel Miller, his successor as speaker, has had to give more and more in order to keep members in line. He has been able to do this by delivering specific programs and projects legislators want in return for their acquiescence. In the Senate, however, Majority Leader Warren Anderson encountered serious problems. In 1988 a bloc of Long Island Republicans challenged his control in an effort to expand their own power within the caucus. Anderson could not hold his party together in negotiating with the governor on the budget. After agreements had apparently been reached, he would announce that all bets were off and that he required another $50 million or so for Long Island school districts. As a consequence, Governor Cuomo was highly critical of the majority leader, charging that he did not have control of his members and could not deliver the votes required to resolve the budget impasse.[43] After that session Anderson stepped down and did not run for reelection to the senate.

Despite a gradual erosion of legislative leadership power in New York, the legislative process here was still a three-person game played by the governor, the speaker of the assembly, and the senate majority leader. In Albany there is a saying, "It takes three to tango." Rockefeller's successors, Hugh Carey (1975-1983) and Mario Cuomo, have had a variety of relationships with the legislative leaders, but throughout it was the leaders with whom they had to deal.

The Party Connection

Among the factors that determine the extent of the relationship a governor has with legislative leaders, the most obvious is party. Whether or not the house speaker or senate president (or president pro tem or majority leader) is of the same party as the governor is important. If control is split, with one party having a majority in the senate and the other having a majority in the house, still another factor enters the equation.

The preferred situation, from the governor's perspective, naturally is to have senate and house majorities. In such circumstances governors tend to work primarily through their own leaders, and only occasionally will they deal with the minority directly. Governor Cuomo, under criticism from Republican minority leader Clarence Rappleyea, reportedly commented: "He's just the minority leader and nothing he says means anything." Governors O'Neill in Connecticut and Perpich in Minnesota also spend little time with minority leadership. Even under such conditions, however, governors cannot expect that legislative leaders will always carry the governor's program. They can count on the leaders most of the time, but not always. In such circumstances, the minority party is seldom consulted and feels few obligations. It can be irresponsible and throw bombs. As one legislative leader described the New Jersey assembly Republicans, who had been in the minority for twelve years: "When you're in the minority, you never have to worry about loose canon. You want your troops to attack, attack, attack."

If governors have to deal with a majority leadership of the opposition, their situation is more difficult. Under such circumstances, leadership is not constrained by party loyalty or mutual partisan advantage. As a Vermont leader put it, "It's easier to serve under a governor of the opposite party because the lines are clearly defined." Indeed, the majority leadership is in a strong bargaining position when it confronts a governor of the opposite party. It is under no obligation to make the governor look good. If it has any strength whatsoever, the minority party also will play an important role here. The governor counts on the minority leadership to keep its members in line, particularly when the governor's veto must be upheld.

When control of the executive and legislative branches is divided, governors generally meet separately with leaders of the two parties. In Iowa, for instance, Republican governor Terry Branstad meets jointly with the senate and house majority and minority leaderships every other week, but he also meets separately on a biweekly basis with the legislative leaders of his own party, who are in the minority. In Maine, Republican governor John McKernan, Jr., meets with the joint leadership once a week, but he also meets separately on a regular basis with the Republican minority leaders and individually with the Democratic leaders.

GUBERNATORIAL ROLE IN LEADERSHIP SELECTION

Another factor that counts, as far as the governor's exercise of power is concerned, is the ties that leaders have—or do not have—to the governor. One of the closest ties results from the governor having been responsible for designating the leaders. It used to be common in the one-party states of the South for the governor to select a legislator in each house to serve as the governor's floor leader. In several states— Alabama, Georgia, Kentucky, and Louisiana—executive control went further. The governor's choice for the top leadership position was accepted by legislators, who were intimidated by the power of the chief executive. Until the mid-1960s the governor of Georgia named the speaker, speaker pro tem, majority leader, and the chairs of the major committees. There was even a direct telephone line between the governor's office and the speaker's rostrum. No wonder, then, that the governor could ensure that favored bills were passed and could bottle up opposed bills in committee.[44]

In Kentucky it was traditional for governors to select leaders (and even committee chairs). When the governor here happened to be slow in announcing his selection in 1966, one legislator remarked: "I wish he'd just go ahead and tell us who he wants. That's what we're all waiting for."[45] Julian Carroll as governor would meet with legislative leaders every day of the session to give them their marching orders. Leadership operated at the pleasure of the governor, and members operated at the pleasure of leadership. They used to have a list of the governor's bills on their desks, which indicated just how they should vote. A couple of bills on the list specified no gubernatorial position, so they could vote however they wanted. Since John Y. Brown's election in 1979, when the governor gave up the prerogative of selecting the general assembly's leadership, the situation has changed dramatically. Brown did not care about the legislature and did not attempt to influence the selection of leaders. He dealt with them at arm's length during his term in office. The Kentucky general assembly now chooses its own leadership independently of the governor's influence, and it is not likely to surrender that authority in the near future.

Not only in the South, but in other states as well, some governors influenced the selection of legislative leaders. New Jersey is an example. As a former chief of staff to a New Jersey governor commented, "The best thing a governor can do in dealing with the legislature is to pick the leaders, and in the old days they used to pick the leaders." It was done behind the scenes, with the governor denying publicly any involvement. Brendan Byrne was one of the Garden State's governors who intervened discreetly, particularly after the elections of 1977, when his candidate was chosen majority leader, which made him next in line to be president of the senate. The chair of the appropriations committee had been expected to move up to the majority leader post. But he had supported a candidate other than Byrne in the Democratic primary for governor, while the chair of the judiciary committee had backed Byrne. If Byrne's candidate were named majority leader, moreover, it would leave the chair of the judiciary committee vacant and thus permit one of the governor's principal senate supporters to move up to that important post. After his reelection as governor, Byrne had sufficient standing to shift people around. He persuaded the appropriations committee chair to withdraw from the contest, and his candidates became majority leader and chair of the judiciary committee.

For the most part, however, governors have eschewed involvement in leadership contests. Even Rockefeller, with all his clout, did not (with a notable exception or two) intrude in the process, acknowledging in his own words that "the members of the legislature are rightfully jealous of their prerogatives." [46] Whatever past practices may have been, the governor's role in the leadership-selection process is much diminished today. Louisiana may be the only state where the governor's influence is still overt and decisive. Governor Buddy Roemer, who was elected in 1987, faced a struggle, but managed to persuade both houses to unseat their old leaders and install the governor's choices as senate president and house speaker. Governor Roemer's leaders, however, had little internal support, and consequently the governor ran into difficulty with the legislature.

A few years ago, in responding to a survey by the National Governors' Association, twenty-five of thirty-one legislative assistants of governors who responded were of the opinion that choosing leaders was strictly an internal matter for the legislature. Yet one observer commented that, although governors will not endorse or comment on struggles for leadership positions, "I think it is unlikely that the Governor actually remains neutral in most situations." NGA concluded that in many states governors continue to exert influence, but the process is often so subtle that it is difficult to pinpoint.[47] This seems to be the case, and a governor's preferences may still weigh in a leadership contest.

If governors do take sides and if their candidate ascends to leadership, it is likely that their legislative programs will benefit. Whether or not a governor actually intervenes in the selection process, if the leader happens to have been on the governor's team, of a similar orientation within the party, and generally in agreement on the issues, then the governor's lot in dealing with leadership will be a happier one. If, on the other hand, the leader is of a different faction or aspires to succeed the governor in office or challenge him or her in a primary, the relationship will be thornier.

OTHER FACTORS THAT SHAPE RELATIONSHIPS

The relationship between governors and leaders depends also upon how much each wants to achieve. The leader's bargaining position is strengthened if the governor has a lengthy program he or she wants enacted. In exchange for the leader's support, the governor may have to give on other matters. Similarly, the governor's bargaining position is strengthened insofar as legislative leaders have their own objectives and require executive support to achieve them. If a leader wants little or nothing, however, the governor has few bargaining chips. One reason for Michael Madigan's power vis-à-vis James Thompson in Illinois is that he does not have his own agenda; thus, it is difficult for the governor to trade with him.

Relationships also vary, depending upon the chemistry between governors and legislative leaders. No matter what issues or partisan matters are involved, some governors and some legislators simply do not get along. In Maryland Schaefer and Mike Miller, the senate president, and Clay Mitchell, the house speaker, started out amicably because of their alliance during the gubernatorial campaign. But their relationship soon soured. Schaefer was such an intimidating force that both Miller and Mitchell felt they had to stand up to him. After a few years, the relationship between the governor and the speaker appeared to reach an equilibrium, but the gulf between the governor and the president continued to be wide, mainly because of Schaefer's unwillingness to bargain or compromise with Miller.

The extent of control that leaders have over members also affects how governors relate to legislative leadership. The more powerful the leaders, the less practicable it is for governors to go to members directly. The governors must deal with and through leaders who mediate, if they are to obtain the support required for their program. Strong leadership can be boon or bane for governors; it can provide them necessary backing, or it can constitute opposition that may be difficult to overcome.

Generally speaking, leadership is more powerful in houses, where the speaker usually is the principal leader, than in senates where leadership is more collegial. Senates have more experienced and individualistic members who rein in strong leadership. In Vermont, for instance, it is far more difficult for the governor to deal with the senate. It is a smaller body, with more independent-minded members, and leadership tends to be weaker. The same is true in Iowa, and in other states as well. But in places where leadership exercises considerable power, as in Illinois, Massachusetts, and New York, differences between the house and senate tend to be somewhat less. Leadership also is more powerful when it is lodged in a single individual rather than in several people. In some states the speaker and the president or president pro tem have the authority to appoint the majority leaders, the whips, and the rest of the leadership team. Connecticut, Florida, Massachusetts, New Hampshire, New York, and West Virginia are among them. In most states, however, the party caucus selects not only the top leader but subordinate leaders too. In such cases, leaders may have the representative of a rival faction among their top lieutenants and their control may be precarious. Governors, then, will probably have to deal with both the leaders and their rivals.

Legislative leaders may also be circumscribed if a governor has prior experience with members and they feel allegiance to him or her. By the late 1970s, Governor Ray of Iowa had been in office longer than most legislators, many of whom were his proteges. He had encouraged them to run and helped them win reelection. In view of this, it was not surprising that a number of legislators, by and large, respected him—his acumen, his tenure, and his savvy. Regardless of leadership, those ties were very helpful to the governor.[48] And, if a governor has in previous years looked with special favor on a legislator, leadership will not be able to intervene in the relationship. No governor has looked as favorably upon as many members of the legislature as John Waihee III of Hawaii. Out of seventy-six members of the senate and house in 1988, he appointed thirteen of them to fill vacant seats. Other governors also have tried and true allies among the rank and file, and they can count on them regardless of legislative leadership.

MEANS OF INTERACTION

Whatever the specific circumstances, governors cannot avoid some involvement with legislative leadership. Most governors interact with leaders on a regular basis. They meet before the session to brief them on the governor's agenda, so that they are not surprised by what comes up. When a governor fails to do so, as happened early in the administration of Governor Bangerter of Utah, leaders become annoyed, and the governor's program may bog down somewhere in the legislature. Governors also keep leaders informed as the session progresses. If they plan to veto an important bill, they know that leaders expect to be notified in advance. Should the governor neglect this, leaders become perturbed. That was the case when Minnesota governor Perpich in 1989 announced his veto of a legislative tax bill at a televised press conference without first informing the leaders.

For most governors today, weekly or biweekly schedule of meetings with leaders is not uncommon. Gerald Baliles and the leadership of the Virginia general assembly meet a few times a week. In Maine Joseph Brennan (1979-1987) breakfasted with the Democratic majority leadership every week. His successor, John McKernan, Jr., meets weekly with both the majority and minority leaderships in an informal and sometimes no-holds-barred discussion. John Ashcroft meets together and separately with Democratic and Republican leaders in Missouri. In Delaware the governor and leaders deal with one another over lunches on Tuesdays. A number of legislative leaders agree as to the utility of regular meetings to discuss issues, review legislation, and plan ahead. "If you have to look each other in the eye every week at the same time, it will keep down the problems," commented the speaker of the North Carolina house. Even when the governor is of the other party, periodic face-to-face sessions contribute to improved relations. New Hampshire's speaker summed up: "Despite our mutual hostility, sitting down in his home and having pancakes with him makes it hard to be uncompromising." [49] Still, in a number of states—Connecticut, Massachusetts, and Rhode Island are examples—regular get-togethers are not the practice. And in North Dakota, the Republican majority leader refused to meet on a scheduled basis with Democratic governor George Sinner, so the governor met only with his own floor leaders.

Meeting practices depend on several factors—partisan alignments, the power of legislative leadership, and the personalities involved. New Jersey illustrates several patterns. Richard Hughes during his second administration held meetings with the assembly speaker, senate president, and the majority and minority leaders before each legislative session. Both the governor's and the legislature's agendas were discussed at these sessions, where leaders on both sides of the aisle frankly discussed what they could and could not do. Leadership meetings continued under Byrne, but they grew in size as assistant leaders were also invited and could share in a sense of high-level participation. "It's impossible to get them in the same room," commented a former legislative leader, "it's like running a caucus."

Kean scrapped the practice of regular bipartisan meetings with legislative leaders. His style was informal, and he preferred to meet with individuals, leaders and rank and file, as the occasion required. Furthermore, his initial relationship with the speaker of the assembly, Alan

Karcher, was a stormy one. Kean described Karcher: "Given a chance between a wise compromise and a good public scrap, he will take the scrap every time." Nor did Karcher refute such a characterization. He believed that in trying to be conciliatory, "you wind up getting kicked in the teeth." [50] Karcher used his early meetings with the governor to further his own partisan agenda, and thus these sessions were soon discontinued and not revived during Kean's governorship. The governor, of course, dealt with legislative leaders, but after his fashion and in a more ad hoc manner.

NOTES

1. James L. Sundquist, *The Decline and Resurgence of Congress* (Washington, D.C.: Brookings Institution, 1981), 19-21.
2. John Maginnis, *The Last Hayride* (Baton Rouge, La.: Gris Gris Press, 1984), 44-45.
3. Edward J. Miller, "Gubernatorial Support in a State Legislature: The Case of Maryland" (Paper delivered at the annual meeting of the American Political Science Association, San Francisco, September 2-5, 1975), 19.
4. Madeleine Kunin (Address to the Center for the American Woman in Politics Forum for Women State Legislators, San Diego, California, November 19-22, 1987).
5. Thad L. Beyle and Robert Dalton, "The Governor and the State Legislature," in *Being Governor: The View from the Office*, ed. Thad L. Beyle and Lynn R. Muchmore (Durham, N.C.: Duke Press Policy Studies, 1983), 125; and National Governors' Association, *Governing the American States: A Handbook for New Governors* (Washington, D.C.: Center for Policy Research, NGA, November 1978), 5.
6. Remarks at Congressional Research Service Symposium, Washington, D.C., July 13, 1989.
7. Jon Bowermaster, *Governor: An Oral Biography of Robert D. Ray* (Ames: Iowa State University Press, 1987), 276, 282, 160-161, 136.
8. National Governors' Association, *Reflections on Being Governor* (Washington, D.C.: Center for Policy Research, NGA, February 1981), 203.
9. Joel A. Thompson, "The 1985 Session of the North Carolina General Assembly," *Comparative State Politics Newsletter* 6 (August 1985): 10-11.
10. *Washington Post*, August 9, 1988.
11. National Governors' Association, *Reflections on Being Governor*, 163.
12. Bowermaster, *Governor*, 288.
13. Miller, "Gubernatorial Support in a State Legislature," 14.
14. Allen Morris, *Reconsiderations*, 3d ed. (Tallahassee: Florida House of Representatives, Office of the Clerk, October 1985), 99; *Gainesville Sun*, May 11, 1986.
15. David R. Colburn and Richard K. Scher, *Florida's Gubernatorial Politics in the Twentieth Century* (Tallahassee: University Presses of Florida, 1980), 182-183.
16. Miller, "Gubernatorial Support in a State Legislature," 14-15.

17. Charles G. Bell and Charles M. Price, *California Government Today*, 2d ed. (Homewood, Ill.: Dorsey Press, 1984), 237-239; Bowermaster, *Governor*, 279.
18. *Gainesville Sun*, May 11, 1986.
19. Eagleton Institute of Politics, Rutgers University, "The Pinelands Protection Act," October 15, 1987 (photocopy), 22; Jeffrey Kanige, "Brendan Byrne on Brendan Byrne," *New Jersey Reporter*, June 1988, 13.
20. *Washington Post*, April 10, 1988.
21. Bowermaster, *Governor*, 87, 289.
22. Robert H. Connery and Gerald Benjamin, *Rockefeller of New York: Executive Power in the State House* (Ithaca, N.Y.: Cornell University Press, 1979), 78, 434.
23. Maginnis, *The Last Hayride*, 46-47; Malcolm E. Jewell and Penny M. Miller, *The Kentucky Legislature: Two Decades of Change* (Lexington: University Press of Kentucky, 1988), 236.
24. Donald Linky, "The Governor," in *The Political State of New Jersey*, ed. Gerald M. Pomper (New Brunswick, N.J.: Rutgers University Press, 1986), 108.
25. Beyle and Dalton, "The Governor and the State Legislature," 127; Alan Rosenthal, *The Governor and the Legislature* (New Brunswick, N.J.: Eagleton Institute of Politics, Rutgers University, 1988), 69; Bowermaster, *Governor*, 289.
26. National Governors' Association, *Reflections on Being Governor*, 189.
27. National Governors' Association, *Reflections on Being Governor*, 65; Charles Kenney and Robert L. Turner, *Dukakis; An American Odyssey* (Boston: Houghton, Mifflin, 1988), 118-119.
28. Ibid., 176-178.
29. Connery and Benjamin, *Rockefeller of New York*, 434; *New York Times*, April 15, 1988.
30. Maginnis, *The Last Hayride*, 23.
31. Bowermaster, *Governor*, 279, 281, 284.
32. Thomas Kean, *The Politics of Inclusion* (New York: Free Press, 1988), 88.
33. National Governors' Association, *Governing the American States*, 278.
34. In many states, tradition would forbid behavior of this kind. In Utah, for example, if the governor came up from his second-floor office to the third floor where the legislature is, members would be shocked. "What is he doing here?" they would ask.
35. Alan Rosenthal, *The Governor and the Legislature*, 11.
36. Both the state press and gubernatorial aides have speculated, somewhat in jest, that racing passes may have passed more of the governor's bills than any other factor. Diane Blair, *Arkansas Politics and Government* (Lincoln: University of Nebraska Press, 1988), 142.
37. Connery and Benjamin, *Rockefeller of New York*, 93.
38. Maginnis, *The Last Hayride*, 99.
39. William K. Muir, *Legislature: California's School for Politics* (Chicago: University of Chicago Press, 1982), 171-172.
40. Connery and Benjamin, *Rockefeller of New York*, 79, 88.
41. Gerald Benjamin, "The Albany Triad," in *Comparative State Politics Newsletter* 9 (February 1988): 7; and Stuart K. Witt, "Modernization of the Legislature," in *Governing New York State: The Rockefeller Years*, ed. Robert H. Connery and Gerald Benjamin (New York: Academy of Political Science, May 1974), 45-57.
42. *New York Times*, July 10, 1988.
43. *New York Times*, July 20, 1987, April 12 and June 17, 1988.
44. Lawrence R. Hepburn, "Georgia," in *The Political Life of the American States*,

ed. Alan Rosenthal and Maureen Moakley (New York: Praeger, 1984), 192.

45. Malcolm E. Jewell, "The Governor as a Legislative Leader," in *The Governor in Behavioral Perspective*, ed. Thad Beyle and J. Oliver Williams (New York: Harper & Row, 1972), 138.
46. Connery and Benjamin, *Rockefeller of New York*, 84.
47. National Governors' Association, *Governing the American States*, 187-188.
48. Bowermaster, *Governor*, 155.
49. National Conference of State Legislatures, *A Guide to Legislative Leadership* (Denver: NCSL, January 1981), 42.
50. Kean, *The Politics of Inclusion*, 84: Alice Chasan Edelman, "John Russo: Born to Run," *New Jersey Reporter*, September 1986, 11.

5

Making Policy

A recent national poll, sponsored by the Council of State Governments, asked people whether they believed the governor or the legislature should take the lead in proposing policies in their states. Despite the visibility of governors and the obscurity of legislatures, 56.9 percent preferred the legislature to take the lead, while 33.2 percent chose leadership by the governor. A comparable question in another poll was asked of citizens in North Carolina: "If you wanted to change a state policy or program, which of the following would you be most likely to contact?" Of those who responded, 31 percent chose the legislature and 25 percent the governor (with 26 percent choosing an organized interest group and 12 percent a state agency).[1]

Although people believe the legislature should make policy, the prevalent belief is that the governor is the one who does make policy. "The governor proposes, the legislature disposes" describes the executive-legislative balance in policy making as perceived by people generally and by political scientists in particular. That perception is not without basis, but while it may have been an accurate description of the balance fifteen or twenty years ago, it is not accurate today. At an earlier time, when demands were made on government, they were made on the governor, and legislatures were content to have the governor deal with the pressing issues.

Nowadays legislatures take on far more than they did in the past. Indeed, they handle many more issues than does the governor, because of entrepreneurial members pushing their own pet bills, a myriad of organized groups lobbying legislators to advance special interests through legislation, and departments and agencies relying on the legislature for bills they need to further bureaucratic objectives. Members, groups, and even units in the executive branch make more demands on the legislature than on the governor.

Legislatures, moreover, have less control over their agendas; and they have a more difficult time in deciding what issues to engage. Just about any interest group, department or agency, standing committee, and even individual member has the means to put something on the legislature's agenda. That is no guarantee of favorable disposition, but it does ensure at least a minimal hearing and consideration. By contrast, governors can and must be, and usually are, more selective. Barring crisis, they have greater choice as to what, or what not, to adopt as a priority item or as part of their program. The tendency of governors is to attend to issues of larger dimensions and to those that lend themselves to thematic treatment. The tendency of legislatures is to take anything or almost anything that comes their way, including of course whatever governors transmit to them as part of their program.

Although the respective roles of the executive and legislative branches in proposing, modifying, ratifying, and rejecting policy are not precisely delineated, one thing is clear. In the policy-making process of the states, the spotlight is on governors and their priorities. Any consideration of policy making in a state must begin with the governor's program, for that establishes a major agenda for the legislature and the focus for the media.

THE GOVERNOR'S PROGRAM

As much as any other device, it is the governor's program that determines what major problems will be addressed by state government. Not every issue requiring attention can be given consideration; thus, the governor's agenda normally consists of a limited number of items. In nearly every state the governor has an identifiable legislative program, and in three-fourths of the states the governor's legislative package is distinguished from the total executive-branch package, which encompasses departmental and agency bills too. The governor's own program, however, includes only those bills in which the executive takes personal interest and to which he or she is willing to commit personal resources.[2]

SETTING THE AGENDA

The National Governors' Association advises governors to focus their energies by picking a limited number of issues on which to concentrate. Some governors would advise their colleagues not to announce an agenda of more than three or four issues, recognizing that they can always add to their agenda once a few issues have been acted on. Most governors heed NGA's advice and undertake no more than a half dozen major legislative initiatives each year, with other subsidiary issues also in their program. They may touch a larger number of bases in their state of the state and budget messages, but their working priorities are more narrowly cast.[3]

In earlier years, governors were less inclined to develop a thrust for their administrations. Marvin Harder, secretary of administration under Robert Docking (1967-1975) of Kansas, described the governor's program as a smorgasbord, reflecting no goal or set of goals and without coherence.[4] From today's perspective, that does not appear to be the most effective approach. In 1971, for example, the initiatives of Governor Dan Evans of Washington were incorporated in sixty-five executive request bills, a high for his administration. After the legislative session, the governor himself noted the inverse ratio between the number of his bills and the passage rate.[5] That was only to be expected.

Other governors have learned similar lessons. At the beginning of his second term as governor of Massachusetts, and with an intervening electoral defeat, Michael Dukakis carefully limited his legislative agenda. The approach worked. Bill Clinton of Arkansas, like Dukakis, also took defeat to heart. In his second term, he focused on two areas only, albeit broad ones—educational reform and economic development. He hoped thereby to give people a sense of direction and gain broad popular support for his program.[6] In each biennial legislative session since then Clinton has selected a single theme encompassing several pieces of legislation. In preparing for the 1989 session, Clinton's staff put together a more comprehensive program than earlier, but still a thematic one that built on education and jobs. Bob Graham of Florida also began with overly ambitious goals when he took office in 1979.

Hoping to attack many of the state's problems in one fell swoop, Graham came to the legislature with as many as fifty separate proposals. He was notably unsuccessful, and soon the governor's office was setting a much narrower agenda that proved to be far more effective.

Most contemporary governors see the wisdom in limiting themselves to a few major priorities for each legislative session. Virginia's Gerald Baliles is exceptionally focused. In Virginia governors are constitutionally permitted to serve only a single term. Baliles had a four-year plan devised when he came into office, with emphasis on the areas of transportation, natural resources, education, and economic development. He established a theme for what he wanted to accomplish, carried the theme into his press conference, and managed to define the policy discussion through the media. He took on transportation first, in 1986, because the problem had reached a crisis. The following legislative session he addressed natural resources and teacher salaries. Then, he confronted economic development, including both the human element and the physical infrastructure of the state.

Minnesota's Rudy Perpich is similarly focused, and since 1983 he has devoted himself primarily to the creation of jobs. The governor's theme, "blueprint for prosperity," includes education, the environment, and taxes. But the main issue is jobs, and every legislative proposal—about twelve in 1988—is framed in relation to employment. William Donald Schaefer has also emphasized economic development in Maryland. According to one member of his cabinet, economic development "is the key to everything in the Schaefer administration, whether we're talking about health or the environment or transportation." [7]

Some governors, however, continue to develop broad agendas, and they still achieve respectable batting averages for their program in the legislature. In Missouri John Ashcroft has taken on education, welfare, and job training at one time and is responsible for thirty to thirty-five proposals at each session. Terry Branstad of Iowa also presents an ambitious program. In 1988, for instance, he advanced forty-four specific proposals in five major areas: economic development and education, environmental quality, human needs, governmental efficiency, and public safety. In New York, Governor Mario Cuomo announced as a theme the "decade of the child," but his 1988 state of the state message and priorities included tax reduction, solid waste, and other major items totaling about a hundred program bills and his 1989 state of the state message included measures that led to the introduction of about one hundred and fifty program bills.

SOURCES FOR THE AGENDA

Governors pick and choose from among a host of possibilities. Not every issue or problem makes it onto the gubernatorial agenda. Relatively few ideas are developed by the governor personally; most percolate up or derive from forces and events that have their own momentum. But governors choose what to respond to and how to respond. One of their immediate challenges is to frame a relatively narrow agenda from all the possibilities. How do governors do that? What factors influence their decisions concerning what to promote and where to focus their energies?

Circumstances play a most significant role, and none are more important than economic conditions. When times are good and revenues are mounting, governors have the wherewithal to propose far-reaching policy agendas. Surpluses allow for innovative programs, shortfalls do not. When times are bad and revenues are in decline, governors have nothing to spend on new initiatives. Instead, they must focus substantial energies on coping with economic crisis. The amount of fiscal resources available, in short, forces governors to set priorities and also constrains their ambitions. Moreover, when governors have a large surplus, they have more resources with which to keep legislators in line. Without a surplus, there are fewer goodies to exchange for critical votes.

Economic recessions necessitate a curtailment of expenditures or an increase in taxes or both. A diminution in the market price of oil, a large revenue-producer in Texas and Oklahoma, had tremendous impact on the states' economies and hence on policy. If economic conditions are bad, if a crisis occurs, or if increased services are suddenly demanded, the chief executive will feel pressure to raise taxes. That is something few public officials care to do, because of the electoral risks involved (especially with the establishment of a new tax). But from time to time, tax increases are unavoidable. In 1981, for example, because of the recession and cutbacks in federal aid, governors called for tax increases, as well as spending cuts, in order to balance state budgets. Thus, sales tax rates rose in four states, motor fuel taxes in twenty-four, severance taxes in twelve, cigarette taxes in six, and alcoholic beverage taxes in eight. Cutbacks in federal aid continued, as did revenue problems. In 1987, revenues were again an agenda item for governors, with four out of five states revamping their tax codes. In 1989 more than half the states enacted tax increases.

The plight of a governor serving when economic conditions are bad is illustrated by Norman Bangerter in Utah. Elected in 1984 on a pledge not to raise taxes, he kept his word during the first two years of his administration despite the state's diminished revenues and increased needs. Finally, as the budgetary situation worsened, he pushed through an increase in taxes in 1987, the year before he ran for reelection. It proved to be costly to the governor, who won reelection with only 40 percent of the vote in a three-candidate race.

Governors cannot plan everything in advance. Emergencies arise and pressures build, forcing them to act legislatively. A scandal involving county commissioners, a court order directed at the state's prisons, a strike, or a flood—each may call for legislation as a solution, and each may induce the governor to devise a program for the legislature to address.

Among the circumstances shaping a governor's choices, political considerations seldom are absent. Governors feel constrained by the partisan balance in the legislature. A Republican governor facing a Republican legislature is likely to propose a somewhat different agenda than the same governor facing a Democratic legislature. Take Republican Terry E. Branstad of Iowa, for example. With the legislature controlled by Democrats for all of his years as governor, Branstad felt that he had to hold back, at least to some extent. Had the Republicans been in control, he would have gone further and asked for more. Given the situation, however, he had to anticipate what the Democratic legislature would be willing to take; that was roughly what he would offer. The same situation faced John Carlin (1979-1987), a Democratic governor of Kansas, who limited his agenda to a few issues because he faced a Republican legislature.

Even where there is little partisan opposition as such in the legislature, political feasibility must enter into governors' calculations. That is because their objective is to succeed in enacting the program that they advocate. To fail is to lose influence. Thus, it could be said about Gerald Baliles, who had a strong legislative record in Virginia: "The governor gets what he asks for, but he asks for what he can get." Most governors behave in similar fashion.

Whether governors are in their first term or their second or final one also affects the types of issues they choose to advance. Many governors tend to be more daring when they are in their final terms and will not have to face the voters again. As a Democratic leader in the New Jersey assembly described the situation in a state where governors after a second term cannot succeed themselves: "The first term is for reelection, the second is for the history books."

On some issues, especially those where emotions are involved and the public is sharply divided, governors will choose not to engage if such a choice is open to them. For example, the abortion issue is one that governors and legislators, too, try to avoid. Yet in light of the Supreme Court's decision in *Webster v. Reproductive Health Services* (1989), it is unlikely that they will be able to steer clear of the prochoice vs. prolife battle that is going on in the states. In fact, governors Bob Martinez of Florida and Robert Casey (1987-   ) of Pennsylvania have chosen to take on the issue. On other issues that might be complex or controversial, governors may be willing to run some risks. Governor Richard Snelling of Vermont, for one, believed strongly that "it is incumbent upon the governor to frequently stick out his neck and do something which is very, very unpopular, but important to the state." According to him, governors can afford the risk, because "the half life of public anguish over those kind of policy decisions is relatively short." [8] Even though many governors normally try to minimize risks, they do appreciate that their involvement is required if certain problems are to be satisfactorily addressed. Only they have the bully pulpit and substantial ability to build support statewide.

Some governors also see their role as issue catalyst, picking up public concern, focusing it, devising a proposal, and pursuing it. Dan Evans of Washington likened the gubernatorial role in this respect to that of a surfer trying to catch the wave that can be ridden to the shore. [9]

Whatever strategic considerations apply in fashioning an agenda, the choice of issues is discretionary and personal. A number of gubernatorial priorities derive from the past campaign and election. As candidates, governors have discussed issues and have made at least implicit promises. They have committed themselves by both word and belief to take action, if they possibly can; and so it is understandable that they try to do so. Florida's Bob Graham, for instance, in his 1982 campaign for reelection as governor promised to raise teacher salaries. His master teacher program, introduced after his reelection, reflected this priority. In Georgia, Joe Frank Harris (1987-   ) stressed education in his campaign and promised to raise educational standards. Once in office, he proposed reforms that resulted in the Quality of Basic Education Act of 1985.[10]

For Graham and Harris, education did not arise as a fresh campaign issue. They had been interested in education for some time. The former had chaired the education committee in the Florida senate, while the latter's wife and sister were teachers and his father was on the school board. For both, education had been a priority before their term of office and before their campaign. Thus, although priorities may take shape because of positions first adopted during a campaign, by and large, they reflect prior interests and concerns. As Reubin Askew reflects, "the major issues were issues which I believed were consistent with my own priorities. . . . I had been in the Legislature for 12 years, and most of the issues just came as my own set of priorities." [11] Such priorities derive from experience, they are embedded in one's political philosophy, and they are, or become, very personal matters.

An illustration is the decision of Governor Brendan Byrne to devote a major effort to legislation preserving and protecting the pinelands of New Jersey.[12] How did the issue of the pinelands arise? Why did Byrne have a particular fondness for the one-million-acre tract of land in the southern part of the state? Could it be, one might ask, because the governor was a hunter, a fisherman, a canoeist, or a hiker? More likely it was because he was a tennis partner of John McPhee, the well-known writer who lived in Princeton and had written a book about the pine barrens. Byrne read McPhee's book, and was moved by it. He then raised the issue with his staff. John Degnan, the governor's counsel, recalls:

> I remember . . . that some time in 1976 the governor told us at one of our Monday morning breakfasts that the Pinelands would be the next issue. I had never even heard of the Pinelands when I grew up. And we all went out with John McPhee's book and we educated ourselves on what the Pine Barrens was.

The issue was then raised in Byrne's 1977 reelection campaign, and that reinforced his desire to take action. After his victory, the governor's staff began work, but could not put together a tenable proposal. Staff members tried to shift Byrne's attention to other measures, but the governor insisted on a program for the pinelands, which resulted in passage of the Pinelands Protection Act in 1979.

In addition to priorities that are long held and ones that seem to arise almost spontaneously, many ideas for legislative programs are borrowed, in one form or another, from elsewhere. Governors may incorporate the ideas of legislators, and particularly legislative leaders, into their agendas. In some instances, this is politically necessary; in others, the ideas have particular appeal, so governors are not loath to adopt them as their own.

Governors not only accept ideas from legislators within their state, but they look to other places as well. A visit to another state may have as a result a major legislative initiative. Governor Schaefer of Maryland on a trip to North Carolina was impressed by an innovative high school for promising math and science students from around the state. He returned to Maryland and made a math-science high school one of the top priorities of his administration. Governors also look to other governors, adopting programs that have earned recognition for their colleagues. Bruce Babbitt of Arizona discovered education in the early 1980s, in part because Governor Lamar Alexander in Tennessee and Jim Hunt (1981-1985) in North Carolina were receiving considerable acknowledgment by virtue of their educational initiatives. Bob Graham also was influenced by what other governors were accomplishing in promoting programs for teachers.

Recently, a new source of ideas has entered the picture: the National Governors' Association, which has come to play a significant role in disseminating policy ideas across state lines.[13] NGA represents the nation's governors and states as a collective force in Washington, and now it also disseminates policy options to the states. Under Lamar Alexander's 1985-1986 chairship, the association grappled with education and presented a policy agenda for the consideration of each governor and each state. "The word in education spread," is how one NGA official described the process. And policy initiatives also spread. A number of governors made education a priority, partly because of the work that had been done by their national association.

NGA repeated the effort in 1986-1987, focusing on economic development and job creation under the chairmanship of Bill Clinton. With only one dissenting vote, NGA adopted an approach to welfare reform that called for mandatory education and a training program for able-bodied welfare recipients. Clinton in Arkansas and other gubernatorial colleagues in their states shortly thereafter put together programs on economic development and jobs that built on their association's efforts.

Still another source of items for the legislative programs of governors is the departments and agencies within the executive branch. Cabinet members, who are governors' trusted associates, have special influence on their priorities. Governors may adopt a cabinet member's program as their own.

Only a few of the numerous departmental and agency proposals, however, are at the core of the governor's legislative package. Rather, they have the governor's formal backing as "administration bills." In Tennessee, for instance, Governor Ned McWherter had eight proposals of his own, but about eight times as many others from his department heads. In Nebraska, Governor Kay Orr concentrated on a handful of issues, but her administration was responsible for another eighty to one hundred bills—measures of a housekeeping nature, fine-tuning of previous legislation, or those providing for reauthorization of a program. Such bills are not pushed by the governor or her chief of staff, but by the departments and agencies themselves. Most are not very controversial, and the overwhelming proportion are enacted into law.

Although the governor's immediate office may have little to do with run-of-the-mill administration bills, a screening and approval process normally is conducted by a department of administration or a planning agency. About 60 percent of the states follow a formalized procedure by which each agency submits recommendations, which are then reviewed and approved or rejected. Most of the other states have a more informal procedure by which agency heads check with the governor's legislative liaison staffer, or occasionally with the governor, on what is appropriate to advance.[14]

If the governor's office refuses to adopt a departmental proposal as an administration bill, the department may appeal to a friendly legislator who will carry its bill. At the outset of an administration, departments and agencies tend to be loyal to the governor. Then, as cabinet members get their bearings, things loosen up and departmental end runs around the governor's office to the legislature increase. Then, cabinet members mobilize their department's clients and seek to have their objectives met in the legislature, in the expectation that the governor will not veto departmental bills when they are sent over to him. Generally, such expectations are confirmed.

GUBERNATORIAL FOLLOW-THROUGH

Legislatures expect governors to lead. They rely on the governor to define issues and set the process in motion. Legislatures need not be weak or a rubber stamp to want gubernatorial leadership. If the issue is significant, the governor's presence and power may be vital in achieving agreement. "What does the governor want?" and "What does the governor want us to do?" are the customary questions raised by legislators in the capitol.

Gubernatorial leadership, at the outset, naturally requires the formulation of a program and the setting of an agenda. But beyond that, it requires that the governor steer the program through and succeed in having it adopted by the legislature. Therefore, as Madeleine Kunin points out, the governor has the ability "not only to define the agenda, but then to develop it, to actually make it happen." To make it happen, governors must have follow-through—the willingness and the skill to appeal to the public, persuade legislators, and do whatever they deem necessary to steer their proposals through the legislative process. Success does not always come on the first push. Sometimes a governor will lose in one legislative session and then reintroduce the proposal in the next. Accomplishment may take a governor's entire term.

Bruce Babbitt, who concentrated on a few issues in each of his years in office, described how he "used everything at my disposal—initiative, referendum, the bully pulpit, the press, browbeating, trade-offs, threats, rewards—to get what I needed." [15] That was Babbitt's way of following through. Other governors do it somewhat differently. There are a variety of ways to succeed, as the following cases of gubernatorial leadership suggest.

THREE CASES OF LEADERSHIP

Byrne and the Pinelands.   Brendan Byrne's advocacy of the pinelands in New Jersey, more than anything else, was responsible for the passage of the Pinelands Protection Act in 1979. Having been influenced by John McPhee's book, Governor Byrne mentioned the pinelands in his 1978 message to the legislature. From then on, he insisted on his goal of protecting and preserving an especially vulnerable area through the establishment of a regional planning and management commission.[16]

During the process, the governor indicated to his staff just how much he wanted the bill. He issued an executive order that established a planning commission and imposed temporary, but stringent, controls on development. That executive order was unparalleled for the reach of executive authority, even in a state where the governor is extremely powerful by virtue of the constitution. The purpose of the executive order was to pressure the legislature into passing a bill rather than face the possibility that the supreme court might uphold the governor's extraordinary action when the case was brought to court. The attorney general and his staff believed that the executive order was unconstitutional. But Byrne did not want to be deterred, so he never asked the attorney general for an opinion; instead, he simply forged ahead.

The process in New Jersey moved forward. Public hearings were held around the state. As a result, amendments were added to the bill to appease various groups, but no substantial changes were made. The governor's staff worked the legislature skillfully and, together with the legislative leadership, persuaded nearly all the members of the senate and enough members in the assembly to go along with Byrne's initiative. Governor Byrne got almost precisely what he wanted, partly because he went all out on behalf of his proposal.

A legislative staffer, Michael Catania, who was involved in the process, describes the role played by Byrne:

> Everybody thought we should preserve the Pines, but nobody thought the legislature would pass a bill until somebody had the guts to say, "I will make this my issue, I will make this happen, and I will make them know that I will not take no for an answer."

The pinelands had many friends, but their protection and preservation were on no one else's agenda. In reflecting on his term as governor, Byrne concluded that the pinelands legislation, like no other measure he proposed, "would not have been passed if I didn't take an interest in it." The governor normally is vital in the enactment of policy; in this case he was indispensable.

Ray and the Bottle Bill. Robert Ray of Iowa was a late convert to a bottle bill, an environmental measure to control litter in the state. But "without the governor's leadership," recalled one senate Republican supporter, "it would have been difficult to pass." [17] As for many other bills, introducing and deliberating the bottle bill in the legislature would have presented no problem, but it is doubtful whether "we would have had the muscle to get the thing passed." A bottle bill was first raised in the early 1970s and was introduced every year by a conservative Republican, but it went nowhere. Late in 1976, the governor's office, in putting together a list of ideas for Ray's annual program, brought up the problem of litter control. The governor responded positively and, after staff review of alternative approaches, he committed himself to a bottle bill.

In order to build support, Ray pursued both an outside and an inside strategy. His backing of the bill put it in the spotlight throughout Iowa. "Suddenly it went from a bill that nobody paid much attention to," explained one of his aides, "to one that was discussed on the talk shows." That was the easy part of the job; the more difficult part was placating the various interest groups and dealing with the legislature.

The Republicans, in the minority for a second term, were anxious to find a measure to back rather than to stand in opposition to the majority Democrats. But beer distributors, soft drink lobbyists, and retailers—a number of whom had contributed to Republican legislators—were adamant in opposition. Organized labor, which was also against the bill, had close ties to the Democrats.

Ray managed to split the opposition. He did not want to hurt Iowa business and worked closely with Alcoa, which subsequently dropped its objections to the bill. That took some of the intensity out of the campaign by both manufacturers and the AFL-CIO and eased the way for passage of the bill. Its final enactment was one of Ray's major accomplishments. "It wasn't his idea, others had introduced it, there was nothing original about it," remarked the Democratic majority leader of the Iowa house. Nevertheless, he admitted, "it is fair for him to take a lot of credit for it." The bottle bill in Iowa would probably not have been enacted without gubernatorial leadership.

Kunin and Growth and Development.   Growth policy in Vermont also demonstrates gubernatorial leadership. Rapid growth and development had caused problems in Vermont since the 1960s, and recent prosperity brought a new surge that appeared to require remedial action by the state. Governor Madeleine Kunin decided that the time was ripe in mid-1987, shortly after she began her second two-year term in office. That summer she held a retreat attended by members of her administration, a few legislators, and several out-of-state experts on the planning process. (She believed that in developing policy and strategy, it was advisable to escape from the daily rhythm of the office.) The strategy devised at that retreat was pursued by means of both outside and inside campaigns. A top-down approach would not work; it had not succeeded in the past. Statewide land-use planning was such a polarizing issue that, without public debate, it would be neither politically nor practically feasible to enact into law. That thinking underlay the subsequent campaign.

Kunin's first step was to appoint a blue-ribbon group, the Governor's Commission on Vermont's Future, to provide a rationale and political cover for legislation. The commission, chaired by the dean of the state university's law school, included the president of the Vermont League of Cities and Towns, a representative of the state's ski resorts, a dairy farmer, two representatives of the business community, the editor of a state business magazine, a member of the governor's administration, the president of a local college, and a veteran legislator. Having to assess the concern of citizens regarding growth, establish guidelines for growth, and suggest mechanisms to help plan Vermont's future, the commission held a dozen hearings and focus groups and conducted several surveys. The process was purposely speedy, so that opposition would have little time to form. The commission, which organized in September 1987, had its report ready by January 1988.[18]

The initial response to the report was positive, and the predictable battle between environmentalists and developers did not take place, at least not at the outset. The ski industry and Vermont business appeared reconciled to some planning process. The public had been alerted and the interested parties had been softened up. It was now in the hands of the legislature, and the strategy shifted to an inside one.

The legislature had its own contribution to make—filling in the details, providing the nuts and bolts. The speaker and Democrats in the house had growth policy as a high priority, so they felt that the governor had chosen the right issue, their issue. They had come into their own, and benefiting from the publicity power of the governor, they stood to achieve their goals. To signal the importance of the issue to members, the speaker appointed a special committee, chaired by the majority leader, to develop legislation and to expedite the process.

Now, with an actual target—a piece of legislation—to shoot at, conflict arose. Opposition organized, and the issue quickly became a partisan one in the senate, with Republicans opposed to the governor's plan. Therefore, the initial thrust was in the house, where the governor worked with the Democratic leadership, and the speaker then dealt with the Republican leadership. One member of the governor's staff spent full time lobbying, with others serving as back-up. The governor, herself, dealt with individual legislators one on one, emphasizing that planning, as required in the proposed legislation, was not a partisan matter.

In addition to explanation and exhortation, bargaining was called for. The growth issue unleashed a concern in the legislature about agriculture. In return for supporting the governor's growth policy, the house extracted as a price the governor's backing of its measure to assist agriculture. The house wanted to provide dairy farmers with a subsidy, but the governor, concerned about excessive spending, refused to go along. Under pressure from Vermont farmers, not one legislator was willing to oppose the subsidy in public. So a compromise had to be worked out. Kunin's office developed as an alternative to a subsidy a tax-abatement program with a temporary subsidy. The house was agreeable to the compromise. Meanwhile, a number of liberal Democrats in the senate were insisting on property tax reform as a quid pro quo for supporting the growth bill. Kunin could not accede to their demand, but she did promise to form a committee to study the issue. The governor's office was prepared with additional inducements. "We had a whole batch of three-digit license plates stockpiled for the occasion," one aide remarked. But the plates were not needed.

During the final stages of the campaign the governor again went public, delivering a television address and meeting with newspaper editors. Not all Democrats were on board and most Republicans were opposed, but the bill passed by a narrow margin in the senate. Without doubt, leadership by the governor had made the difference.

OUTSIDE AND INSIDE STRATEGIES

As indicated by these cases, and especially the Vermont growth legislation, on major and controversial issues governors are likely to deal with the public and relevant groups outside the legislature before dealing with leaders and rank and file within the fold. The two strategies are complementary. Going outside facilitates the bargaining that dominates the legislative process. The approach of many governors today may be thought of in terms of *conditioning, coalition formation,* and *consensus building.* The first step is to let the public know about problems that need to be addressed. A second step, combining outside and inside elements, is to involve interest groups and to begin discussions. A third step is to negotiate with legislative leaders and legislators, and perhaps other groups, in order to arrive at a program with sufficiently broad support.

Governors' appeals to the public do not mean that they are going over the head of the legislature. While they may occasionally do so, more frequently their appeals to the public are for purposes of laying a groundwork for a campaign. Many modern governors are in the habit of going public by establishing a theme and a program, packaging the issue so people will understand it, repeating the message continuously, and scheduling events to highlight the particular issue being promoted.

Some governors see themselves as educators. Minnesota governor Rudy Perpich is foremost among them. He takes issues to the public as a matter of principle, traveling throughout the state in the fall, holding hearings, and opening up major issues for public debate. Other governors think less of public education per se and more of accomplishing designated purposes. They go to the public on a few issues only—ones where a major change is being proposed or support is required or both, or where a governor can benefit politically by identifying his or her administration with a particular issue. Often these governors conduct their issue campaigns as if they were running for office themselves, hiring outside consultants and attempting to manage coverage in the press. Lamar Alexander of Tennessee, for example, raised money to retain the firm of Bailey, Deardorff for public relations. He was interested in developing labels and themes for his programs, and shaping people's perceptions accordingly. John Sununu, who served as governor of New Hampshire before moving to the Bush White House as chief of staff, maintained that in order to be successful in office, governors need the same communication skills that they need as candidates. "In the 1990s," he states, "a governor will be governing almost entirely in public, on stage." [19]

It is not surprising, then, that today's governors devote time and energy to speaking to the public. Governor Mike Hayden and his transportation secretary flew around Kansas and argued (unsuccessfully as it turned out) that both safety and economic development required adoption of his program.

In Vermont, Madeleine Kunin focused on educational finance in 1987, so that it was the only subject of her state of the state address. Her objective was to direct attention to funding for the schools, and that is what she talked about with whatever groups she met. Even though her audiences would groan as she belabored the topic, Kunin managed to create a public climate in Vermont that was favorably disposed toward dealing with the educational funding problem.

Over the years, Bill Clinton of Arkansas has become particularly adept in appealing to the public. His approach and techniques vary according to the legislative package or issues involved. On themes central to his administration, he spends months educating the public before the legislative session. In 1988 he succeeded in winning support from the public for a tax increase before a special session. Later that year, in anticipation of the 1989 session, he took his dog and pony show from one corner of Arkansas to another preparing people and the legislature for his "year 2000" program.

When governors neglect going outside on major issues, they risk failure. Kentucky's Martha Layne Collins proposed a tax program in 1984 to finance educational reform, but she never had a chance to engage in a speaking and media campaign or to mobilize public support. She lost in the legislature, but for the next sixteen months she went public before succeeding with her program in a special session the following year.

The real contest occurs on those relatively infrequent occasions when the governor appeals to the public over the head of the legislature. Sometimes the threat of appeal is enough to pressure the legislature into compliance. That was the case in a western state whose governor delivered the following ultimatum to his legislature.

I believe that water policy is our most serious problem. I am willing to work with you on a solution, but whether or not you address the issue,

I plan to. If we have not been able to act together during the coming two years, I will act alone, taking my case to the people.[20]

From time to time, there is cause to do battle. Governor Mario Cuomo of New York, for instance, appealed to the public over the head of the legislature on several occasions, most notably on ethics legislation. Objecting to a weakened ethics bill that emerged from a compromise between the senate and assembly, Cuomo took the high ground and with righteousness cast a veto. He then focused public attention on the issue through constant comment in the media, delighting the press and making legislators look bad. Given the nature of the issue and Cuomo's resolve and oratorical skills, there could be little question as to the outcome. The legislature was forced to agree to a bill that satisfied the governor's objections.[21]

Appealing over the head of the legislature will not always work, and the strategy itself entails risks. As a legislative leader in the New Jersey assembly put it: "If you go to the public, you better win; otherwise you'll lose your pants in the legislature." Whether they lose their pants or lose face, governors cannot afford to be bested once they throw down the gauntlet in a challenge to the legislature.

An outside strategy usually entails engaging the state's opinion leadership and its organized interests, as well as appealing to the mass public through the media. Governors travel across their states to meet with editorial boards of newspapers in an attempt to secure their endorsement for an incipient proposal, and thereby impress legislators who are not yet committed. They also work at wooing influential special interests, who in turn may help persuade legislators that the governor is on the right track.

One device that is frequently employed combines elements of both strategic approaches. Governors appoint commissions, task forces, committees, or the like, which pave the way for the governor's priorities with the public and also with the legislature. The blue ribbon commission has become a most popular device at the national level, used largely to furnish the president and Congress with political cover, a way to avoid blame. Special panels to address the social security system, obsolete military bases, federal criminal sentencing, and the budget deficit are examples. At the state level, governors have also made use of such bodies—sometimes to avoid dealing with a problem, sometimes to shield the executive from political heat, but increasingly to fashion programs and develop consensus. Moreover, such entities facilitate longer range planning, insulate discussion from the political maneuvering of a legislative session, and permit broad participation by representatives of business, academia, and other groups.

In resorting to a commission, governors cannot be certain as to what exactly will emerge, but they can have a reasonably good idea of the general dimensions of the product. At the very least, they can count on their interest being expressed by members of their administration whom they appoint to the commission, and probably by other appointees as well. The objective of many commissions—not all, since some are intended to shelve problems—is to come up with proposals, to accomplish something specific. The tendency is for members to endorse the governor's initiatives. In any case, members recognize that their recommendations will not get far without gubernatorial backing. All of this accounts for the governor's influence at this stage of formulation.

As a rule, a commission will include not only a member or two of the administration, but also representatives of significant and relevant interest groups, usually including business, and several key legislators. Once the commission has made its report, the governor can take the package of proposals to the press and the people for their endorsement. Meanwhile, commission members from the interest groups can be expected to become advocates and to line up their organizations and perhaps engage them in a campaign on behalf of the governor's package. Finally, the legislators who served and who approved the package will be responsible for providing leadership in moving legislation through the house and senate.

Commissions are widely used in the states, taking on economic development in Maine, transportation in Virginia, unemployment in New Jersey, and tort reform in Missouri. But probably no policy domain has been as well served by blue-ribbon commissions as elementary and secondary education. With the publication of *A Nation at Risk* in 1983, educational reform accelerated throughout the nation. In many of the states that underwent reform, commissions spearheaded the drive. Arkansas governor Clinton made use of a legislatively created citizens' committee on new educational standards and appointed his wife as chair. She took the committee on the road, holding hearings in all seventy-five of the state's counties. On the basis of the committee's recommendations, Clinton backed a teacher-testing bill and tax increases to pay for an expanded teaching force and for higher salaries. With the governor's firm leadership, the package passed the legislature.[22]

Reform began in Florida with a commission on secondary schools. The governor, speaker of the house, and president of the Senate knew what they wanted from the commission and agreed on a chair who would seek their objectives. As a result, a comprehensive education package, including many of the commission's proposals, was passed by the legislature. In Georgia, Governor Harris established the Educational Review Commission, on which business would play a predominant role.

He embraced the commission's report, championed it throughout the state, and managed its recommendations through the legislature, where the Quality Basic Education Act of 1985 passed without challenge.

Legislators' participation at this early stage appears highly desirable. In order to enhance their chances, governors give legislators a sense of ownership, encouraging their participation in the initial formulation of a program or a share of the credit for what is finally achieved or both.

Governor Kunin, for example, welcomed legislative involvement in educational finance and in growth and development from the very outset. She established a summer study commission on school funding, which included legislators as well as her own secretary of administration. Legislators were the ones to take the lead, hammering out a revised school aid formula. Because of their vigorous participation, they could help steer the governor's proposals—and their own—through the process. One of the products of Kunin's Commission on Vermont's Future was proposed legislation, presented not as a package of bills but rather as a set of working documents. It was left to a special legislative committee to transform these documents into bills. The committee did so, and as a result almost everyone's hand had been on the legislation by the time it came up for decision. That proved decisive in the struggle that ensued.

Ownership can also come about when a governor, such as John Ashcroft in Missouri, develops proposals on job creation, rural development, and education and divvies up the initiatives among individual legislators and interest groups, all of whom sign on and advocate the governor's program.

Governors, however, cannot rely completely on their appeals to the public, on blue-ribbon commissions, and on legislators having a sense of ownership. They still have to exercise leadership within the institution, and that entails intervening in the process and using the resources of gubernatorial office. Whatever the popularity of individual governors, as far as state legislatures are concerned, a time comes to shut the door and cut a deal.

Governors must deal first with leadership, and then with rank-and-file members. Occasionally leadership can accomplish whatever is necessary, but frequently governors must be personally involved. In Arizona, for example, Governor Babbitt could not leave such matters to anyone else. He proved effective, largely because he threatened to veto members' bills unless they backed his proposals. In Louisiana, Governor Edwin Edwards needed a two-thirds vote from the legislature for a constitutional amendment to make the superintendent of education an appointive officer. In the senate, the governor's bill failed by one vote. After a night of intense lobbying by Edwards, the bill was recalled under the rules the next day and passed with a vote to spare. In the house, it was defeated initially, but the governor overnight succeeded in changing six votes. Once again, the next day the legislation was recalled and passed.[23] It was the governor's doing, no one else's.

THE BOTTOM LINE

If governors are selective in what they propose, make use of the commission device, take their case to the people, and work the legislature from inside, we would expect them to achieve considerable success in having their programs enacted into law. Their cumulative powers surely give them a head start.

Officials of both the executive and legislative branches agree that today's governors are highly effective in steering their proposals through the legislatures. The record bears them out, as the following examples show.

- In Arkansas, governors since 1979 have succeeded with more than three-fourths of their major policy proposals.[24]
- In Hawaii, Governor Waihee had about 80 percent of his bills pass.
- Governor Branstad in Iowa had about an 85 percent success rate.
- Maine's McKernan steered through twenty of twenty-four initiatives in 1987.
- Maryland's Schaefer had twelve of fourteen important administration bills pass in 1988, including major breakthroughs in higher education, prisons, and transportation.
- In Minnesota, Governor Perpich was successful on ten of twelve initiatives.
- In Missouri, Governor Ashcroft managed to ensure that 80 to 85 percent of his priorities were enacted.
- Governor Kean of New Jersey won on such issues as an alternate route to teaching, high school proficiency examinations, minimum teacher salaries, school takeover, ocean clean-up, civil service reform, and inheritance tax changes—roughly 80 to 90 percent of his priorities.
- Governor Lamar Alexander of Tennessee, despite being a "lame duck" Republican with a Democratic legislature, managed to steer nearly all of his proposals through the 1986 session.[25]
- Tennessee governor Ned McWherter received legislative approval for all his initiatives in 1987 and 1988, although his program was limited to relatively few measures.

One of the poorest records—statistically, at least—was that of Mario Cuomo in New York. Only about 50 to 60 percent of his program bills were enacted into law by a divided legislature during the 1988 session. But Cuomo did well by comparison to his predecessor, Hugh Carey, who got only about 25 percent of what he wanted from the legislature.

A high executive batting average should not suggest that the legislature is a rubber stamp. Nothing could be further from the truth. One of the principal reasons gubernatorial success rates are impressive is because governors know how to accommodate their legislatures. And usually the legislature leaves a heavy imprint on the governor's initiative.

Such an imprint may not even be discernible when made early, before the start of the formal process. Many governors consult with legislative leaders and other key members before the opening of a session, and at that time they take into account legislative priorities and views. The process of modification is already under way before the process formally begins. Modification by the legislature continues through review by the standing committees of house and senate, sometimes through amendments on the floor, and occasionally occurs as late as a conference committee between the two chambers. The process of negotiation is a continuing one.

If governors prove stubborn, they may lose. For example, in 1987, Governor Ashcroft of Missouri rejected a legislative change in his proposal for college savings bonds. As a result, nothing passed. The next year Ashcroft accepted the grafting onto his plan of a Michigan-style prepaid tuition plan. The two notions were married, and the proposal was enacted into law. In other instances, too, governors have had to give way. Governor Edward DiPrete of Rhode Island wanted a new department of environmental quality, with the consolidation of a number of commissions, and a department of environmental management. He got some of what he wanted, but by no means everything. Instead of a new department, he had to settle for a new deputy commissioner, the establishment of a study commission, and the possibility that he would get more of what he wanted in the future. DiPrete also had as a priority affordable housing. He could not persuade the legislature to require towns to allocate land to low-income housing, but he did succeed in obtaining a loan and grant program that accomplished some, if not all, of his objectives.

While most recent governors have been relatively successful, a few have not fared well at the hands of their legislatures. Mike Hayden of Kansas was beaten on some of his top priorities, and those of his proposals that became law in 1988 passed in "one battered form or another." [26] In New Mexico, Toney Anaya was about as unsuccessful as a governor could be with a legislature that rejected major parts of his revenue package and killed his plan to invite out-of-state banks into New Mexico.

Even in places where governors have compiled positive records, legislatures have drawn the line on one issue or another. Iowa's Branstad lost on criminal justice, tightening of the drunk driving laws, and caps on medical and tort liability, and he was not able to reach agreement with the Democratic legislature on workmen's compensation. Vermont's Kunin could not persuade her legislature to enact a parental leave bill, and Maine's McKernan was defeated on a reorganization plan involving energy resources. In Missouri, Ashcroft's big loss was an economic development measure, which failed on the last day of the session, and a secondary loss was a welfare reform plan.

Even Governor Schaefer, who surely dominated in Maryland during his first two years in office, suffered setbacks. He wanted to have savings and loan depositors paid at a faster pace; the legislature turned him down. He proposed a plan to revise the appointment of circuit judges; like governors before him, he lost on that issue too. But Schaefer's most important and bitter defeat was on his proposal for a residential "super" high school for math and science, to be called the Maryland School for Science and Technology. The governor argued that such a school would be a boon to economic development in the state. In the 1987 session the legislature put the governor's scheme on hold, setting aside $100,000 for planning rather than starting immediately. The following year Schaefer went all out, appealing to the public. But the teachers' associations questioned the school, the senate budget and taxation committee was firm in its opposition, and finally legislative leadership came out against it. The governor made the issue a very personal one—"you're for the high school or you're against me"—and confronted the legislature. But the general assembly stood its ground, and Schaefer could not prevail, however vigorously he fought.

Governors are more likely to suffer losses on tax measures, or on proposals that require additional revenues, than on anything else. Bill Clinton, for instance, has been beaten on tax issues on several occasions. One reason for this is that in Arkansas, as well as in several other states, revenue bills require more than a majority vote in the house and senate. Clinton has been able to raise the "sin" taxes somewhat, but has not succeeded in capturing the revenues needed to fund the programs he believes are necessary.

Another governor who has had a particularly difficult time with taxes is James Thompson of Illinois. In his second campaign against Adlai Stevenson III, Thompson omitted any mention of taxes. Then right after reelection he called for the largest tax increase in Illinois history. With little preparation or campaigning, the proposal failed. Recently, the governor made two more attempts to put a tax package through the legislature. After taking office in 1987 for a fourth term, he proposed higher income and gas taxes and a new tax on services. He lost again in what was called "the single greatest defeat Thompson had suffered in a decade in office." [27] While he managed to obtain the support of the minority leaders and of Phil Rock, the Democratic president of the senate, he could not persuade the house speaker, Michael Madigan, to go along with his plan.

The Illinois general assembly finally enacted a tax package, increasing revenues by about one billion dollars, in 1989. It was not Thompson's income tax, but rather Speaker Madigan's, that passed. In May Madigan had suddenly announced his own tax-increase plan, which was smaller than the governor's. In a display of raw power, the speaker had his plan passed in the house that same day. Significantly, the new monies were earmarked for local governments and schools, and not for state agencies. Senate support for Madigan's bill could not be put together until the last day of the session, and the speaker obtained most of what he wanted. Governor Thompson signed the bill into law. Although the governor did not get the permanent tax increase that was part of his proposal, he did get gasoline and cigarette taxes that were part of his overall package. But the speaker and the legislature had prevailed.

Even with defeat in the legislature, governors still have recourse. If they persevere, there is a good chance that they will prevail in time. For example, Schaefer refashioned his proposal for Maryland's math-science school. No longer did he seek a high school per se; instead he sought a program to train math and science teachers. William F. Winter, one of Mississippi's new breed of governors, had as his principal goal educational reform. In the 1982 session his proposal for public kindergartens came up on the last day of the session. The speaker, C. B. (Buddie) Newman, adjourned the house, and the bill died. Thereupon, the governor launched a statewide campaign and managed to pass his measure in a special session of the legislature.[28]

Defeat for a governor is not the end of the line. "Defeat doesn't mean as much as a lot of people think," said a chief of staff to a New Jersey governor. "If the governor is persistent, he can win most of his battles." And most governors do.

THE LEGISLATURE'S AGENDA

If governors have programs, legislatures have an agenda. It may not be as readily identifiable with a single individual or group, but the legislature's agenda includes many important items that are not initiated by the governor. It also represents many smaller items that comprise the

wish lists of constituents in members' districts, interest groups throughout the state, and legislators themselves.

LEGISLATIVE INITIATIVES

The conventional wisdom, as propagated by political scientists,
accords the legislature a subordinate role as "arbiter" or "legitimizer"
rather than as an initiator of public policy. The governor is credited with
almost exclusive power over policy initiation. "He sets the agenda for
public decision making, and he largely determines what the business of
the legislature will be in any one session," writes Sarah McCally
Morehouse. "Few major state undertakings get off the ground," she
asserts, "without his initiation." [29] If that is an accurate description of the
respective roles of the governor and the legislature in the past, it no
longer applies today.

Growth of the Legislative Role. The initiating role of state
legislatures with regard to major policy has expanded considerably. The
enhancement of legislative capacity has given legislatures the where-
withal with which to initiate policy. The development of independence
and assertiveness has given legislatures the confidence. And the New
Federalism of the Nixon, Carter, and Reagan administrations has given
legislatures cause to initiate policy, as they endeavor to fill the vacuum
left by the diminution of federal control.

The motivation for legislatures to initiate policy increases when
control of government is divided, with both houses of the legislature
dominated by one party and the office of governor dominated by the
other. For example, when Virginia had Republican governors—Mills
Godwin (1966-1970, 1974-1978), Linwood Holton (1970-1974), and John
Dalton (1978-1982)—most initiatives came from the Democratic general
assembly. When Iowa recently elected a Democratic legislature, while
the governor remained Republican, initiative shifted to a noticeable
degree. Legislative initiatives can also be expected when governors
themselves do not take the lead. California Governors Ronald Reagan,
Gerry Brown, and George Deukmejian all believed in minimal government, leaving it to the legislature to lead on a variety of issues.
Moreover, if a governor is a lame duck and transition is under way, the
legislature may fill in while the incumbent governor is winding down
his administration and before a new one has been selected.

Finally, the rationale for legislative initiative increases when economic conditions are good and a state surplus is in the cards. When
money is available, legislatures (as well as governors) can be more
creative in devising new programs. But when the economy is in a

downturn and deficits loom, the focus must be on balancing the budget by cutting expenditures or raising taxes. There is less play for policy initiation.

Whatever the particular partisan or economic conditions, the secular trend has been for greater initiation of policy by the legislature, just as it has been for greater legislative involvement in policy initiated by the executive. Phil Rock, the senate president in Illinois, could claim with justification: "We do not any longer wait for the executive to recommend; we're out in front on a lot of these things." [30] It is not unusual, moreover, for the legislature to move onto ground where the governor has already planted a stake. In New York, for instance, when a number of items on the governor's agenda and the legislature's agenda coincided, both would take the lead. In Iowa, too, the legislature had its own agenda, but usually it overlapped substantially with the governor's. Recently, for example, the Iowa legislature called for a big increase in welfare benefits, while Governor Branstad was interested in welfare reform. The quid pro quo of reform for benefits was obvious.

Leadership Programs.   At a 1988 workshop session of legislative leaders from the northeastern states, a Republican from Vermont asked, "At what point as leaders do we determine the agenda, or do we let the governor set it?" Increasingly, in states throughout the nation leaders are taking on the responsibility for helping to determine the agenda. John Martin, the Democratic speaker in Maine, describes the development of a leadership program for the house. First, leaders put together a program and distribute it to members of the legislative party. They review it, and then Democrats caucus on it. After members provide their inputs, the leadership writes a document that is then revised before final adoption of what is called "the Democratic legislative plan." Running about thirty pages or so, and including both long- and short-term measures, the document becomes the alternative plan to the governor's. In fashioning the Democratic alternative, Martin exercises care so that members feel that they are part of the process. "It is a mistake," he says, "for leadership to try to separate itself from the members in policy-making, in terms of issues and programs." [31]

In a number of states, legislative leaders have not waited on the governor, but have fashioned their own priorities. Oregon offers an example. At the beginning of the 1987 session, the Oregon leadership specified three contentious issues as priorities: reconnecting to the federal income tax code, reform of workers' compensation, and changes in the tort and liability system. In New York, it was the assembly Democratic leadership that in 1988 first raised several of the major issues of the session: a capital rebuilding program for New York City's

Metropolitan Transportation Authority, increased aid for local schools, an environmental bond issue, and a billion-dollar program to rebuild the state's roads and bridges. In Kansas, a Republican legislature took the lead on economic development, establishing a special legislative commission and enlisting the support of Democratic Governor John Carlin.[32]

Perhaps in no other state has legislative leadership developed as broad a program as in Florida. For almost two decades house speakers, in particular, and senate presidents, to a lesser extent, have initiated major legislative programs. Florida's leaders rotate, with no one remaining in the top position for longer than two years. Thus, speakers and presidents, wanting to leave their mark on policy, have had only the brief period during which they held power to do so. Together with their leadership teams, including the chairs of the major committees, they have drafted an overall program for the legislative session. Because of the power of leadership office and the tradition that evolved, they have been able to have most of their initiatives enacted into law.

A leadership program such as Florida's is the exception. Nevertheless, initiatives do come from elsewhere. The standing and interim committees of the legislature develop proposals within their areas of jurisdiction. Their efforts make up part of the legislative agenda. However dominant governors may appear when it comes to initiation, the fact is that in certain areas legislatures are actually in the vanguard. Gun control is an example. Maryland's handgun control law of 1988 was a skillful compromise, which was initiated in and negotiated by the general assembly. The legislative role came first, the governor's involvement later. After enactment, when repeal of the law was on the ballot for decision by the voters of Maryland, Governor Schaefer took the reins. But the enactment itself was attributable mainly to the legislature, not the governor. The gun ban in California, passed in 1989, also arose in the legislature and was not part of the governor's program.

Education Policy. In the domain of elementary and secondary education, initiatives are just as likely to come from the legislature as from the governor. There are some states, such as Georgia, where governors have traditionally led. And there are some where governors have played a principal role setting the agenda and mobilizing the public, but have worked closely with their legislatures. Minnesota is an example.[33] In other states, such as Pennsylvania, both the governor and the legislature are primarily reactive, responding to the state board of education, the department of education, or teacher groups. But in a number of places legislative leadership in education has become institutionalized.[34]

Florida is one such state. Here since the 1970s the legislature has made major changes or tinkered with education each biennium. It has exerted strong policy leadership, enacting mandate after mandate and specifying requirements, because of a continuing distrust of the department of education.

Arizona is another state where the legislature, rather than the governor, exercises educational leadership. When Bruce Babbitt served as governor, he and the Republican-controlled legislature each had their own educational agendas. Babbitt responded to the teachers, through their educational association, while the legislature was intent on preserving local control for the state's school districts. Although the governor had intermittent success, over the years the legislature's overall agenda prevailed. In effect, the legislature through the education committee leadership of the senate and house acted as the preeminent policy maker in education, a "super school board." Its major concern tended to be fiscal, its secondary interests were in the areas of student performance and teacher policy. To a large extent, however, it delegated to the state board of education and left many specific decisions to the state's local school districts.

In California, too, the legislature has dominated the education scene, while governors have expressed lesser interest. Neither Pat Brown, Ronald Reagan, Gerry Brown, nor George Deukmejian held elementary and secondary education as a high priority. Reagan was mainly concerned about higher education, and Deukmejian became involved because of the public's support for educational reform and the pressure for additional school funds. At the most, California's governors have emerged from time to time as "show horses" in the field. As issues approached resolution, they would become involved and claim their share of credit, but they have seldom been in the thick of decision making throughout the process.

The tradition in California is that of large-scale educational initiatives by the legislature: compensatory education in 1964, early childhood education in 1972, school finance reform in 1972 and 1977, and school improvement in 1979. The legislature, including a few key legislative leaders and staff, has consistently been the principal locus for policy ideas. Typically, the legislature devotes two years of work to a variety of subjects and then aggregates a number of items into an omnibus proposal. During the past decade, it has been even more active than earlier and has become known as "the great school board in the sky." Consider the 1983 educational reform initiative, SB 813, an omnibus bill with more than eighty separate reform items. Included were mentor teacher and alternate route programs, graduation requirements, and increased beginning salaries for teachers. Bill Honig, California's superintendent of public instruction, was a major player in the process, acting as a cheerleader for education with the public. Governor Deukmejian, however, climbed aboard the reform train only at the last minute, when SB 813 was in conference. Legislators refer to the governor as a "reluctant bridegroom." Meanwhile, the ideas for the omnibus bill had developed among legislators and staff, and legislative leadership built the coalitions necessary for passage by grafting a variety of items together. There is little question that California's SB 813 was a legislative achievement.

Pressures on the Legislature. One reason why legislatures are as involved as they are in the formulation of policy is that they are subject to more, and more constant, pressures and demands than are governors. They, rather than the executive, are the main focus for constituents and for lobbyists. Anyone who is unhappy with the current state of affairs or anyone who has an idea for a new policy or program is likely to appeal to the legislature. And legislators, as representatives of constituencies and interests and as policy entrepreneurs, are happy to adopt a cause and seek legislative satisfaction. The legislature welcomes demands and converts many, if not all, into policy initiatives of greater or lesser significance.

As a result, hundreds and even thousands of bills are introduced in the legislature during a regular session. For example, in 1987 over 15,000 bills were introduced and about 850 were enacted in New York, about 4,500 were introduced and nearly 800 were enacted in Illinois, over 4,000 were introduced and over 1,000 enacted in Texas, nearly 4,000 introduced and 700 enacted in Connecticut, and about 2,700 introduced and 570 enacted in Florida. Even in far less active states, such as Wyoming, Oklahoma, Vermont, Utah, and Nebraska, bill introductions ranged between 500 and 1,000, with several hundred being enacted into law.

Many of the bill introductions are duplicates, many are trivial, and many are not meant to go anywhere. But a large number are important—to a district, an industry, a group, or one or a number of legislators. And some have potential impact throughout the entire state. Thus, only a small proportion of the legislative workload consists of the governor's priorities or even administration bills. On most bills requiring legislative action, the governor has no position and exerts no influence.

With regard to regulation and licensing and the many issues affecting special interests, the legislative role is surely the predominant one. In the 1989 session of the California legislature, for example, many of the four thousand bills introduced were designed to settle an economic squabble or to give one group or another an edge. There were bills that would force restaurants to hire animal renderers to haul away kitchen grease for recycling, protect rate structures of large moving van companies, provide exemptions on weight limits for tow trucks, length-en the schedules for horse racing tracks, and change the sardine fishing quotas.[35] Legislatures usually do not initiate policy independently of groups in these areas, but frequently they are caught between compet-ing demands. Governors can remain relatively aloof, while legislatures mediate the group struggle that makes up a significant part of the agenda in most states.

Liability insurance is an example of an issue in which legislatures have been playing the predominant policy role. That is because as rates soared, the medical and business communities appealed to legislatures for limitations on the claims that could be made. Legislators heard the horror stories about the cost of medical malpractice premiums and their unavailability. Cities and counties, for which insurance coverage was becoming a major problem, also appealed. The result of the insurance "crisis" was that in 1986 more than ten thousand bills were filed and forty-four states enacted legislation of one sort or another. Trial attor-neys lined up against insurance companies, and all-out struggle ensued nearly everywhere. Florida and Michigan, for instance, passed omnibus bills that tied tort reform to insurance regulation. The next year the states again debated legislation on tort law, sovereign immunity, medi-cal malpractice, and liability insurance. Further legislation was enacted.

Legislatures may not always desire to address these contentious issues, but often they cannot avoid having to do so. Generally, they manage to reach temporary settlements, if not solutions, to the thorny problems posed by conflicting groups and to contentious matters like insurance in the states. The problems do not go away.

GUBERNATORIAL RESPONSE

Just as governors need the legislature's support for items on their priority list and for administration bills, so the legislature needs governors' support, or at least acquiescence, in order to effect its agenda.

On major legislative initiatives governors are usually involved at an early stage. Many are flexible, accepting legislative initiatives when they can be accommodated within the bounds of executive policy. They realize that such accommodation is necessary to win legislative backing for their own agendas. In Arkansas, for instance, a number of important items were proposed by legislators, seeking the endorsement and assistance of Governor Clinton. He was generally supportive, particu-larly if the proposals came from influential legislators, although on some he did ask that changes be made. Governor Waihee of Hawaii operates in similar fashion. When the legislature initiated a telecommunications bill, the governor was brought in early. Negotiations began before the bill's introduction and continued throughout the process; the governor was on board all the way.

Missouri's Ashcroft has also been supportive of policies initiated by the legislature. The way the process works in Missouri is that usually both the governor and the legislature agree that a problem exists, that it is significant, and that something has to be done about it. The two branches may have somewhat different responses, but they manage to work out a compromise. The governor frequently winds up endorsing the legislative initiative. On a bill concerned with Acquired Immune Deficiency Syndrome, for example, Ashcroft worked with the legislature and interested groups in advance and suggested provisions before the bill was introduced. On some legislative initiatives, Ashcroft kept a greater distance from the process, but eventually he went along. If he had a significant objection, he would signal it to the legislature in advance of having to cast a veto, and the legislature would normally make modifications needed to secure the governor's assent. The relationship apparently worked.

On matters that are less critical, the governor's office still keeps track of the progress of legislation. Take New Jersey as an example. Here Governor Kean's office did not take positions on bills while they were still in committee, because it was too early and the administration was waiting to hear from the concerned groups. By the time these bills reached the Republican caucus in the assembly, however, one of the governor's assistant counsels would intervene. He or she would announce the governor's position, which might be "full support," "support," "let pass," "do not oppose," or "oppose." The governor might try to have a bill that he opposed kept off the board or amended at second reading. And he always had the conditional veto and absolute veto available.

Hundreds of bills must be reviewed before the governor signs or vetoes them. Relatively few are significant legislative initiatives or items with which the governor has been directly involved. Some screening process is required to separate the bills that governors will sign from those that they will permit to become law without their signature and from those that they will veto. The National Governors' Association, in a 1976 survey of the legislative assistants to governors, found that in nearly all of the thirty-seven states responding:

- The governor or his staff requested comments on legislation from the agencies.
- Legislative liaison staff to the governor examined the legislation and made recommendations.

- Legislative liaison staff requested comments on the legislation from affected parties and interest groups.

In addition, in almost half of these states the governor routinely received opinions from the attorney general.[36]

The process varies in its details by state. In Minnesota, for example, it is highly formalized. The planning agency and attorney general conduct a review of each enacted bill, the finance department joins in reviewing bills with a fiscal impact, and the departments are called upon to recommend that the governor approve or veto. All of the reviews are then forwarded to the governor's office. Once the reviews have been completed, it is up to the governor to sign, not sign, or veto. The governor will usually be briefed by the person responsible for legislative liaison, who sometimes holds the title of "governor's counsel."

The process that took place on the last day for bill signings at the end of the 1986 legislative session in Florida is not atypical of the procedure. Governor Graham sat at his desk with Gene Adams, one of two people responsible for liaison with the legislature. The governor and his aide discussed a number of bills. Since they were not among gubernatorial priorities or administration bills, Graham was not familiar with them. Adams briefly explained their substance. On the first two: "Having read both bills, I see no reason for you not to sign them," advised Adams. Another bill would have allowed the Department of Agriculture and the Department of Natural Resources to enforce rules regarding the burning of materials. "Is the Department of Environmental Regulation also okay on the bill?" asked Graham. "Yes," he was assured. He signed the bill. Another bill involved poultry disposal, which had been backed by an executive department and an interest group. After assurance that both environmental and public health concerns were being met, the governor penned his signature to this one. The next bill, according to which "respiratory care therapists" were renamed "respiratory care technicians," received a quick signature. Then the discussion turned to legislation defining "poultry" and specifying that pigeons could not be sold as meat, and legislation that allowed participants in a "crime watch" program to put a scanner in their automobile. The governor signed both.

The overwhelming majority of bills that reach the governor's desk are signed into law. But in some instances governors may not like a bill sent over by the legislature They may go along, nonetheless; veto might cost them elsewhere. Under such circumstances, governors will normally sign the bill in private. New Jersey's Kean, for instance, reluctantly signed legislation—the so-called Ford bill—to provide a tax deduction to homeowners and tenants on their state income tax bills.

The governor was tempted to exercise his veto, but the Democrats who controlled the legislature threatened that they would give him no other property-tax relief measure. Kean signed the bill in private, regretted having done so, and toward the end of his administration called for its repeal.

HANG TOGETHER OR HANG SEPARATELY

The enactment of public policy, in practically every instance, requires the assent of both the governor and the legislature. The legislature can refuse to go along with the priorities of the governor, and the governor can veto items on the legislature's agenda. Neither can achieve their purpose in the face of opposition from the other. The two branches of government come into frequent conflict, but if settlements are to be reached and issues resolved they must work together. The more controversial the issue, the greater the need for collaboration.

The battle over the sales tax on services in Florida highlights the critical nature of executive-legislative collaboration, not only through the actual policy-making process itself but beyond it as well. This is a story of initial cooperation, which turned into bitter conflict and led to an embarrassing defeat for both branches of government, scars that would take some time to heal, and a severe setback for the conduct of government and the provision of public services in Florida.

The idea for a services tax arose in the 1980s as a response to state needs estimated at almost $53 billion over the next ten years. The tax was set in motion by the Democratic legislative leadership, which in the 1986 session pushed through legislation to allow most existing exemptions to the state sales tax to expire as of July 1, 1987. Sunsetting the sales tax exemptions meant that unless the legislature acted at its 1987 session, previously exempted services would be subject to a 5 percent sales tax, as were most items in Florida. The strategy behind sunsetting the exemptions was to shift the burden from the legislature, which otherwise would have had to make the case for imposing a tax on each service individually, to the special interests, which would then have to persuade the legislature to exempt a specific service from the normal sales tax. Governor Graham, in his last year in office, approved the legislature's objective and happily signed the bill.

The problem facing those who saw the need for a new and expanding tax base was that a Republican was succeeding Graham as governor. Bob Martinez, the mayor of Tampa, had campaigned in the 1986 election on a promise to trim $800 million in government waste. He had blasted his Democratic opponent as "the biggest taxer this state has ever seen." His rhetoric did not suggest that he would support a services tax. Yet upon taking office he quickly came to support legislation extending the sales tax to most personal and professional services. He apparently realized that as governor he would need new revenues to provide necessary services.

With agreement between the governor and Democratic leaders in the senate and house, and with legislative Republicans reluctantly cooperating, the tax on services passed with amazing speed only three weeks into the 1987 session. This new tax expanded the levy on consumer services, such as laundry and dry cleaning, and on business services, such as legal, accounting, advertising, and construction services, and imposed a use tax on services provided from other states. The estimate was that it would raise $760 million in fiscal year 1988 and $1.2 billion the following fiscal year. Everyone was pleased with the achievement, and the warmth between the Democratic legislature and Republican governor reached a high point.

In signing the tax bill, Martinez stated: "I'm concerned about Florida's future and how we're going to pay for it . . . I think in the long run, the people are going to understand that I didn't come here to preside over the sinking of a ship because it couldn't float itself." A month later, he was quoted in the Republican party newsletter defending the tax as "responsible" and explaining that, "I chose to do what was right for Florida rather than what was easy for me politically, and I accept the responsibility for my choice." [37]

The tax went into effect on July 1. The opposition, which had not had time to mobilize when the governor and Democratic leadership coalesced earlier, mounted a campaign to repeal the tax. A citizens' group organized and sought to gather enough signatures to put on the 1988 ballot a constitutional initiative prohibiting such a tax. A loose alliance of powerful groups, including advertisers, broadcasters, publishers, realtors, home builders, and attorneys, formed to fight the tax. The broadcasters and newspaper publishers editorialized against it. National advertisers canceled radio and television commercials in Florida. Where a television ad would have run, a blank spot or thirty-second video of a metronome appeared, with an explanation that an advertiser had chosen not to sponsor a commercial in the state. The realtors had seventy-five thousand of their members contact legislators. The attorneys, along with other professional groups, brought a case in court challenging the constitutionability of the services tax.[38]

Ironically, the strength and ambition of the Florida legislature helped to account for the ultimate defeat of the tax. As Speaker Jon Mills reflected later on, "We took on everyone. When you have a coalition of national advertisers and piano teachers mad, you're in trouble." Had the legislature not included the advertisers (and perhaps the realtors too) in the tax on services, it might have been able to hold out. But legislators did not want to be perceived as giving in to powerful special interests; they wanted to apply the tax evenly and also raise as much revenue as possible. One lobbyist described legislators as having had "their hearts and minds set for passing as broad-based a tax as they could." However, they did not realize that the reaction would be as relentless as it was. "They went for the big banana and they missed," the lobbyist concluded.[39]

The legislature failed in its quest, in part because Governor Martinez failed to stand his ground. The campaigns against the tax were proving highly effective. Moreover, the way the bill had been rushed through in April and the report that a deal had been cut over pizza in a private residence behind closed doors began to sour the public on the entire affair. Legislative Republicans were turning against the governor. Martinez wavered, but still wanted to head off the petition drive which over the summer had collected two hundred thousand signatures for the constitutional initiative. He suggested to legislative leaders that they call for a referendum of their own at a special election in March so that the people could decide. He would still campaign for the tax before the vote. Martinez continued to hold to the view that the services tax was "a great tax for the people of Florida."[40] The legislators, however, were unconvinced by the governor's strategy and were not willing to go along with his idea for a referendum.

The situation deteriorated rapidly. The media, spearheaded by the advertising industry, focused on the governor rather than on 160 legislators. Martinez traveled around the state defending the tax, but both the tax and the governor plummeted in the polls. A statewide poll conducted by Bill Hamilton and paid for by the Democratic party showed that 78 percent of Floridians blamed Martinez for the new tax, while only 8 percent blamed the legislature. As many as 77 percent of the public wanted the tax repealed. Whereas in March, before its passage, Martinez's job performance rating had been 64 percent favorable and 24 percent unfavorable, by September his rating was reversed, 26 percent favorable and 65 percent unfavorable.[41] By the middle of the month, the governor capitulated; he followed the interests, the public, and the polls and came out for repeal.

With the governor's reversal, it was up to the legislature to deal with what had become a very messy situation. The legislature met for four weeks in special session, as support for the services tax eroded and the deadlock between the legislature and the governor hardened. The legislature enacted a plan revising the tax and putting it on the ballot for the voters to decide between the revised tax and a general sales tax increase. Martinez vetoed the bill, and in mid-October the legislature adjourned.

By December, with the next election less than a year away, legislators were beginning to run scared. The speaker of the house and president of the senate held public hearings around the state to try to educate the public and rally support. But they were met with adamant opposition. The legislature was in disarray: the Republicans had defected, following their governor, and the Democrats were splitting. "It was just sort of a gradual erosion," said Sam Bell, the house appropriations committee chair and a supporter of the tax. "I don't fault anyone who caved in. It was inevitable." [42] On December 8, 1987, another special session of the legislature convened. Quickly, the legislature repealed the services tax, replacing it with a one-cent increase in the sales tax on goods.

The services tax ended on January 1, 1988, and was replaced in February by the increased sales tax. The change hit the poor harder than the rich, cost average taxpayers more money, and raised less revenue for Florida's future. Moreover, state government was left in shambles as an aftermath of the battle. The executive and legislative branches of government had been damaged—not irreparably, but damaged nonetheless. The chair of the house finance and tax committee predicted that "we are witnessing the beginning of what I believe will be a period of strife for Florida." [43] That prediction would prove correct.

The lack of leadership by the governor and then his reversal on the services tax had left the Florida legislature vulnerable to pressures outside and to dissension within. Although the leadership tried to hold the line, in the face of the governor's opposition, it could not. The services tax contingent fell apart. Republicans, whose hearts had never been with the tax, peeled off first. Conservative Democrats and those who felt impending threat to their reelection followed suit. Legislative leaders used their muscle and managed to hold the troops together, hoping that the public clamor would die down and that in the meantime they could weather the storm. But with the governor beating the drum for repeal and with the interest groups working over the public, there was little chance to hold a majority in support of the tax.

On an issue as controversial as the services tax, the governor might possibly have been able to withstand a reversal by the legislature. But the legislature could not withstand the governor's desertion. It could not take all of the heat alone. The governor and the legislature did not hang together; and although they may not actually have hanged separately, each felt the noose tighten.

NOTES

1. Council of State Governments, "Public Opinion and Policy Leadership in the American States: A National Survey" (presented at 1987 annual meeting of CSG, Boston, Mass., December 5-9), 10; Institute for Research in Social Science, University of North Carolina, Fall 1986, Carolina Poll.
2. National Governors' Association, *Governing the American States: A Handbook for New Governors* (Washington, D.C.: Center for Policy Research, NGA, November 1978), 179.
3. National Governors' Association, Office of State Services, *Transition and the New Governor* (Washington, D.C.: NGA, November 1982), 29. What governors say and what they do are not exactly the same. Governor Richard Snelling of Vermont mentioned that you can always find "inclusionary pages" in governors' documents. Such pages, he noted whimsically, can be inserted at the beginning, middle, or end and "make reference to all subjects which are not fully addressed or referenced and acknowledged anywhere else in the document as being important and vital to the planning for the future of the state." Alan Rosenthal, ed., *The Governor and the Legislature* (New Brunswick, N.J.: Eagleton Institute of Politics, Rutgers University, 1988), 45.
4. Marvin A. Harder, *Can Governors Govern? Managing the Policy Process in Kansas* (Lawrence: University Press of Kansas, forthcoming), 218-219.
5. Manuscript, titled "Legislator," by George Scott.
6. Charles Kenney and Robert L. Turner, *Dukakis: An American Odyssey* (Boston: Houghton Mifflin, 1988), 187; David Osborne, *Laboratories of Democracy* (Boston: Harvard Business School Press, 1988), 92.
7. Blair Lee, "Schaefer's 'Superschool': A $20 Million Gimmick," *Washington Post*, January 17, 1988.
8. Rosenthal, *The Governor and the Legislature*, 33.
9. National Governors' Association, *Reflections on Being Governor* (Washington, D.C.: Center for Policy Research, NGA, February 1981), 107.
10. Information on educational policy is taken from a project conducted by the Center for Policy Research in Education (CPRE), a consortium of Michigan State, Stanford, Wisconsin, and Rutgers universities, under a grant from the U.S. Department of Education.
11. National Governors' Association, *Reflections on Being Governor*, 23.
12. Eagleton Institute of Politics, Rutgers University, "The Pinelands Protection Act," October 15, 1987 (photocopy), 20.
13. Thad L. Beyle, "From Governor to Governors," in *State of the States*, ed. Carl Van Horn (Washington, D.C.: CQ Press, 1988), 56, 61.
14. Thad L. Beyle, "The Governor as Chief Legislator," in *Being Governor: The View from the Office*, ed. Thad L. Beyle and Lynn R. Muchmore (Durham, N.C.: Duke Press Policy Studies, 1983), 133.
15. David Osborne, *Laboratories of Democracy* (Boston: Harvard Business School Press, 1988), 139-140.
16. The following section is based on Eagleton Institute of Politics, "The Pinelands Protection Act."
17. This section is based on Jon Bowermaster, *Governor: An Oral Biography of Robert D. Ray* (Ames: Iowa State University, 1987), 169-176.
18. Report of the Governor's Commission on Vermont's Future: Guidelines for Growth, January 1988.
19. Rod Paul, "John H. Sununu, New Hampshire's Governor Preaches High-

Tech Solutions to Age-Old Problems," *Governing*, August 1988, 52.

20. National Governors' Association, *Transition and the New Governor*, 30.
21. Gerald Benjamin, "The Albany Triad," *Comparative State Politics Newsletter* 9 (February 1988): 9-10.
22. Osborne, *Laboratories of Democracy*, 92-94.
23. Charles D. Hadley, "Louisiana," *Comparative State Politics Newsletter* 6 (August 1985): 4.
24. Diane Blair, *Arkansas Politics and Government* (Lincoln: University of Nebraska Press, 1988), 139-140.
25. Steven D. Williams, "The 1986 Session of the Tennessee State Assembly," *Comparative State Politics Newsletter*, 7 (June 1986): 18-19.
26. The characterization is from the *Wichita Eagle-Beacon*, quoted in Sharon Randall, "From Big Shot to Boss," *State Legislatures*, July 1988, 36.
27. John M. Dowling, "Robert L. Mandeville: The Financial Wizardry (Or Sleight of Hand) of a Fiscal Spin Doctor," *Governing*, January 1989, 46.
28. Peter J. Boyer, "The Yuppies of Mississippi—How They Took Over the Statehouse," *New York Times Magazine*, February 28, 1988.
29. Sarah McCally Morehouse, *State Politics, Parties and Policy* (New York: Holt, Rinehart & Winston, 1980), 243.
30. Diane Ross, "Phil Rock—Holding Together a Raucous Caucus," *Illinois Issues*, April 1985, 12.
31. Rosenthal, *The Governor and the Legislature*, 61-62.
32. Vera Katz, "The Leader and the Public," *Journal of State Government* 60 (November/December 1987): 253; *New York Times*, July 10, 1988; and Lucinda Simon, "The Vocabulary of Business Speaks to Both Branches," *State Legislatures*, March 1989, 12.
33. Tim L. Mazzoni, "Governors as Policy Leaders for Education: A Minnesota Comparison," *Educational Policy* 3 (March 1989): 83-86.
34. This section on education is based on information collected by the Center for Policy Research in Education.
35. James Richardson, "When Authors of Bills Know Little About Them," *Sacramento Bee*, March 20, 1989.
36. Beyle, "The Governor as Chief Legislator," 140.
37. *St. Petersburg Times*, September 3, 1987.
38. *Gainesville Sun*, December 26, 1987.
39. *Florida Times Union*, December 13, 1987.
40. Ibid.
41. *Orlando Sentinel Star*, September 10, 1987.
42. *Gainesville Sun*, December 26, 1987.
43. *Florida Times Union*, December 13, 1987.

6

Determining the Budget

Few if any bills that the legislature acts on are as critical as those appropriating monies for state government. The budget allocates taxpayer dollars to the departments and agencies for administering policies promulgated by the legislature, delivering services to people throughout the state, and providing for the regulation of a host of operations. Whereas the governor and the legislature may choose whether or not to place most issues on the state's agenda, they have no choice in the case of the budget. Constitutionally, a budget must be enacted either annually (as in twenty-nine states) or biennially (in twenty-one others).

As a rule, the executive and legislative branches participate in different phases of the budgetary process. Usually the executive has responsibility for preparing the budget request and submitting it to the legislature. The legislature has responsibility for reviewing the request it and adopting it in the form of an appropriations act or acts. Then, the execution of the budget is an administrative function, while overseeing it and attempting to exercise some measure of control are legislative prerogatives.

BUDGETARY CONSIDERATIONS

The budgetary process takes place regularly, and although it varies from state to state and time to time, several considerations normally pertain.

First, not all the funds that state government raises and spends are reflected in the budget, or the general fund portion of the budget. Not all are under the immediate control of the governor and the legislature. Expenditures on capital construction that derive from bonding may be included in the executive budget, but generally they are dealt with

131

separately and are not subject to the same types of controls. The income and expenditures of special authorities, which generate revenues from their activities, are also excluded. Thus, removed from the budget process are housing authorities, port commissions, toll highway authorities, college dormitory construction agencies, and the like. Federal aid is reflected in the state budget, but in a special section, and control by governors and legislatures is limited by specifications laid down by Washington. Finally, there are dedicated funds that have been constitutionally or statutorily restricted for particular purposes—for education, highways, senior citizens, local aid, and so forth. It is estimated that states dedicate or earmark about 21 percent of their revenues, which, although down from 50 percent in 1954, is a substantial sum nonetheless.[1]

Second, a relatively small amount of the general fund budget itself is, practically speaking, controllable. Though it is theoretically possible for the governor and legislature to end programs, discontinue services, and make significant shifts in the allocation of funds, commitments are in fact observed from year to year. The "big ticket" items within the general fund—elementary and secondary education aid, higher education, welfare and Medicaid, and state employee pay and pension funding—command a large portion of a state's resources, with little left over for new policies and programs. The funds over which governors and legislatures really have discretion amount to only 5 to 15 percent of the budget. It is over these monies that the contest is waged, at the margins of the budget but still over significant amounts.

Third, unlike the federal budget, state budgets must be balanced. That is, revenues must at least be equal to expenditures when the budget is enacted, and normally additional funds are left in a reserve in case there is an economic downturn or other unforeseen need. Every state except Vermont has a constitutional or statutory requirement for a balanced budget, and Vermont also follows the practice of balancing its budget, although not mandated by law to do so. Another one-third of the states are bound by constitutional or statutory spending limits, which also restrict the discretion of state policy makers.

It should be noted, however, that a state can balance its budget in various ways, including some that do not require additional revenues. Bookkeeping devices, tapping into special funds—the stuff of blue smoke and mirrors—all are employed from time to time. Illinois, for example, has had a balanced budget. Yet if appropriations from the general fund are compared with revenues, the state ran a deficit of $310 million in 1982 and $357 million in 1983.[2]

Fourth, the greatest force affecting the budget and the budgetary process, and what governors and legislatures can or cannot do, is the economy itself. When the national and state economies are good, revenues from income, sales, and other taxes are greater. Given a projected surplus of revenues, governors and legislatures have leeway for additional spending—increasing ongoing programs, establishing new ones, expanding agencies, or putting more funds in local aid formulas. In such a situation, both the governor and the legislature can share in divvying up the extra monies. But since everyone feels entitled to a piece of this larger pie, the pressures on available funds increase. Saying no becomes very difficult for governors and for legislators in particular. As a chief of staff to one governor expressed it, "the burden of a surplus is tougher to live with than the burden of a deficit."

Therefore, in years of prosperity, governors and legislatures tend to say yes to new and expanding programs, nearly all of which have merit. They may do this without taking into account the likelihood of an eventual downturn in the economy. Commitments are made and clienteles created; however, should the economy take a turn for the worse, revenues will be insufficient to keep pace with promises and expectations. Michael Dukakis's "Massachusetts miracle" suffered this fate.

When economic conditions are poor, because of high inflation, interest rates, or unemployment, budgetary politics are much different. Under such circumstances, most of state policy making turns on fiscal issues. "Cutback management" becomes the mode. The choice is to raise taxes, cut expenditures, or manage some combination of the two. It is not a pleasant choice for people in public office, who in most cases will be seeking reelection. It is one, however, that will bring the governor and the legislature into the closest kind of involvement, as they try to meet the deficit while displeasing the fewest citizens and shouldering the least political blame possible.

BUDGETARY POWER

Every year, or every other year, the battle over who gets how much takes place. The claimants for public resources are many—the schools, universities, institutions, transportation, health, law enforcement, the young and the elderly, business and labor, and countless others. The budget pits agency against agency, client group against client group, cities against suburbs, and frequently Democrats against Republicans. It also provides a major test in the struggle between the governor and the legislature to determine who has control over how much is spent on what for the benefit of whom.

Executive-legislative rivalry over the budget can manifest itself in various ways—loudly or quietly, publicly or privately, confrontationally or diplomatically, but just about everywhere the two branches do clash on budgetary issues. A spokesman for Warren Anderson, New York's senate majority leader, referred to the process by which the governor and legislature work out a budget agreement as "the annual dance of the budget flamingoes," with an opening gambit "where the birds bow, then strut around flapping their wings." [3] By the end of the legislative session, the birds will have squawked and pecked at one another, but they will also have resolved the issue, at least for a time.

The ability to formulate the budget is certainly one of the governor's principal powers.[4] "There is no question that the most important single thing that any Governor does . . . is the preparation of the budget for the coming fiscal year," according to Governor Blair Lee of Maryland.[5] The ability to review the budget is certainly one of the legislature's principal powers. Joe Clarke, the veteran chairman of the house revenue and appropriations committee in Kentucky, expressed the legislative-power perspective clearly: "If you grab them by their budgets, their hearts and minds will follow."

Who has the upper hand? In part, it depends on whom you ask. A survey of executive budget officers and legislative fiscal officers found that the former tended to rank the governor as more influential, while the latter tended to rank the legislature as more influential. In fourteen states both ranked the governor as more influential, while in nine both ranked the legislature higher. In the remaining fourteen that were surveyed, the two respondents divided on this question.[6]

The budget is key for governors, in part because it provides them with the mechanism for controlling the departments, agencies, and personnel of the executive branch. But, even more important, most governors' policy and program goals require money for their execution. Thus, gubernatorial proposals for education, drug enforcement, tourism, or whatever are incorporated into the budgets they formulate. Governors may also cut budgets, as a means of achieving programmatic objectives, and some do. In California, Governor Deukmejian, for example, advanced an ideological budget in 1987-1988, eliminating Cal-OSHA, squeezing Medi-Cal, and setting spending priorities contrary to the desires of the Democratic legislature.

In addition, more and more gubernatorial policy initiatives, and legislative initiatives as well, are finding their way into the budget without resort to legislation. This has happened in Maryland, where Governor Schaefer inserted light rail, dropout prevention, and reorganization of higher education proposals in the budget, although they had not been separately considered and authorized by the legislature. Probably nowhere has this practice advanced further than in Wisconsin. Here, a single budget bill encompasses all agency and local aid expenditures, as well as all revenue measures. And since, unlike many other states, Wisconsin has no constitutional prohibition against combining unrelated measures in a single bill, the budget bill has also come to be a vehicle for numerous policy initiatives.[7] Unrelated bits of legislation are jumbled together for political, practical, and administrative reasons. Thus, the appropriations act in the past decade or so has become a vehicle for policy matters that have nothing at all to do with financing state government. A veritable Christmas tree, the appropriations act has included provisions covering tavern licensing as well as a major revision of Wisconsin's drunken driving laws.[8] Both the governor and legislators believe they have a better chance of advancing their policy agendas and pet projects through the budget, rather than by the normal legislative means. Indeed, the budget has become the governor's prime policy document. The governor prefers this approach because it is easier to work with the leadership in managing a more contained budget process and there is greater opportunity for compromises when a number of policy initiatives are up for consideration in the same bill. Legislators prefer this approach, because it enables them, as a price for their vote on the entire budget in the majority caucus, to insert legislation for which they could not ensure passage separately.

The governor and the legislature both have substantial weapons. The former has the power to item veto legislative items, and the latter has the power to eliminate gubernatorial items in the committee, caucus, and floor stages of deliberation.

BUDGET FORMULATION

The governors' upper hand in the contest with the legislature for budgetary power derives from their ability to formulate the budget, to put together in a policy/expenditure document just what they want and then to send it to the legislature for review and adoption. In formulating budgets, governors usually have some room for maneuver. Depending on revenue projections and the fiscal climate, they can decide where expenditures will be increased, where they will be reduced, and whether changes in taxes will be sought.[9] Governors at this stage can decide on their goals and policies and what it will take to achieve them through the budget. Let us say that a governor is faced with the decision either to cut the budget significantly or to raise taxes. Under such circumstances, he or she may make the strategic decision to cut local aid programs, such as school aid, which are traditionally favored by legislators. That way the governor has the ability to force legislative leaders to agree to higher taxes to pay for restoration of the funds. Thus, the blame for taxes can be shared. Another governor may put additional monies in the budget and not in an aid formula. That way he can decide where to direct the funds, rather than have them automatically allocated. Under an executive budget system, the governor sets the agenda, deals the cards, and dictates what game is to be played.[10] The governor is in an enviable position; nevertheless, practical considerations limit what he or she can actually do.

THE BUREAUCRACY AS A CONSTRAINT

The first constraint on the governor's ability to formulate an executive budget is the executive bureaucracy. As mentioned earlier, the base of an agency budget is seldom questioned and obligatory expenditures are seldom up for grabs. The field of play is limited, and the governor is only one of many executive contestants, albeit the most powerful. The bureaucratic process in the executive branch runs generally as follows. In the summer the governor, with the assistance of the executive budget staff (in the governor's office, the department of administration, the office of budget and management, or the bureau of the budget), sets agency targets, and the budget staff sends out guidelines for agency expenditures. In August, September, or October, the agencies submit their recommendations for spending, and the details are processed by the budget office. During this period, budget hearings are held where agency heads make their appeals for funds.

The governor's involvement in the budgetary process varies from place to place, from person to person, and over time. Some governors preside over the budget hearings of each agency. Others delegate the task to their budget directors. Robert Ray of Iowa spent considerable time listening to agency heads explain and plead their budgets; he played a decisive role. So did James Thompson of Illinois, at least at the outset of his long career as governor. During his first three months in office, he attended twenty-eight meetings on the state budget; but by his eleventh year, he attended only four.[11] In Maryland, Governor Schaefer also involves himself in the budgetary process, which he finds fascinating, even in the most minute details. During 1988, for instance, he spent ten to twelve working days reviewing the requests of his agency heads.

The development of the budget in the executive branch is an intensely political process, as everyone fights for a share of scarce resources and the chief executive attempts to keep the budget in balance and have gubernatorial priorities reflected in state spending. The agencies, of course, have their own agendas and their own resources. They look at the long term and have what they deem to be deserving clienteles to satisfy. In pursuing their objectives, they can be extremely effective in persuading the budget staff and governor to adhere to their spending provisions. They may not receive as much money as they would like, but normally they can resist significant interference in their allocations. A former New Jersey treasurer, Cliff Goldman, described a variety of agency strategies: (1) agency budgeters will begin with a program at a low budget figure and then make it grow; (2) they will use a fashionable label for a program they want to initiate—one, such as "high technology" as a euphemism for education, that is in vogue with the governor; (3) cabinet officers will personally try to persuade the governor to include agencies' requests; and (4) agencies will activate their constituent groups, who can bring pressure to bear on the governor and on the legislature. Thus, although the budget that is drafted within the executive branch will no doubt include the governor's priorities, it will also reflect the political strength and resourcefulness of the agencies of state government. In recognition of the power of the bureaucracy, a seventeen-year veteran of the legislature and cochair of the joint finance committee in Wisconsin declared that "the fight in the budget is really between the legislature and the bureaucrats." [12]

THE LEGISLATURE AS A CONSTRAINT

The second constraint on the governor's ability to formulate an executive budget is the legislature. The National Governors' Association recommends that governors not allow the legislature too much influence early in the process, lest they lose leverage later and jeopardize their image as strong executives.[13] While this may be sound advice from a gubernatorial point of view, it cannot always be followed.

Some governors manage to exclude legislators from the initial stages of budget formulation, holding power as tightly as possible. In Wisconsin, for example, Republican Tommy Thompson puts the budget together privately with his aides. He does not invite leaders of the Democratic majorities in the senate and assembly. But other governors operate much differently. They invite legislators to sit around the table or they anticipate legislators' desires. Ned McWherter of Tennessee welcomes input from the legislature when putting his budget together; not surprisingly, the legislature is positively oriented toward the governor's spending priorities when it engages in its review later on.[14]

In Virginia, too, the legislature works from the governor's budget bill. But the budgetary process is "wired," in the sense that the governor will not send over a budget that will make key legislators unhappy. The budget is worked out beforehand. Governor Baliles has an open process in developing the executive budget. Legislators come to the governor with their wish lists. The leaders, more often than not, have their priorities included in the governor's budget. If they do not, the governor will usually figure out an alternative way of funding their priorities. Throughout the budgetary process, Baliles maintains contact with legislative leaders and committee chairs, so that they are familiar with the recommendations he will make. Therefore, few public confrontations take place.

The dominant pattern is for the governor to take the lead in the formulative stages and for the legislature to react to his submission. "I'm chairman of the board. It's the executive budget bill. It's not the Legislature's budget bill." That is how Governor Thompson describes his authority in Wisconsin. Although the Democratic-controlled legislature has vigorously contested the Republican governor's budgets, going so far as to challenge his use of the item, or partial, veto, executive primacy is understood. The speaker of the assembly, Tom Loftus, acknowledges the disadvantages under which the legislature operates. It is an "executive budget" put together in private by the governor and his aides.[15]

The executive budget pattern applies to a large majority of states, where legislatures play little role in the budget preparation stage. Their role comes later in the process. But this is by no means the pattern everywhere. In a number of places, a comprehensive budget is prepared by the legislature separately from the executive budget and, in some other states, legislatures prepare separate budgets at least in part.

Take the case of Texas, where an independent legislative budget process is probably most advanced. Through an independent Legislative Budget Board—which has as members the lieutenant governor; the speaker; the chairs of the house appropriations, house ways and means, and senate finance, and senate state affairs committees; and two other legislators from each chamber—the senate and house develop a separate legislative budget. The governor's budget competes as a set of priorities, but is not necessarily the most authoritative one. While the governor's Budget and Planning Office develops the executive budget proposal, the Legislative Budget Board develops its own omnibus appropriations bill. The appropriations committee in the house and the finance committee in the senate develop their bills on the basis of both the executive and legislative alternatives before them.

In Arkansas, also, the legislature participates to a significant extent. Here, the governor proposes a comprehensive state budget to the Legislative Council, a house-senate interim committee, which holds its own budget hearings throughout the fall to consider the governor's recommendations and make its own. When the legislature goes into session, the Legislative Council's recommendations are the ones forwarded to the joint budget committee, which then develops and introduces the appropriations bills. Only recently has the legislature begun inviting gubernatorial budget recommendations. Some observers now classify the Arkansas budget as "executive," others as "legislative," and still others as an "executive-legislative hybrid." [16] It can probably best be regarded as the last, since it is a joint product initially (and ultimately) of the governor and senior legislators. They are the ones with the real power, balancing the budget under the Arkansas Revenue Stabilization Act, with its A, B, and C priorities, whereby if a request fails to be included in the A budget, it is unlikely to be funded.

In South Carolina, the Budget and Control Board includes the chairs of the house ways and means and senate finance committees, as well as the governor, treasurer, and comptroller general. This board conducts hearings, analyzes agency budget requests, and directs its staff to prepare an appropriations bill. The general appropriations bill in Louisiana usually reflects the governor's recommendations, but it also shows input from the joint legislative budget committee. After the bill has been drafted, the house and senate appropriations subcommittees revise it. [17]

Elsewhere, too, the legislature refuses to settle for a reactive role. The executive budget prepared by the governor in Colorado is said to have about as much status as a child's letter to Santa Claus. It is largely ignored by the legislature, whose six-member joint budget committee requires state agencies to submit their requests directly to the legislature, as well as to the governor, and then drafts its own budget on that basis. About the same happens in Florida, where the governor's position in the budget process is weak compared with that of the legislature. As described by the chairman of the house appropriations committee:

> We do have a recommended bill from the governor, but we do not introduce a governor's bill in the legislative process. Instead, we develop the committee bill through the legislative process itself. The governor's document is only an advisory document and represents his best suggestions on how we should develop the state's budget and spending effort.

The two appropriations committees may refer to the governor's budget recommendations, but they rely on what their subcommittees have put together essentially from scratch. [18]

The competition between the governor and the legislature over control of the budget, even in the initial stages, is not as one-sided everywhere as is popularly believed. In a majority of states—such as California, Illinois, New Jersey, New York, and Wisconsin—the governor, along with the executive bureaucracies, clearly controls the formulation of the budget. But elsewhere, as in Colorado and Texas, the legislature has more of a say than the governor. And in still other places the two engage in developing the state budget on roughly equal terms.

THE LEGISLATIVE RESPONSE

The legislature's principal budgetary role is not formulation, but review and modification. It is based on constitutional provisions, such as Article II, Section 22 of the Ohio Constitution, which provides that "no money shall be drawn from the treasury, except in pursuance of a specific appropriation, made by law." The requirement that a budget bill or bills be enacted allows the legislature ample room to exercise influence. The legislature, in reviewing a governor's budget proposal, can be as involved and aggressive as it chooses.

A few legislatures may be limited in their action, particularly with regard to increasing the amount of the governor's recommendations. In Nebraska, for instance, a three-fifths vote is needed to effect an increase, while only a majority is needed to reject or decrease a recommendation. The Maryland general assembly is probably the most restricted in the action it can take. Although the legislature may decrease items in the operating budget, it may not add, increase, or transfer items. (It may, however, increase items in the capital budget.)

For the most part, legislatures can add, subtract, or eliminate funds, programs, and projects as a consequence of their review. Even in a state like Pennsylvania, which has a strong executive, the legislature makes its weight felt. Governor Milton Shapp, in reflecting on his years in office, recounted:

> In Pennsylvania, as the Governor I prepare a budget, but the Legislature can take my budget and throw it into the wastepaper basket and start from scratch. We have 203 members in the House, 50 members in the Senate, and all 253 of these people think they have more information about what should be in the budget, more data and more understanding of the state's problems than the Governor does. So, one of the biggest problems we have every year in Pennsylvania is the battle over the budget.[19]

LEGISLATIVE RESOURCES

During the past twenty years, the legislature has made remarkable progress in developing the resources that would be necessary to contest the budget with the executive. The growth of specialized fiscal staff agencies, the development of computerized fiscal information systems, and the establishment of revenue-estimating capability have all contributed to the expansion of legislative capacity and influence in budgetary matters.

When he served in the Maryland general assembly, Blair Lee sponsored a bill to create a Department of Legislative Services, which included a fiscal staff. Shortly after the bill was enacted, Marvin Mandel succeeded Governor Spiro Agnew, who left to become vice president in the middle of his term. Blair Lee became secretary of state, doing the work of lieutenant governor, and later he became governor. "So ironically," Lee recalls, "I was hoisted by my own petard." He regards the legislature as stronger and more active than it used to be, a body that keeps the governor on his toes: "The legislative staff is now much larger and much better equipped, and when they review a Governor's budget they really review it. In the old days it was sort of hit or miss." [20]

At present, fiscal staffs vary in how they are organized. In some states, each appropriations committee has its own staff. Florida is one such state, where the staff director of the appropriations committee is responsible jointly to the presiding officer and to the chair of the committee. In other states the appropriations committees have their own staffs, while a central, nonpartisan fiscal agency also serves them with fiscal assistance. California, with the Office of Legislative Analyst, typifies this pattern. Elsewhere, as in New Jersey, the appropriations committees are served by partisan fiscal consultants as well as by a nonpartisan legislative services agency. In most states, however, the major—if not exclusive—reliance of the legislature is on a fiscal agency that serves both houses, both committees, and members of both parties. Maryland, Virginia, and Colorado exemplify this pattern.

Fiscal staffs also vary in their size. The largest staffs are in California and New York, which have over a hundred professionals, and in Michigan, Illinois, and Texas, which have over fifty apiece. Relatively large staffs are also found in Pennsylvania, Maryland, and Wisconsin, each with between thirty and fifty analysts. At the other end of the continuum are Idaho, Wyoming, South Dakota, North Dakota, Tennessee, and Vermont, each with a staff of fewer than ten professionals. [21]

Whatever its organizational pattern or precise size, fiscal staff has made an enormous difference to the legislature's performance on the budget. These analysts contest with the governor's budget experts, matching the latter in skill and earning their respect. [22] Thanks to staff, the contemporary legislature has an independent source of information—its own numbers derived by its own people. The governor's budget is now taken apart for analysis, even if it is eventually put back together. As one fiscal staff director commented: "We've given the legislature a stronger information base from which to hang tough."

Staff, legislators, and technology together have been responsible for providing additional, better, and more usable information than legislatures have had available before. Typically, the legislature seeks information conveying the following: (1) the percentage increase of a request over last year's program; (2) justifications for new and expanded activities; (3) the effectiveness of an agency's programs and activities; (4) the efficiency of an agency; (5) support of clientele groups for the agency; (6) the significance of an agency's programs for the districts of legislators; and (7) the willingness of an agency to abide by legislative intent.[23] Without adequate staff, the legislature could neither obtain nor analyze most of these items.

In earlier years, the legislature had access to much less information. Governors had far greater control of the flow. Nowadays, legislatures receive even the budget requests made by executive agencies of the governor. In fact, in forty-one states the legislature receives the agency budget request before the executive budget is prepared. In only three states—California, Hawaii, and Illinois—is the legislature denied the agency request, even after receipt of the executive budget.[24] Governors like Bob Martinez in Florida are now making an effort to recapture control of the flow of information in order to regain an upper hand with their legislature. But legislatures are unwilling to give back what they have struggled to gain.

Probably the most important advance in the intelligence capacity of legislatures has been the undertaking of revenue projections and forecasts. Traditionally, legislatures and their staffs focused on expenditures. In recent years, however, legislatures have realized that the power to establish revenue levels gives the executive branch a significant advantage in the competition to determine expenditures. Today, legislative fiscal staffs in three-fifths of the states prepare their own revenue estimates, and these estimates become part of the budget negotiations the legislature conducts with the governor. Predicting revenues is considered to be "the nuts and bolts of the whole game."

State spending decisions obviously depend on the amount of revenues available. If revenues are high, a larger pot can be shared among agencies, programs, clienteles, and constituencies. If revenues are low, then expenditures must be held down or cut, taxes have to be raised, or some combination of the two must be put into effect. Revenue estimates will differ, depending on economic assumptions. If economic growth and higher tax revenues at the same rates are assumed, then money can be expected to flow in. If an economic downturn, or worse, is assumed, tax revenues can be expected to decline, and the treasury will likely have less money to spend.

Projections are part art, part science, and part politics. As a rule, the executive branch tends to be conservative in its estimates, while the legislature is more optimistic. In Iowa, for example, Governor Ray's philosophy, according to a legislative fiscal officer, was that "you can't trust the legislature," at least not with surplus funds. So the governor usually estimated lower, while the legislature estimated higher. Only toward the end of the legislative session would both sides meet to hammer out an agreement on the amount of revenue that could be anticipated. Governor Shapp of Pennsylvania was particularly skillful at underestimating revenues. Often his projections were off by more than 5 percent, and thus he wound up with substantial surpluses. And when Edwin Edwards was governor of Louisiana, the civil servant responsible for estimating revenues would come up with any figure the governor wanted. Edwards would ask him to lowball his estimates, so that the legislature could not overspend and he would not have to veto as many projects.[25]

In sharp contrast to the executive, the legislative branch tends to highball its numbers. "Cooking" revenue estimates so spending can rise is a normal legislative posture in Illinois, according to an aide to Governor Thompson. It is typical in other places as well, where legislatures want to have sufficient monies to allocate to programs and projects and to clients and constituents.

Occasionally, however, the roles are reversed. For example, the New Jersey legislature saw a deficit looming for 1990-1991, months before the executive acknowledged any gap. And the Louisiana legislature in 1985 estimated a $30 million shortfall, while the governor's Division of Administration projected a $90 million surplus. In this instance, the legislature accepted the executive's figures, because it was unwilling to buck special-interest pressures and make the hard decisions to cut programs.[26]

Although executive and legislative staffs conduct their own analyses, in a growing number of states the two come together as experts in formal sessions to negotiate their respective estimates and reach agreements. Typically in these revenue forecasting conferences, representatives of the governor and the legislature, and sometimes of the agencies, thrash out their estimates and work toward consensus. The process has been under way in Iowa for the past few years. The director of the Office of Management, the director of the Legislative Fiscal Bureau, and an outsider meet in December, and have to come into agreement. They meet again the following March and produce an up-to-date figure; thus, the governor's requests to the legislature are altered by means of new data and further negotiation. The process—known as the revenue estimating conference—has also been used for a number of years in Florida, where it now works quite effectively.

LEGISLATIVE REVIEW

The process of legislative review takes place after the formulation stage, and normally follows the governor's budget message, which sets forth priorities and policies in terms of budget allocations. The legislature then deals with the appropriations bills that have been introduced—going over the bills item by item, making additions, deletions, and other modifications, and enacting a state expenditure plan.

In twenty states a single bill is introduced and passed into law, not including supplementals that may come later and are dealt with separately. Other states differ in the number of appropriations bills. In New York appropriations are contained in between ten and thirty bills, in Oklahoma in almost a hundred bills, in Oregon and Idaho over a hundred, in Illinois between one hundred fifty and two hundred, and in Arkansas over three hundred. The bills are prepared by the executive branch in the majority of states, but by the appropriations committee and fiscal staff in a number of others. These bills in sixteen states are introduced in the house only, and then they make their way to the senate. In fifteen states they are handled by both houses simultaneously. In another twelve, where there are multiple bills, they are divided up between the bodies. In the rest, the house of origin alternates from session to session or varies depending upon the executive's strategy.[27]

Appropriations Committees. Whatever the number and the precise routing of appropriations bills, the principal legislative actors in the process are the appropriations committees. At one time many such committees may have been rubber stamps for the executive. Now, they have knowledge and power and are extremely hard-working groups.

In fifteen states joint committees act on appropriations; in the remainder separate house and senate committees take action. Three-fourths of the committees are responsible for appropriations only, but one-fourth also have jurisdiction over revenues. These committees range in size from Utah, on the one hand, where all seventy-five members of the house and twenty-nine members of the senate serve on one of the appropriations subcommittees, to Wisconsin, where only eight senators and eight representatives are members.[28]

Appropriations committees in every state but six are organized into subcommittees, which are responsible for much of the work and have major influence over budgets within their jurisdictions. Generally, the various subcommittees are given allotments by the leadership and the committee chairs, and then it is up to them to divide the sums among the agencies and programs within their areas. In Florida, for example,

the house and senate appropriations committees have generally operated through three subcommittees for purposes of putting together the
appropriations bill. On the basis of revenue projections, the speaker of
the house and the president of the senate, together with the appropriations committee chairs, determine the total amount to be appropriated
and how it will be divided up among the three subcommittee jurisdictions. It is up to the subcommittees, then, to live within the limits and
divvy up the funds as they see fit. Here, as in most places, debate over
the appropriations bill goes on until the last few days of the session. The
final, and probably most critical, stage in Florida is the conference
carried on by members of each pair of subcommittees from the house
and the senate. To reconcile differences, the conferees meet for several
days during the last week or two. Once conferees from the two
chambers agree, the bill is reported to the floor. Leadership is firmly in
control. The appropriations act is passed largely in the form shaped by
the subcommittees and committees, with the assent of the speaker of the
house and president of the senate.

The appropriations committee ranks as the most desirable committee assignment in most legislative bodies. As described by a Democratic
staff member in the Pennsylvania house:

> One of the first things nearly every member wants is a letterhead that
> says he is on the Appropriations Committee. It is a prestigious
> committee, it is a committee that legislative leaders come out of, and it
> is also a committee that sometimes allows members to bring certain
> projects to their districts. This committee also may get involved in
> bargaining with the Governor. It is power and it is fun.[29]

Those legislators who are not on the committee tend to feel shut out of
the most important part of the process. Take the case of Wisconsin,
where fiscal power is very narrowly held by the eight of ninety-nine
representatives and eight of thirty-three senators who are on the joint
finance committee. Speaker Loftus has been trying to open up the
process on the grounds that the ninety-one members of the assembly
who are not on the panel "really resent that these people have that
much power."[30]

In some states an effort has been made to integrate substantive
policy and appropriations and to placate legislators who do not serve on
appropriations committees. Kentucky is an example. The house appropriations and revenue committee is divided into subcommittees, each of
which has three liaison members from substantive standing committees,
as well as four members of the appropriations and revenue committee.
The liaison members can vote in the full committee, which makes final
budgetary decisions.

Recently, as more policy issues are addressed in the appropriations act, criticism of the appropriations committees has increased. Other committee chairs feel that their prerogatives are being usurped. But appropriations committees, where supported by legislative leadership, have managed to keep their turf intact.

Appropriations Hearings.   An important part of legislative review is the hearings held by the appropriations committees. The hearings perform a variety of functions. As enumerated by a legislative fiscal officer in Ohio, appropriations hearings allow the committees: (1) to understand the objectives of each program; (2) to determine what the governor eliminated from each agency request; (3) to discover weaknesses in the budget request of the executive; (4) to provide oversight of agency performance on behalf of the legislature; and (5) to determine the competency of agency heads and to raise pet gripes with them. Hearings also afford the agency the opportunity to present its case to the legislature and to the public. Finally, they provide a forum for different groups and clienteles to express their views.[31]

Hearings before the appropriations committees constitute a major test for an agency's top personnel, whose budget request is at stake. Understandably, they are intent on making a strong showing defending their programs and their performance. Hearings differ from state to state, chamber to chamber, agency to agency, and year to year. Still, an idea of their nature can be obtained by considering the hearings of the New Jersey Department of Transportation before the appropriations committee of the assembly in April 1988.

A few days before their scheduled appearance at the legislature, the commissioner, Hazel Gluck, and about twenty-five of the transportation department's senior managers and staff met to prepare for the hearing. Anticipating questions that legislators would pose, their discussion touched on fare-box policy; bridge conditions in New Jersey; unexpended balances that the department held in large amounts for planning, maintenance, and equipment; and personnel levels. Discussion then turned to concerns that individual members of the assembly appropriations committee would be sure to bring up, because they had brought up such matters in the past.

A few days later, the commissioner, her assistant commissioner, the executive director of N.J. Transit (an independent agency, whose board the transportation commissioner chaired), and other staff (from the communications, policy, and legislative liaison sections) attended the assembly committee hearing. Department of Transportation and N.J. Transit personnel practically filled up the fifty-seat hearing room in the State House Annex. The meeting was held in the morning, with the department appearing first at Commissioner Gluck's request. (Some cabinet members in New Jersey are of the opinion that it is preferable to be scheduled later in the day, when committee members are tired and ask fewer questions.)

Before the hearings, the minority Democrats on the committee had been briefed by their staff, who prepared questions on transportation policy, the Transportation Trust Fund, transportation department operations, and the N.J. Transit fare increase. Members chose the listed questions that they would feel most confident asking.

Republican member of the assembly Anthony Villane chaired the hearing, and only two other members were present at the start. But several members arrived as the hearing progressed. Commissioner Gluck made her presentation, announcing that the transportation department would launch no new or significantly expanded programs, indicating the FY 1989 projects, and requesting thirty-five new positions because of growth stemming from the Transportation Trust Fund. Villane began the questioning, asking Gluck to justify the new positions. He also asked about her role vis-à-vis the New Jersey Parkway Authority, giving her the opportunity to suggest that the commissioner of transportation should sit on the Parkway Authority as well as the New Jersey Turnpike Authority. The chair very obviously was helping Gluck press ahead on one of her major items.

The next line of questions pursued by Villane dealt with federal aid and how the decrease in federal funds would affect the Transportation Trust Fund. The problem was that the cuts in aid would affect mass transit more than highways, the commissioner pointed out. The closing of New York City's Williamsburg Bridge came up next, and Gluck turned to an assistant commissioner for his expert opinion. "I can assure you that our bridges are safe," he said. The chair then questioned the cleanliness of the state's highways, and the commissioner blamed its lack on the legislature's habit of cutting maintenance.

The ranking minority member, Democratic assemblyman John Watson, then took over, asking how many consultants the department had employed since 1981. He indicated that employees, rather than outsiders, should be doing the work. Gluck replied that it was difficult to recruit engineers, and thus the department resorted to consultants. The chair, backing Watson, then asked the department to provide information on the costs of consultants versus employees.

As anticipated, Watson than brought up a constituency concern of his.

WATSON: I don't like to get parochial, but my Rte. 129 situation in the city of Trenton. What is the status of that?

GLUCK: We're right on schedule.
WATSON: Anything in the Transportation Trust Fund to help defray the cost?
GLUCK: We can talk.

Watson then raised another district issue, asking how the city could have residents transported to the suburbs for jobs. The next issue for the black assembly member was affirmative action at the department, and especially the issue of hiring minority contractors.

Republican member of the assembly Walter Kavanaugh, from the northern part of the state, took over the questioning at this point. "How do we improve access to the Lincoln Tunnel?" he asked. The commissioner responded that she was thinking of a high occupancy vehicle lane and that she would allow two lanes for buses. Kavanaugh then asked the executive director of N.J. Transit about new seats on the commuter trains, because riders had been complaining to him. He expressed his concern about fare increases for his constituents. After Kavanaugh, Democratic member of the assembly Byron Baer took over and criticized the fare-box increase. The questioning concluded with Democratic member of the assembly Wayne Bryant, who expressed concern about the percentage of the fare-box increase for his constituents and for the poor in other areas. At about that point in the early afternoon, the assembly went into session, and the committee adjourned for the day.

The Department of Transportation had anticipated many of the issues that would be brought up by committee members. The testimony of its personnel served departmental purposes. Also during the morning's hearings, the legislators accomplished their objectives. They had spoken on behalf of their constituencies, who were interested in lower transit fares, highways, minority hiring, and local projects. Their questions were frequently parochial, sometimes nit-picking, and occasionally partisan, but they also raised policy issues and made specific suggestions for administrative action.

Negotiations. The appropriations committees and subcommittees are the crucial and focal bodies during the legislative process. Their hearings, mark-up sessions, and conferences are among the most important stages in budget making. These work units of the senate and house make the specific decisions as to who gets how much for what, and they provide the main feedback and direction to the department and agency heads who come before them hat in hand. As important as they are, often their efforts take place within parameters set by legislative leadership and the negotiations of leaders with the governor. Not everywhere, but in many states, legislative leadership—which may include the appropriations chairs—resolves the major issues of spending and taxing directly with the governor.

Although each round of negotiations between the legislature and the governor over the budget is unique, an examination of the resolution of the budget during the 1986 session of the Florida legislature can be instructive. Governor Bob Graham delivered his $15.9 billion budget to the legislature in February. It called for increases in spending and higher taxes to produce the necessary revenues. The next step was the presentation of the governor's budget to the appropriations committees. Glenn Robertson, director of planning and budgeting in the governor's office, made the presentation to the senate committee early in March. But his appearance was for the record more than anything else. All the committee members attending were chatting with one another, reading, or preparing for budget workshops scheduled to follow the brief full committee meetings. Once the subcommittees began meeting, the real work would begin. For the record, and for the media, the senators asked Robertson questions on their pet subjects—Karen Thurman on growth management, Jack Gordon on human services, Malcolm Beard on salaries for state troopers, Mary Grizzle on terrorism, and Arnett Girardeau on education. Pat Neal, who chaired the committee, concluded that while the governor could simply assume new taxes, the legislature would have to raise them. The problem, according to him, was to find money for high-priority programs by cutting existing programs. This would be the task of the three senate subcommittees.

Neal urged his colleagues to use either a sharp knife or blunt instrument to cut Graham's budget, while expressing criticism of the governor's unrealistic approach:

> He is able to raise taxes in his little green book and spend them easier than we can raise taxes in the Florida Legislature and appropriate them. It is a privilege that the governor has when he draws his budget to make people feel good throughout the state . . . but we don't have the capacity to make them feel as good as the governor has.[32]

The appropriations committee staffs of the Florida house and senate and the six subcommittees began putting together their appropriations bills, and meanwhile negotiations between the legislative and executive branches came to a virtual halt.

By mid-May, with only three weeks left in the session, the governor began to lobby the legislature on behalf of his budget priorities. He declared publicly that both the house and senate versions of the budget had "serious deficiencies," and it was reported in the press that he wanted more money for schools and for medical care for prison inmates, among other things.[33] But for the most part, Graham called leaders into his office one by one for informal discussions to try to convince them of the need for more revenues.

On May 19, for example, he had the house leadership in to discuss the budget. James Harold Thompson, the speaker; Sam Bell, chairman of the appropriations committee; Herb Morgan, chairman of the rules committee (and a former chairman of appropriations); Elaine Gordon, speaker pro tem and chairwoman of the human services subcommittee; Fred Breeze, the speaker's chief of staff, and Tony Carvalho, the staff director of the appropriations committee, represented the house. With Graham were Buddy Schorstein, his chief of staff, Gene Adams, one of his legislative counsels, and Glenn Robertson. Speaker Thompson thanked the governor for inviting them in for private criticism before meeting with the press. Graham indicated where he wanted additions, admitting that the house budget came much closer to his figure than the senate budget. "I like your bill better," Graham said. But there were amendments that he wanted introduced.

Although house leaders listened attentively to the governor, they were not moved by his appeals for more money. They believed they had gone as far as they could. Nor were they terribly concerned about the implicit threat that Graham might make public his criticism of the legislature. At this late stage in the appropriations process, the house and senate were traveling their own paths. As expected, however, Graham persisted in his efforts; he continued to lobby lawmakers and he also appealed to the public. He wanted an eight-cents-a-pack cigarette tax to finance aid for poor and infirm children, strengthen child support enforcement, and meet other human services needs. The theme he developed was that of neglect of children, the poor, and the elderly.[34]

With the session due to end within a week, the pace of negotiations between the governor and the house and senate quickened. June 2 was a busy day for Governor Graham, as far as lobbying for his budget was concerned. He met again with house leaders, who did not seem to care about his priorities nearly as much as they did about their own. The speaker's response to Graham's pleas was simply: "We're working on it." The governor argued for taxes he favored, such as a tourism tax and, now, an additional five cents on cigarettes. House leaders responded with their mix of revenue producers. The meeting ended inconclusively, with House leaders resistant to pressure or interference by the governor.

Senate leaders were a friendlier group; they had been more cooperative with the governor throughout the 1986 session. They met with him that same day, reporting that certain revenue increases were politically out of the question. The best possibility, as far as they were concerned, was raising the cigarette tax from two cents to five cents (still two cents less than the governor's reduced demand). Ken Jenne, the rules committee chairman, indicated that the Senate had already added $28 million to the human services budget. But Graham countered that although the money went to the Department of Health and Rehabilitative Services, it was not directed specifically to his own priorities. "We're just not funding the programs you want us to fund," rejoined senate president Harry Johnston. "It's a legislative responsibility to raise and spend this money." Senate leaders were not sure whether the governor wanted additional revenues or a redistribution of the funds that they had already allocated. But, in any case, the senate's principal problem was not the governor. Rather, the leaders saw most of their difficulties stemming from disagreements with the house.

That same day, after a bill-signing ceremony to commemorate the seatbelt law that had just been passed, the capitol press corps inquired into Graham's meetings with legislative leaders and the status of the budget and taxes. The governor made an eloquent appeal for his programs and maintained that at least $50 million more was needed in taxes (although he would have liked about $100 million more than the legislature was planning to raise). He was applying pressure for greater funding of social programs. But he did not specify to the press exactly how additional funds should be raised. The cigarette tax was a good possibility, but the governor said he would not lobby for one revenue package or another. He would consider any mix from a "cafeteria of revenue items." It was up to the house and senate to negotiate a package; he was willing to be a mediator in the process.

Neither the house nor the senate, however, could work out a revenue plan to which the other body and the governor would agree. An impasse had developed. On the evening of June 4, in an effort to settle the budget, Graham hosted a meeting of house and senate leaders at the mansion. He affirmed at the outset that about $100 million more was still needed, but the discussion of taxes went nowhere. Senate and house leaders decided to go off into separate rooms to see if they could agree among themselves on a position. The governor and his staff were left behind. House leaders quickly came up with a plan and invited the senators into their room to negotiate. Four members of the house and four members of the senate huddled in the dining room. The house proposal was presented, and immediately the senate president said, "We accept."

At that point, the leaders rejoined the governor, ready to present a united front. Speaker Thompson opened the conversation, declaring that they all wanted to stay together and give Graham credit for the settlement. The governor responded that the $45 million the agreed-on plan would raise was not at all sufficient for human services. When he began to lecture the legislators, Thompson became furious. He laced into the governor, saying that whatever the legislature did would not matter, it would never be enough for Graham. Senator Ken Jenne followed with sharp words on behalf of the senate. Then, the legislators rose, took leave of the governor, and left the mansion. Graham followed them out and hinted that he would settle for the legislature's plan, if there were a reallocation of funds with more going to human services. The leaders made no promises, but said they would look into the possibility. That night two of the governor's top aides arrived at the speaker's office with the proposal that $20 million be reallocated internally to the Department of Health and Rehabilitative Services. They had a list of specific items the governor wanted increased.

The result of the struggle over the budget between Governor Graham on the one hand and the Florida house and senate on the other was a settlement nearer to the legislature's desires than to the governor's. According to Gene Adams, the governor had three priorities as the 1986 legislative session began: "Budget, budget, budget." Yet, the budget was where Graham took his worst licks. He had pressed for an eight-cents-per-pack cigarette tax increase that would have raised $112 million a year for social welfare and education. But the legislature would only accept three cents, leaving human services $60 million short of what Graham wanted. One of Graham's few major budgetary initiatives was $30 million to establish a minimum statewide salary for teachers. That proposal, however, went nowhere because of its cost.

Arenas for Legislative Action.   The legislature's shaping of the budget takes place in several arenas. The committee and subcommittee arenas are always significant, and that in which governors negotiate with legislative leaders is usually critical. Party caucuses or conferences also count in many places, and in some states they may be the key locales for legislative decisions on the budget. Although the joint budget committee in Colorado has great influence, the majority party caucuses in the house and senate essentially determine the final shape of the budget. In Wisconsin the bill fashioned by the joint finance committee nowadays needs additional support, so the majority party caucus in the assembly redrafts much of it. The process in which the caucus engages, referred to as "auctioning off," involves giving enough members projects for their districts to achieve the fifty-one votes needed to pass the bill on the floor.

Deliberations over the budget, like deliberations over other issues in the legislature, go on throughout the session and in numerous places—the subcommittee and committee meetings and hearings, the leadership conference rooms, the governor's office. The process includes communications among legislators, staff members, lobbyists, constituents, heads of state agencies, and the governor and staff. Not many people who want in are left out; yet it is the governor, legislative leadership, and the appropriations committees that normally share principal control.

LEGISLATIVE IMPACT

Twenty years ago, a political scientist who studied the budgetary process in Illinois concluded that "legislative participation in the determination of state expenditures is virtually nonexistent." That characterization would probably have fit the large majority of states, at least at that time. More recently, however, a study of the budget behavior of 671 executive agencies in 18 states indicated that the role of governors was by no means as dominant as before.[35] The legislature had challenged their power.

Process.   The change in the legislature's participation in determining the state budget did not occur overnight. The trend toward greater legislative involvement has been gradual, but seemingly inexorable. Furthermore, in a number of states today the legislature is not hesitant to go its own way from time to time. The appropriations and revenue committees in Kentucky in 1984 wrote the budget after the governor's plan for a tax increase failed. In Massachusetts the budget presented by Governor Dukakis in 1989 was considered irrelevant. The governor was relegated to the sidelines because of his support for increased taxes, and the senate and house ways and means committees played the principal budgetary role.[36]

A study of the budgetary process in Wisconsin concluded that the legislature is neither marching to the beat of the governor nor "merely rubber stamping proposals emanating from the line agencies, but is significantly shaping the final budget product." The legislature here has managed to exercise influence by delegating responsibility to the governor and the agencies on matters dealing with agency operations, involving little of policy significance, and costing relatively little. But on "big ticket" items or when local units of government are affected, the legislature decides on its own.[37]

The expansion of legislative influence can be demonstrated by, among other indicators, the legislature's relatively recent insistence on having some say on the use of federal funds by state departments and agencies. Before the 1970s most legislatures ignored the federal aid coming into their states, which then accounted for a substantial portion of their budgets. But executive agencies were initiating programs with federal funds, thus requiring immediate state matching funds and later on increased state financing. As categorical grants proliferated, legislative control over the purpose and amount of state agency spending diminished. Education departments, for example, became semi-autonomous, more beholden to the U.S. Department of Education than to the governor and the legislature in their own states. The weakness of legislatures was shown in a 1980 report by the General Accounting Office. The GAO found that in nearly all of the grant programs it examined, legislatures were shut out while governors and executive agencies decided on the state's federal assistance proposals. In fact, federal officials would not give information to legislative committees, even if requested to do so.[38]

Legislators were annoyed at what they felt was a humiliating situation. In Pennsylvania, for example, many legislators felt that administrators were deceitful, arrogant, and overbearing in attempting to exclude them from participation in the policy-making process. Agencies had expanded their staffs by means of federal money, thus forcing the legislature to pay the tab when federal funds dwindled or expired, as they usually did. They had also overestimated federal receipts, forcing the legislature to make up the difference. Finally, they had shifted funds around, further upsetting legislators who might have intended that the funds be expended otherwise.[39]

During the mid-1970s legislatures began to assert themselves, with California, Oregon, Pennsylvania, and South Dakota among the initiators of what became a national movement to increase state legislative control of federal funds. Legislatures took steps to appropriate federal grant-in-aid monies in order to: (1) assure that legislative priorities were advanced; (2) guard against the commitment of future state funds without prior legislative approval; and (3) avoid state executive pursuit with federal authorities of programs the legislature had disallowed. In addition, legislatures undertook to review agency applications for federal funds and to track the disposition of federal funds that had been granted to the state.[40]

As might have been expected, the legislature's assertion of power was resisted by the executive branch. In some states open conflict broke out, and in a number of cases the courts were called upon to resolve disputes between the two branches. In considering whether state legislatures may appropriate federal funds, the state courts have reached a variety of decisions. Courts have supported governors in Arizona, New Mexico, Oklahoma, and Massachusetts. By contrast, in *Shapp v. Sloan* (1978), the Pennsylvania Supreme Court upheld a statute requiring all federal funds to be deposited in the state's general fund and to be available for appropriation by the legislature. In *Anderson v. Regan* (1981) a New York court of appeals also determined that federal funds deposited in the state's treasury were subject to legislative appropriation.

With President Reagan's New Federalism initiatives, Congress in the Budget Reconciliation Act of 1981 consolidated over fifty categorical programs into seven new block grants. The authority of the states to set program priorities, allocate funds, and develop regulations was thereby increased. In most places the governor and executive agencies took the lead in responding; yet legislatures in a number of states insisted on sharing responsibility for the new block grants and for the replacement of lost federal aid.[41] Legislatures took further advantage of the opportunity to assert their role.

Colorado's legislature took especially forceful action. After the annual meeting of the National Conference of State Legislatures in 1981, the legislative leaders and staff of the joint budget committee met to plan an assertion of legislative appropriation authority over federal block grants. A year later a report by Colorado's state auditor recommended that the legislature exercise such authority. In response, the legislature in a headnote to the budget bill (referred to as the "long bill" in Colorado) listed eight federal block grants and specified that they were appropriated. Governor Lamm vetoed the headnote and the legislature commenced litigation. In 1987 Colorado's supreme court approved legislative control of state funds to match federal funds, by means of a headnote setting a maximum amount that the state would match. Thus, the legislature could determine the amount of federal funds spent for a specific program by appropriating the state share.[42]

Today, over three-fourths of the states have some provision for legislative review of federal funds, although often that power is limited. In eleven states legislatures actively appropriate federal funds, but in the majority legislative scrutiny of federally financed programs is considerably less intensive than that of state-funded programs. Much discretion still resides with the executive branch. Furthermore, the expansion of legislative involvement has not been without drawbacks. In Pennsylvania, where the legislative role is strong, it has produced cumbersome procedures, more paperwork, minor conflicts, occasional policy confrontation, and some politicization of state administration. And there is always the danger that legislators, who receive much more information as a result of their involvement in this area, will be deluged by detail and consequently lose sight of larger policy questions.[43]

While acknowledging the downside of legislative participation, there still can be little doubt that legislative influence over the budget has increased, owing to the fact that the legislature has assumed responsibility for federal as well as state funds. As proof of this increased power, federal agencies and officials now deal with legislatures as well as with governors and state agencies. Together with the increase in the amount and intensity of committee and staff participation in the appropriation process, this development has enlarged the legislative role considerably.

Policy.   If one takes a macroscopic view of budgets, legislatures can be seen giving governors most of what they want by way of policy and funding. Take Iowa, for instance. Governor Robert Ray, during his several administrations, would shape the budget according to executive preferences. "The legislature massaged it, played with it, and normally adopted 95 percent of it," Cal Hultman, a Republican legislative leader, reported.[44] When Terry Branstad succeeded Ray, it is estimated that the legislature still accepted 90 percent of his budget. "When all is said and done it's usually close to the governor's recommendation," estimates a member of Branstad's staff. The situation is not very different in other states.

If one takes a closer look, however, the legislative role in shaping the budget can be seen as far more influential. The Kentucky legislature rejected Martha Layne Collins's budget and passed its own instead; then it challenged her successor, Wallace Wilkinson, on spending and taxing levels. Governor Buddy Roemer of Louisiana, who was unable to get a tax increase in the 1989 session, had to cut the state budget in order to balance it. Prominent among the cuts were reductions in higher education and charity hospitals, which would have resulted in institutions being closed in the districts of a number of senators. These senators resisted, and the governor eventually had to compromise with the senate.

Even in Maryland, where legislative budgetary power is curtailed by its constitutional inability to add to the governor's proposal, the general assembly plays an important budgetary role. The common perception is that the budget rests entirely in the hands of the governor, although it may take a new chief executive a while to discover the principal levers of control. But the legislature took an independent stance when the somewhat passive Harry Hughes was governor, and it has remained remarkably independent even with a very assertive William Donald Schaefer as governor. Maryland's Spending Affordability Act, passed in response to California's Proposition 13 and Massachusetts' Proposition 2½, provides the framework for legislative influence. On the basis of a review of economic indicators, primarily personal income, a spending affordability committee established by the general assembly decides on a percentage of growth for the state budget. The legislature has insisted on adherence to the limit, while Governor Schaefer has maintained that the state's needs are too great to be so restricted.

Thus, the Maryland general assembly, and in particular the senate's budget and taxation committee, have been tough on Schaefer's budget. For example, in 1988 the legislature made more changes and deeper cuts in Schaefer's budget than in any other in recent years.[45] One hundred million dollars were cut, which may not seem much, considering that the budget totaled just short of $9 billion. But if one excludes fixed costs and attends only to "discretionary" funds, legislative action assumes far greater significance. There is little question that in Maryland, where the legislature cannot increase the budget, it has acted as a restraint on the governor.

Wisconsin offers another example of legislative influence in this domain. Here, the legislature amends or deletes executive initiatives, as well as initiating its own policy proposals. A study of the Wisconsin budgetary process, which examined 538 decisions for 14 major state agencies in the 1977-1979 biennial budget, found that the legislature had notable impact. Nine out of ten of the joint finance committee's proposals were incorporated into the budget, as were 85 percent of the proposals made by amendments on the floor. The committee and floor amendments contributed 38 percent and 18 percent of the approved decision items of major policy significance and relatively high cost.[46]

Although patterns vary, the tendency appears to be for the legislature to add more than it cuts from the governor's budget. Indeed, there are greater incentives for responding positively to clientele groups and other interests that request additional monies than for responding negatively. Normally, for instance, the New York legislature raises the amount the governor requests for state aid to local schools, by $100 to $200 million. Governor Cuomo's objective, keeping the general fund budget at the level he recommends, is not always achieved. And he has accused senators publicly of trying to raise the budget so that they can deliver more to their constituents. In 1989, for example, the legislature increased spending by $300 million over the governor's budget, cutting about the same amount from his proposals, and including many provisions that he opposed.[47]

Vermont also witnessed disagreement over spending, with the legislature preferring to dole out more and Governor Madeleine M. Kunin less. The legislature wanted to give a subsidy to dairy farmers; the governor refused. The compromise that resulted was a tax abatement provision for farmers. Fearing that the revenue situation would worsen in the 1988 session, Kunin resisted increases for human services. The legislature, however, rewrote the formula for special education, with higher costs for the state. The legislature was disposed to commit all the surplus to spending, while the governor would have preferred putting it into a "rainy day fund." In the end, the governor had to accept several budgetary items. Nevertheless, according to her chief of staff: "We kept it within limits, and they think they got what they wanted." Neither branch prevailed, but both had some measure of success in achieving their objectives.

It is difficult, if not impossible, to determine who comes out ahead in the budgetary rivalry between governors and legislatures. For one thing, often there is agreement between the two on priorities. Not only do governors and legislatures perceive similar needs and respond to similar pressures, but the governor's budgetary formulation is likely to reflect the legislature's own priorities. There may be relatively little to contest, but whatever is subject to dispute can be hard fought.

New York illustrates how the battle over the budget is waged by skilled politicians. In the budget enacted in 1989, Governor Cuomo refused to budge on a few issues, but he gave in on many others. The legislature rebuffed him on a number of his initiatives: it refused to shift the costs of many programs to local government; it added $300 million to what the governor proposed, plus another $80 million in pork; it restored funds for jobs he proposed eliminating; and it refused to increase local government's share of long-term Medicaid costs. But the governor managed to keep the spending rate down, which he had declared to be his major goal. According to his aides, Cuomo's strategy required him to propose a budget that slashed state programs severely, so that the legislature could make increases and still keep within his actual spending goals. The governor did not expect many of his proposals to be accepted, but "he had to take the heat in order to achieve the objective," according to one of Cuomo's advisers. The governor prevailed on the overall rate of spending, but the legislature decided where the additions and cuts would be made.[48] Power truly was shared on the 1989-1990 budget, as it is generally between the governor and the legislature in New York.

Pork.   As representatives of their constituencies and as candidates for reelection, legislators are deeply concerned with the amount of state aid they secure for their districts. In what has been called "the politics of formula manipulation" or "the politics of printouts," their objective is to obtain as much state revenue sharing funds as possible for their districts. Depending on the state, that would include monies provided by formula for schools, local transportation, mental health, and other local assistance. Thanks to modern technology, each member can see, on a computer printout, how his or her district will fare under a proposed budget, as compared to other districts and as compared to past budgets. Since the state aid formula is where much of the money is, it naturally becomes a bone of contention among members, between the two houses, and between the legislature and the governor in the budgetary process.

As representatives and as candidates, legislators also are concerned with obtaining appropriations for special projects located in their districts and which benefit their constituencies. Referred to generally as "pork," and in Florida as "turkeys," such projects appropriate state monies for parks, museums, monuments, roads, and other facilities located in a legislator's district. What chiefly differentiates pork or turkeys from other projects is that they are not recommended by the agencies of the executive branch. They may be worthy items on which to spend monies, but they have circumvented the executive planning and budgetary processes. Pork barreling, as it is called, thus substitutes a political process of decision making for the normal bureaucratic processes in which need and merit are said to count. Although these projects may well have merit, the question is whether they have more or less merit than competing claims on the state's budget. From the point of view of legislators, "the difference between a turkey and a worthwhile project hinges upon whether it is in their own district." [49] From the point of view of the administration, pork barreling is a poor way to allocate scarce resources.

Take the 1988-1989 budget in Florida as an example. Out of a state budget of $21.1 billion that passed the legislature, about $150 million, or less than one percent, was for turkeys. These turkeys included an orchid show in Orlando ($25,000), purchase of weed-eating fish by a drainage district ($100,000), and an international tourism exhibition and bowling tournament in Miami ($2 million). In addition, a catfish farm, an access road for a shirt factory, and a convention for the busing and travel agent industries were included in the appropriations act. The delegation from St. Petersburg pushed a $30 million package for a new domed stadium to help lure the White Sox from Chicago to Florida.

Individual members brought the bacon back to their districts. W. D. Childers, a senator from Escambia County, obtained a $3 million convention center and a $1 million naval aviation museum. The senate appropriations committee chairman, Jim Scott, and the house speaker-designate, Tom Gustafson, combined to get $10.3 million for an arts and science center and another $700,000 to plan a university tower in Broward County. The house appropriations committee chairman, Sam Bell, obtained an $8 million project for Daytona Beach Community College.[50]

Not every legislator has as ample a diet of pork. Those in the minority party receive relatively little. Those who have opposed leadership on key issues are also likely to go undernourished. Others do better than average. Leadership obviously receives more than its fair share, since it parcels out the turkeys. Members of the appropriations commit-tee also do well as far as pork is concerned. Then, if the majority party caucus plays a decisive role, as in Colorado and Wisconsin, additional pet projects will be included as necessary political deals are struck in order to ensure passage of the budget bill. In some places, such as North Carolina (where the governor cannot veto items), legislators are allo-cated relatively equal sums. Each representative receives $50,000 to $70,000 and each senator $85,000 to $100,000 worth of projects for the district. All are in a bill that moves through the process separately from the appropriations bill.[51]

Legislators—at least in such states as Florida, New York, North Carolina, and Wisconsin—appear to be more demanding than in earlier years and leadership resorts to pork as an inducement to keep members in line. The quid pro quo is that the leadership agrees to a member's project in return for a member's vote on a larger issue, such as the overall budget. Pork thus serves as a relatively inexpensive method of keeping the legislative wheels greased for consensus building. A governor may invoke the item veto and excoriate the legislature on its Christmas tree of an appropriations bill with presents for everyone. But a number of governors—Cuomo of New York, Thompson of Illinois, and McWherter of Tennessee—also recognize pork to be a necessary staple of the legislative diet and important to the executive, as well as to legislative leadership, for trading purposes.

BALANCING THE BOOKS

In constructing their appropriations bill, legislatures try to sidestep the governor's budgetary scalpel, the item veto. Either they work matters out before the budget's enactment or they try to circumvent the veto in one way or another. In some states they manage to hide individual projects in the lump sum appropriations of departmental accounts, so that the governor cannot item veto them without eliminating his or her own proposals as well. Practically speaking, legislatures have little recourse if the governor invokes the item veto. Overrides are rare, although from time to time a legislature will rise up and successfully challenge the governor's authority.

In any case, legislators have little to lose in risking the removal of their projects by the governor. Indeed, the item-veto power may encourage legislators to act irresponsibly—loading the budget with pork, passing the buck to the governor, denouncing the governor's action when their projects are vetoed, and taking credit in their districts for having given constituents their best effort.

Governors make use of the item veto for a variety of reasons. In Wisconsin they have used it to bring the state's law in line with their views of acceptable policy more than to exercise fiscal restraint. Partisanship has also been a consideration, with the veto exercised more frequently when the governor's party did not control the legislature.[52] They have also made use of this power to cut the pet projects of legislators out of the budget.

Wisconsin, during the tenure of Tommy Thompson, demonstrates the furthest limits of gubernatorial power in the appropriations process. Here, the constitution provides for more than an item veto, it provides for a "partial veto." An amendment in 1930 to Article V, Section 10 reads: "Appropriation bills may be approved in whole or in part by the governor." According to this provision, as upheld by repeated state supreme court decisions, the governor has the authority to veto "sections, subsections, paragraphs, sentences, words, parts of words, letters, and digits included in an appropriation bill." Governor Thompson in the 1987-1989 budget bill exercised 290 partial vetoes, going so far as to veto parts of words, while saving letters to create new words. For example, one section of the bill would have allowed a court to place in detention for "not more than 48 hours" a juvenile who violated a court order in a delinquency proceeding. Thompson vetoed the provision in such a way that "48 hours" was turned into "ten days" by selective vetoes of words and letters from another sentence in that subsection. "He's like a kid with an alphabet," commented the speaker of the assembly, who challenged the governor, but without success, in court.[53]

Thompson was willing to take on the legislature, and do it with a vengeance: "I'm not going to allow the budget bill to be porked up and have every individual special-interest bill placed in there or buy votes by letting them throw their own special legislation into the budget bill."[54] His vetoes were all sustained.

Florida's governors have directed their item vetoes at the legislature's flock of turkeys, or at least at the ones the executive found particularly objectionable. Graham took his veto responsibility seriously. On one occasion, he was counseled by a supporter that the legislature was sure to override his veto on a particular measure. The governor's attitude, according to a member of his staff, was that "It's the governor's job to veto, if he feels it necessary. It's the legislature's job to override it, if they feel it necessary. I'll do my job and let them do theirs." Graham did his job. But though he spoke loudly and threatened the veto frequently, he used it sparingly.

Graham and his chief of staff, legislative counsels, director of planning and budgeting, and others would meet to discuss what to let stand and what to item veto in the appropriations act after the session ended. A meeting on June 1, 1986, is illustrative. In reviewing items for the governor, staff would be guided by the following questions: (1) Is the item in the governor's recommended budget? (2) Is the item related to the governor's key policy initiatives? (3) Is the item related to an important issue dealt with during the legislative session? (4) Is the item in the budget solely for the purpose of providing one geographic area a prize without relating it to a special need or priority? (5) Is the item one that was vetoed the year before and is appearing again?

After a discussion of almost a hundred projects totaling over $80 million, the governor decided to veto four even though they were not very costly. On other projects, he requested additional information from his staff. The following day, Graham met with his staff again to review further a list of potential item-veto candidates. It included fifty-six projects at a cost of almost $68 million. One by one, items were taken off the list until only a few were left for veto.

That year, with an election approaching, Graham made only limited use of his item-veto power. He deleted items such as: $75,000 for a University of Miami Fire Fighters Health Clinic; $1 million for a four-year liberal arts college in Broward County, which had not been requested by the Board of Regents; and $1 million to the Northeast Florida Water Management District for a water restoration program, which had not been requested by the Department of Environmental Resources.

Governor Martinez speaks as loudly as his predecessor, but he carries a bigger stick. In deciding what to veto, Martinez weighs several factors: (1) whether the project has been reviewed and requested by one of the executive agencies; (2) whether local governments should pay for the project instead of the state; and (3) whether the legislator is an ally of the governor.[55] In 1988, his second year in office, some of the legislature's turkeys managed to make the grade, but a remarkably high number did not. The governor cast 136 item vetoes, cutting about $150 million from the 1988-1989 budget of $18.5 billion. With the state facing fiscal problems on the one side and a Democratic-controlled legislature on the other, Martinez showed little reluctance to throw down the gauntlet and use his item-veto authority to the fullest. In 1989, Martinez continued on his turkey shoot, vetoing about 250 items in the budget bill.

NOTES

1. For an overview of budgetary practices, see Tony Hutchison and Kathy James, *Legislative Budget Procedures in the 50 States: A Guide to Appropriations and Budget Processes* (Denver: National Conference of State Legislatures, September 1988).
2. John M. Dowling, "Robert L. Mandeville: The Financial Wizardry (Or Sleight of Hand) of a Fiscal Spin Doctor," *Governing*, January 1989, 44.
3. *New York Times*, March 9, 1988.
4. Senators who were surveyed in eleven states ranked it as the most important of a governor's powers, ahead of the ability to muster popular support. This was over a decade ago, before governors had acquired the machinery to win popularity. E. Lee Bernick, "Gubernatorial Tools: Formal vs. Informal," *Journal of Politics* 41 (May 1979): 656-664.
5. National Governors' Association, *Reflections on Being Governor* (Washington, D.C.: Center for Policy Research, February 1981), 153-154.
6. Glen Abney and Thomas P. Lauth, "Perception of the Impact of Governors and Legislatures in the State Appropriations Process," *Western Political Quarterly* 40 (June 1987): 335-342.
7. David Adamany, "Wisconsin Gov. Lucey: Successful Hands-Off Management," *Journal of State Government* 62 (July/August 1989): 142.
8. Justice William Bablitch, in *The Courts: Sharing and Separating Powers*, ed. Lawrence Baum and David Frohnmayer (New Brunswick, N.J.: Eagleton Institute of Politics, 1989), 69.
9. National Governors' Association, *Governing the American States: A Handbook for New Governors* (Washington, D.C.: Center for Policy Research, NGA, November 1978), 164.
10. This characterization is of the governor's authority in Wisconsin, as expressed by Speaker Tom Loftus, "The Wisconsin Budget Process" (Lecture for the University of Wisconsin—Whitewater, Political Science Department, March 17, 1986), 3.
11. National Governors' Association, *Governing the American States*, 164; Alan Rosenthal, ed., *The Governor and the Legislature* (New Brunswick, N.J.: Eagleton Institute of Politics, Rutgers University, 1988), 13.
12. Representative Marlin Schneider, quoted in *Milwaukee Sentinel*, August 31, 1987.
13. National Governors' Association, Office of State Services, *Transition and the New Governor* (Washington, D.C.: NGA, November 1982), 82.
14. Loftus, "The Wisconsin Budget Process," 3; Sharon Randall, "From Big Shot to Boss," *State Legislatures*, July 1988, 35.
15. *Milwaukee Sentinel*, August 31, 1987; Loftus, "The Wisconsin Budget Process," 3.
16. Diane Blair, *Arkansas Politics and Government* (Lincoln: University of Nebraska Press, 1988), 248-250.
17. Until recently executives in Mississippi and North Carolina were also severely limited in their budgetary roles, but a 1982 state Supreme Court decision gave responsibility to the governor of North Carolina, and 1984 legislation gave similar responsibility to the governor of Mississippi. The legislature's role was diminished, but by no means eliminated.
18. Fred Brown, "Colorado Citizens Rewrite Legislative Rules," *State Legislatures*, August 1989, 18; Herbert F. Morgan, "Need for Legislative Oversight

and Legislator Expectations of Legislative Staff," in *Proceedings of the Conference on Legislative Oversight*, Joint Legislative Audit and Review Commission, Virginia General Assembly (Richmond: JLARC, October 13-15, 1985), 18.

19. National Governors' Association, *Reflections on Being Governor*, 204.
20. Ibid., 163-164.
21. Data as of April 1989, furnished to the author by the National Conference of State Legislatures.
22. See, for example, the case of California in William K. Muir, Jr., *Legislature: California's School for Politics* (Chicago: University of Chicago Press, 1982), 114-115.
23. Abney and Lauth, "Perception of the Impact of Governors and Legislatures in the State Appropriations Process," 335-342.
24. Hutchison and James, *Legislative Budget Procedures in the 50 States*, 43-44.
25. Jon Bowermaster, *Governor: An Oral Biography of Robert D. Ray* (Ames: Iowa State University Press, 1987), 229; Paul B. Beers, *Pennsylvania: Politics Today and Yesterday* (University Park: Pennsylvania State University Press, 1980), 389; Richard G. Sheridan, *State Budgeting in Ohio*, 2d ed. (Columbus: Ohio Legislative Budget Office, 1983), 88-89; and John Maginnis, *The Last Hayride* (Baton Rouge, La.: Gris Gris Press, 1984), 76-77.
26. Charles D. Hadley, "Louisiana," *Comparative State Politics Newsletter* 6 (August 1985): 5.
27. Hutchison and James, *Legislative Budget Procedures in the 50 States*, 49-53.
28. Ibid., 58-60.
29. Sidney Wise, *The Legislative Process in Pennsylvania*, 2d ed. (Harrisburg: Bipartisan Management Committee, House of Representatives, 1984), 93.
30. *Milwaukee Sentinel*, October 10, 1987.
31. Sheridan, *State Budgeting in Ohio*, 151-152.
32. *Tallahassee Democrat*, March 7, 1986.
33. *Tallahassee Democrat*, May 14, 1986.
34. *Tampa Tribune*, May 25, 1986.
35. Thomas J. Anton, *The Politics of State Expenditure in Illinois* (Urbana: University of Illinois Press, 1966), 34, 35; Joel A. Thompson, "Agency Requests, Gubernatorial Support, and Budget Success in State Legislatures Revisited," *Journal of Politics* 49 (August 1987): 756-779.
36. Malcolm E. Jewell and Penny M. Miller, *The Kentucky Legislature: Two Decades of Change* (Lexington: University Press of Kentucky, 1988), 139; *Boston Globe*, April 3, 1989.
37. James J. Gosling, "Patterns of Influence and Choice in the Wisconsin Budgetary Process," *Legislative Studies Quarterly* 10 (November 1985): 478-479.
38. Advisory Commission on Intergovernmental Relations, *The Question of State Government Capability* (Washington, D.C.: ACIR, January 1985), 117-120.
39. James E. Skok, "Federal Funds and State Legislatures: Executive-Legislative Conflict in State Government," *Public Administration Review* 40 (November/ December 1980): 563.
40. Advisory Commission on Intergovernmental Relations, *The Question of State Government Capability*, 117; Carol S. Weissert, "State Legislative Oversight of Federal Funds," *State Government* (Spring 1980): 77.
41. Fred C. Doolittle, "State Legislatures and Federal Grants: An Overview," *Public Budgeting and Finance* 4 (Summer 1984): 9, 11.
42. *Colorado General Assembly v. Lamm* (1987).

43. Advisory Commission on Intergovernmental Relations, *The Question of State Government Capability*, 120-121; Hutchison and James, *Legislative Budget Procedures in the 50 States*, 108-111; and Skok, "Federal Funds and State Legislatures," 566-567.
44. Bowermaster, *Governor*, 155.
45. *Washington Post*, April 10, 1988.
46. Gosling, "Patterns of Influence and Choice in the Wisconsin Budgetary Process," 469-470.
47. *New York Times*, March 9, 1988, April 19, 1989.
48. Elizabeth Kolbert, "Cuomo's Budget Strategy: Sticking to Some Issues, Giving in on Others," *New York Times*, April 2, 1989.
49. David Dahl and Tim Nickens, "Talking Turkey," *St. Petersburg Times*, June 24, 1988.
50. Ibid.
51. See Joel Thompson, Bringing Home the Bacon: The Politics of Pork Barrel in the North Carolina Legislature, *Legislative Studies Quarterly* 11 (February 1986): 91-108.
52. James J. Gosling, "Wisconsin Item-Veto Lessons," *Public Administration Review* 46 (July-August 1986): 296-298.
53. Baum and Frohnmayer, *The Courts*, 74-99.
54. Randall, "From Big Shot to Boss," 36.
55. Dahl and Nickens, "Talking Turkey."

7

Running Government

After policies and appropriations have been enacted, the business of implementation begins. Rules and regulations are promulgated, programs initiated, services delivered, and funds allocated. The conventional wisdom is that the legislature has done its job and the governor can now run the show. Indeed, there are few governors who do not breathe a sigh of relief when the legislature goes home and they can devote their full energies to doing their executive job. William Donald Schaefer of Maryland regards the end of the legislative session with special glee: "I don't want the legislature to get in my way, but they do—for 90 days—and then after that we go ahead.... I can't do anything until the legislature's out of session—and then I go wild!" [1] Schaefer can then run state government as he ran Baltimore when he was mayor, actively and without interference.

Whatever the state, governors have principal responsibility for the direction of departments and agencies of the executive branch, for implementing legislative enactments, and for the day-to-day management of government. They are the chief administrators, while legislatures are supposed to have little or no role in this domain. Yet state legislatures have become increasingly concerned with matters of administration—how and for what purposes appropriated funds are expended, what rules and regulations are applied, how programs are administered, and how effective they are. Legislatures no longer stand on the sidelines; they have become players in the game of government.

SHARING CONTROL

The governor's formal powers and putative role as chief administrator ought to ensure ascendancy over the legislature in terms of controlling

167

the departments, agencies, and bureaucracies of the executive branch. Surprisingly, perhaps, governors do not always exercise predominant control. Frequently control is shared rather evenly. And in most cases, it appears that legislatures have somewhat greater influence in this respect. According to a recent study by one of the leading scholars in the field, the legislative branch, not the executive, is the most powerful force in the bureaucracy's external environment.[2]

A number of studies document the legislature's challenge to gubernatorial preeminence in the administrative arena. The American State Administrators Project surveyed about fourteen hundred administrators in all fifty states periodically over the course of two decades, asking who exercised greater control over their agency—the governor or the legislature. In the 1978 and 1984 surveys, 39 percent said the governor had greater control, 37 percent said the legislature, and the remaining 24 percent said each had about the same. (When asked whose control was preferred, three times as many administrators expressed a preference for gubernatorial rather than legislative control.) The 1978 data formed the basis for another study, which examined the degree of influence attributed by heads of different types of agencies to the governor and legislature, as well as to clientele groups and professional associations. In human resources, natural resources, economic affairs, criminal justice, and independent agencies, the influence attributed to the legislature was higher. Only in the case of staff agencies, such as offices of finance, budgeting, planning, and personnel, which are closest to the governor, was the legislature's influence ranked lower.[3]

Another survey asked top agency officials in ten states to assess the influence of governors and legislatures, as well as other institutions, on a variety of important decisions. In five of six instances, the state legislature was perceived by officials as the most important actor in the agency's external environment. Still another study of the fifty states reached the conclusion that governors do not dominate the administrative branches of government. Asked to rank governors and legislatures in terms of their impact on agency programs and objectives, 43 percent of the respondents cited the legislature as most influential and 38 percent cited the governor. The distribution of the states in terms of whether the governor or legislature was perceived to have most influence is shown in Table 7-1. One of the states where the governor has the edge is Illinois. A study here asked sixty-six agency heads from the Thompson and Walker administrations who had influence over their agencies. The governor ranked at the top, with his chief of staff and budget director near the top, and the speaker of the house and president of the senate somewhat below.[4]

TABLE 7-1   Relative Influence of Governors by State

States Where Half or More of Respondents Ranked Governor as Most Influential	*States Where One-Quarter to One-Half of Respondents Ranked Governor as Most Influential*	*States Where Less Than One-Quarter of Respondents Ranked Governor as Most Influential*
Maryland (91%)	Kansas (47%)	Oregon (24%)
New Jersey (82%)	Massachusetts (47%)	Arkansas (21%)
Kentucky (81%)	Wisconsin (47%)	Alabama (20%)
Rhode Island (73%)	Tennessee (43%)	Delaware (20%)
Hawaii (69%)	Nevada (42%)	Florida (20%)
California (60%)	Washington (42%)	Mississippi (17%)
New York (59%)	North Carolina (40%)	South Dakota (17%)
Louisiana (58%)	Georgia (40%)	Iowa (15%)
West Virginia (57%)	Minnesota (38%)	Texas (15%)
Alaska (55%)	Vermont (38%)	Arizona (14%)
Illinois (54%)	Nebraska (37%)	Virginia (12%)
Connecticut (53%)	Missouri (36%)	Montana (8%)
Oklahoma (53%)	New Hampshire (36%)	Colorado (0%)
Maine (50%)	Utah (36%)	South Carolina (0%)
New Mexico (50%)	Indiana (35%)	
Pennsylvania (50%)	North Dakota (33%)	
	Ohio (28%)	
	Idaho (28%)	
	Michigan (27%)	
	Wyoming (25%)	

Source: Glenn Abney and Thomas P. Lauth, "Legislative Influence in the Appropriations Process: A Comparative Analysis" (Paper presented at the annual meeting of the American Political Science Association, Chicago, September 1-4, 1983), 41.

Note: Percentages are calculated by dividing the number of respondents from a state citing governor as most influential actor by the number of respondents from that state.

The Extent of Gubernatorial Management

The governor is supposed to be a manager. Indeed, the "governor as manager" emerged not too long ago as a dominant theme of the contemporary governorship and a major civic cause of state government.[5] Governors themselves articulated their managerial responsibility:[6]

> James B. Edwards (South Carolina): I think personally that the management role is really where the meat of the governor's office is.
>
> J. James Exon (1971-1979, Nebraska): To me, that's number one—being a good manager. Being a good manager of a state is more important, I think, than programs or anything else.

CALVIN L. RAMPTON (Utah): I think if a governor is going to do his job, he has got to be the manager.

DAN WALKER (Illinois): What counts is management, and there isn't enough emphasis on management in government.

HARVEY WOLLMAN (1978-1979 South Dakota): But if a governor doesn't devote a high percentage of his time—over half of his time—just to executive management functions, he is really missing the boat.

Despite these testimonials from governors who served between 1965 and 1979, it is doubtful that governors even during that period did very much in the way of managing, other than intervening sporadically in response to crisis. On the basis of a study of the administration of Francis Sargent (1969-1975), a Republican governor of Massachusetts, one scholar concluded: "Governors do not manage in the customary sense of the word, that is, they do not direct or oversee the affairs of agencies over some period of time."[7]

More recently, governors have been downplaying their role as managers. That is understandable, because there are few incentives for governors to expend their energy and power on management. Greater rewards derive from the pursuit of other functions—formulating policy, steering programs through the legislature, building popularity and support among the public, helping develop the state economy, and engaging in a host of entrepreneurial activities. Today's governors seem more inclined to exert leadership beyond the executive branch than to exercise management within it. James Thompson of Illinois probably spoke for many of his colleagues when he said: "Governors really, especially in the latter part of their service, don't manage the state. If they're still managing the state after their first term, they ought not to be governor."[8] Except in a few cases, such as that of Richard Lamm of Colorado, governors regard management as of secondary concern.[9]

Someone, then, must be managing for the governor. The job is done mainly by the governor's cabinet officers or department heads or both, who are overseen by the governor's office staff. Management is in their hands. Thus, the power of appointment is critical for governors, so they can choose people they trust and upon whom they can rely. Although the appointment powers of governors have been increased over the years, their control over top personnel is still limited. Of the top two thousand administrative positions in state governments today, only 46.8 percent are appointed by governors, while another 38.2 percent are appointed by boards, the legislature, or agency heads, and the remaining 15 percent are separately elected. The variation among the states in the proportion of officials a governor can appoint is tremendous, ranging from 20 percent in South Carolina to 87 percent in New York.[10]

Among those officials appointed by governors throughout the nation, about two-thirds must be confirmed by the senate. Normally, the governor's nominations are confirmed without controversy. But the confirmation requirement gives the legislature its initial grip on the administration of government. The power to reject is always implicit; sometimes it is actually threatened, and on occasion it is exercised. Governors have to concern themselves with legislative wishes when it comes to nominating candidates for top administrative positions. It is not always easy for the governors. In California, for instance, most of the 230 key administrative appointments are subject to senate confirmation. In recent years, the senate has become quite critical of the governor's nominees, going so far as to propose changes that would give the senate greater authority over appointments.[11]

The significance of the legislature's role in the appointment of executive-branch personnel is illustrated by a confrontation between Governor Thornburgh and the Pennsylvania general assembly. The governor wanted to get rid of the state's Liquor Control Board, a $750 million monopoly that retailed wines, liquors, and spirits. Thornburgh recalled:

> In order to facilitate getting rid of the liquor control board, I needed to get control of the board so that the appropriate environment and climate could be created for getting them out of business. That required a two-thirds vote on my appointees in the senate; yet, the same guys were serving when I left office as served when I first got in there.

The same proved true in the case of Pennsylvania's Turnpike Commission, which Thornburgh also wanted to change. He could not gain control of its membership. "The point that I'm getting to," Thornburgh argued, "is that it is sometimes very difficult, if not impossible, to enact major initiatives when there is an undertow of resistance among those people who are in charge of the day-to-day operation of government."[12]

Even when governors succeed in naming their choices to head a department or agency, there are no guarantees. The appointments may not work out. For one thing, his political appointees have to manage in a very different environment from that of the governor. Each department operates in an essentially independent fashion, and each defines the goals of state government from its own perspective.[13] Nor is it unusual for a department head to wander from the reservation, responding more to the agency's clientele and professional employees than to the governor and his or her staff. And no matter how strenuously the governor's aides try to rein in some of these officials, the pulls from the departmental domain often are stronger. These political executives have been coopted; they have "gone native."

Nor can department heads be depended upon to manage on behalf of the governor, or even on behalf of themselves. They, too, are likely to have programmatic agendas to accomplish, and management offers fewer rewards than policy. As a top political administrator in New Jersey described the problem: "Cabinet officers have to decide if they're going to pay attention to the inside of the organization. A lot of people aren't interested." Nor are they forced to take an interest, unless mismanagement or scandal becomes a public issue.

The civil service also restricts the chief executive's ability to manage. After the triumph of civil service reform, governors have had fewer appointments to make in the departments and agencies of state government. Generally, they would like greater flexibility and the removal of more of the top levels of personnel from civil service protection. But such wishes are seldom indulged. The political troops upon whom governors and their department heads can depend are very few, compared to the armies of career servants. What happened in Pennsylvania is not uncommon. Here fifty thousand state jobs were pure patronage positions in 1963 when William Scranton (1963-1967) became governor. In the sixteen years between then and 1979 when Richard Thornburgh took office, the pool of appointive jobs was reduced to about eight hundred. Thornburgh achieved welfare reform legislation, one of his priorities in 1982. But in the Department of Public Welfare, with its forty thousand employees, there were only eight or ten over whom the governor had the power of appointment. Given the symbiotic relationship that had grown up between welfare recipients and welfare dispensers, disruption of the status quo was an extremely difficult task. "So a lot of foot dragging and a lot of internal sabotage was apparent from the outset in trying to effect this welfare reform program," Thornburgh recalls.[14] It was not possible to bring in a new group of people to work toward the governor's goal, so progress was slow indeed.

All of this does not mean that governors and their appointees cannot gain control. It just means that the task may be more difficult than anticipated. Governors have made strides in the right direction, largely by dint of their authority to reorganize state government. Since 1965 the executive branches of nearly two dozen states have undergone comprehensive reorganization. Thirty years ago, in only two states did governors have the power to reorganize subject to legislative veto, a process whereby a proposal automatically went into effect after a specified period unless both legislative houses adopted a resolution of disapproval. By 1986 there were twenty-four states where governors had such reorganization authority. Yet that authority is not unlimited. Governors cannot create or abolish departments unless the legislature assents by means of law. And legislative assent cannot be taken for granted. Governor Brendan Byrne, for instance, wanted to abolish New Jersey's Department of Community Affairs. The commissioner of the department simply refused to go along, and she, and an assortment of interests, managed to sway the legislature. The governor failed, and the department continued in existence.

A new administration is apt to attempt at the outset to take charge of the departments and agencies of the executive branch. The New Jersey experience is revealing in this regard.[15] One method of taking charge is for governors to set an agenda for each department, indicating what they wish to accomplish during the four-year term. Governors must make clear to the career service that it is a gubernatorial direction, and not just the commissioner's or the legislature's. According to a former member of Byrne's cabinet, "I think that's the only way you can manage any group of people. Give them a sense of direction." Alternatively, governors can take dramatic action. If a new governor wants to abolish an agency, reorganize it, or change the qualifications for its head, he or she must do so early, taking advantage of the so-called "honeymoon period," before the glow of victory at the polls has worn off.

One such across-the-board action was taken by Thomas Kean when he first came into office. He inaugurated the Governor's Management Improvement Program (GMIP), in an effort both to trim $100 million from the budget to make up for a shortfall he had inherited and to enable his commissioners to make organizational changes they thought necessary. GMIP required substantial efforts—by the governor's office itself, the commissioners and their top managers, and a panel of business executives whose time was contributed by the private sector. The results of the exercise were mixed. "I think it shook everybody up, and maybe from that perspective it was helpful," was the assessment of one cabinet officer. "It wasn't worth the effort," summed up another. At the least, the program served the governor's political and public relations purposes. At the most, some commissioners took advantage of the process to achieve organizational objectives they had in mind anyway, and some learned much about the internal life of their agencies from the experience.

BASES OF LEGISLATIVE INVOLVEMENT

Although the governor is chief administrator, it is not unusual for the head of a department to spend as much time relating to the legislature as to the governor and the governor's staff. Nor is it unusual for those at the top of the ladder in the career service to spend more time trying to pacify the legislature than trying to figure out what the governor might want to do. The governor's concern is episodic, the legislature's—through one house or the other, a single committee or several, and any number of individual members—is continuous. Some legislator is always on the bureaucracy's back. Moreover, "bureaucrats fear legislators," writes one expert on bureaucracy, because legislators are "important, abrasive, insistent, and vindictive." [16]

The trend since the period of legislative modernization has been for legislatures to become more involved in administrative matters. Only in a few southern states—such as Kentucky, Mississippi, North Carolina, and South Carolina, where individual legislators had statutory memberships on executive boards and commissions—has the trend been in the other direction. As the courts have ruled in recent years that such membership was a violation of the separation-of-powers clause of the state constitution, legislators have been removed from these positions, and gubernatorial power has thereby been enhanced. Legislative involvement in these states now occurs in a more orthodox fashion as it does elsewhere.

Given the contemporary rivalry between the two branches, when governors pull back from administration, legislatures will move in. Thus, if governors eschew management because of scanty payoffs, legislatures will take on management because of opportunities to exercise power. Moreover, legislators have learned—from the litany of legislative reform—that oversight of the implementation of policy and administration of government is one of the legislature's major functions. In challenging management by the executive, therefore, legislators can feel that they are now exercising a responsibility they had neglected in the past. As for legislative oversight, they now do it and sometimes overdo it.

Not only does the rivalry between the branches stoke the fires of legislative involvement, but in many places the distrust legislators feel toward both political administrators and bureaucrats provides additional fuel. A common feeling is that executive agencies will either try to thwart the intent of the legislature or operate in ways the legislature never contemplated. If the legislature insists over agency objections that funds be used for a given project, there is a good chance that they will be used for a different one. And if, as is often the case, the price for building a majority coalition for a policy is to leave legislative intent unclear, whatever the agency does can be criticized. One side or the other will be unhappy, since its intent may not have been fully served. Except in places like Minnesota and Virginia, where trust, civility, and respect are part of the political cultures, suspicion of bureaucracies runs deep in legislative bodies (and disdain for legislatures runs deep in bureaucratic bodies). It has become more and more common for legislators to bash bureaucrats.

The legislative division of labor into standing committees and committee jurisdictions that parallel the organization of the executive branch also encourages involvement. True, legislatures are fragmented; but it is important not to equate a fragmented legislature with a weak one. Indeed, a fragmented legislature is in an even better position to intrude on the executive branch, engaging in what one observer referred to as "hit and run" attacks on the bureaucracy.[17] Moreover, the legislature has enough committees and staff to ride herd on the departments and agencies; the governor lacks the same extent of coverage.

Departments and agencies have no recourse other than to appeal to the appropriations committees and subcommittees for their budgets. As noted earlier, hearings offer the committee's members the opportunity to exercise influence on administrators. Members are not reluctant on these occasions to provide cues or explicit directions as to how management should behave, particularly with regard to operations in local districts. If administrators want to satisfy their budgetary needs, they must take into consideration or comply with legislators' directions and cues.

Departments and agencies also have to go to the standing committees within whose jurisdictions they fall, if they hope to have their legislative programs enacted into law. Sometimes their legislative priorities are of major scope, and they receive help from the governor. But many of their legislative proposals are amendatory, cleaning up previously enacted laws that had unforeseen glitches in them. And many proposals are of a purely housekeeping nature, necessary to the internal life of the organization. The measures are not important in the larger scheme of things, and the governor cannot be bothered; but they are very important to the operations of the department or agency. To achieve their specific objectives, administrators need the support of their committee chairs and of rank-and-file members. So they will naturally be attentive to explicit directions or implicit cues that pertain to administration and, if at all possible, they will comply with them.

Administrators often need legislative support more than gubernatorial support. Even if governors try to screen agency requests to the legislature, it is difficult for them to do so completely. They cannot monitor all the relationships between agency bureaucrats and legislative politicians. Minnesota, for example, has a loyal bureaucracy and a generally effective clearance system for legislation. But it is not perfect.

The Office of Planning reviews agency legislative requests on behalf of the governor. After executive approval, bills are parceled to senators and representatives who act as sponsors. If the planning office rejects the bill, that is ordinarily the end of it. But many transactions continue. Agencies make end runs and take what are known as "bootleg bills" to legislators who are willing to sponsor them. Although the governor's staff members know which bills are bootlegged, they may not be willing to force the issue and oppose them. In return for such legislative cooperation, administrators can be expected to heed the managerial advice of legislators.

Individual members may also intrude on administration for reasons of constituency and career. A complaint from a constituent may prompt a legislator's inquiry into a matter of administration and even a legislator's suggestions for administrative change. Such service is part of the member's job as representative; and it is also one of the strategies employed by incumbents to win reelection. Moreover, if a member can capture the attention of the press and present an image of ombudsman or reformer, there is further incentive for intervening in administration. Being critical is a low-cost enterprise, but it may pay off, in the media and beyond.

Legislative participation in administration is pervasive today. The practice has become embedded in the system, and it engenders greater conflict between the two branches. Governors are trying to hold their own, while legislatures refuse to back off.

THE STRUGGLE OVER SPENDING

One area of conflict involves spending. If the budget is a device that the governor uses to help manage government, it is also one of the methods the legislature uses to exercise control over management. The budgetary struggle between the two branches does not conclude once the appropriations bill has been enacted; it continues well beyond that and through the stages of execution. It continues because the legislature is reluctant to entrust the allocation of appropriated funds to the governor and staff. Except in emergency situations and where there is fiscal crisis, the legislature is unwilling to have the governor unilaterally wield such power.

GUBERNATORIAL DEVICES

The fiscal contest between the governor and the legislature has been as intense in New York as anywhere in recent years. The legislature adds its items to the governor's budget; the governor casts his line-item veto. The legislature responds the following year by circumventing the veto with lump-sum appropriations that mix spending desired by the legislature with that desired by the governor. If the governor were then to use the veto, it would be like throwing out the baby with the bath water. So to avoid the designated use of authorized expenditures, the executive must resort to administrative discretion.

Transferring funds from one place to another is one device for thwarting the legislature. In New York, the governor's budget implementation authority is delegated to the Division of the Budget. Section 49 of the State Finance Law prohibits expenditures from any lump-sum appropriations (except for the legislature and the judiciary) without approval of the budget director. Section 51 grants the budget director total discretion to approve the transfer of funds among items within an agency's program and limited discretion to approve a transfer between an agency's programs. This section provides the executive branch with the flexibility necessary to respond to a variety of unforeseen circumstances.[18]

Impoundment is another device. Not only do governors resort to the line-item veto to keep the budget in balance, but they also withhold appropriated funds to achieve the same purpose. And sometimes they withhold funds because they question the merit of such expenditures. Section 42 of the New York State Finance Law, for example, permits the expenditure of less than the amount appropriated, if the amount to be expended is "sufficient to accomplish in full the purposes designated by the appropriations." The Division of the Budget reduces expenditures when it foresees a prospective budget deficit. But that cannot be justified by law.[19] Thus, a New York court ruled that the executive had no authority to impound mandated appropriations in order to achieve a balanced budget. On the other hand, a Massachusetts court acted in contrary fashion, upholding the governor's prerogative to spend less than the full amount of the legislature's appropriation.

LEGISLATIVE TECHNIQUES

Legislatures have tried to restrict the authority of the executive branch to manage expenditures, and they have made significant progress in this endeavor. Today, in practically every state the executive's authority to transfer funds among departments is limited; in forty states its authority to transfer funds between programs within a department is also limited.[20] Some examples of how legislatures ride herd over transfers are instructive.

In Florida a transfer has to be authorized by the administration committee of the state, which is made up of the governor and members of the cabinet. If an agency requests a transfer, a consultative process takes place, during which the legislature can object in writing. If it does so, two-thirds of the administration committee is required to override the objection. But the governor generally will respect legislative wishes, because he cannot be sure of getting the votes of enough of his colleagues for an override. In Ohio executive authority is limited by means of a body aptly titled the Controlling Board. It is composed of six legislators and a single representative of the executive. The board is authorized by statute to make certain transfers of funds upon the request of a state agency or the director of the Office of Budget and Management.[21]

Wisconsin's joint committee on finance not only reviews the executive budget proposal, but has significant power after its enactment. Among other things, the committee approves the transfer of funds between appropriations and programs within a department. It may also authorize changes in position levels within state agencies and may require agencies to report to the committee before the release of new money for a program. For example, the committee has required representatives of the University of Wisconsin to inform members of proposed revisions of the procedures for instruction before they could receive the money to go ahead with them. Finally, the joint finance committee has enacted laws that require committee approval in sixty different instances of financial management, including any expenditures from the prison industry account for construction or purchase of equipment as well as any sale of surplus state land worth $20,000 or more.[22] There can be little question that in these cases the legislature is very much involved in the administration of the state.

In addition to committees that exercise control over executive spending, the legislature attempts to direct the spending of state money specifically through language inserted in the appropriations bills and accompanying documents. Such directions may occur in line items, in footnotes, in the concluding section, or somewhere else in the bill or in the committee report, letter of intent, or other message to the executive. Ohio is one of a number of states where a "budget provision" has become a method to specify legislative intent in detail. For example, in the so-called "language bill" of 1977-1979 that accompanied state appropriations, the legislature adopted the following provisions:

- With regard to subsidies for the Arts Council, no grant shall be used to eliminate or reduce an existing deficit of an arts group.
- With regard to the Department of Public Welfare, there shall be no reduction of grant levels to Aid to Dependent Children recipients below 1977-1978 levels.

- With regard to the Board of Regents, a report shall be submitted on the impact of part-time student service costs.

If legislative intentions are not described in appropriations legislation, the Legislative Budget Office will describe them in a document prepared after the session. "While these have no force or effect," the Ohio legislative budget officer wrote, "agencies are put on notice of what took place when their appropriations were formulated, and legislators can address deliberate departure from any assumed legislative intent through the Controlling Board or during budget hearings for the next biennium." [23]

The New York legislature has tilted with governors over the budget for years, but recently it went further than it ever had before. Discontent over executive impoundment of appropriations for staff caused the legislature to include language in the 1984-1985 budget that explicitly mandated staffing levels and reporting requirements for the City University of New York, the State University of New York, and two other agencies. Governor Cuomo permitted the language to stand, despite its undermining effect on his management authority. The next year, however, Cuomo vetoed similar language in several measures. He maintained that provisions in appropriations bills that required agencies to report to the legislature on progress toward administrative goals interfered with the governor's legal authority to evaluate agency performance.[24]

Even if the legislature in New York does not insert language into the appropriations act itself, for the past few years each house has adopted by resolution a statement of legislative intent. The itemized expenditures in this statement reflect an accord negotiated between the legislature and the executive. "This is significant," writes the counsel to New York's senate Democrats, "since the Report [of the Fiscal Committee on the Executive Budget] may be more specific than the budget bills themselves, and thus, may represent a limitation on executive power over and above that contained in the bills." Executive failure to abide by the report is not subject to legal sanction, but it is subject to political remedy.[25]

Maryland's general assembly also endeavors to exert control over executive behavior. Along with the budget bill, which includes directive language, it issues a joint chairs' report. This document contains a description and explanation of the cuts made, a description and explanation of language in the budget bill, and a committee narrative that covers legislative intent and requests that particular studies be conducted by agencies. The size of the report has grown tremendously, from 80 pages in 1982 to 200 pages in 1989. The report is voted on in committee, but is not debated on the floor and is not subject to amendment. It is a political document, without the force of law, and one to which the governor objects vociferously. Agencies do not have to pay attention to it, but they do have to come back to the committees. For that reason, the report has weight.

THE POLITICS OF CONTROL

The Florida legislature has gone as far as any other in demonstrating control over executive functions in the fiscal domain, and Florida governors have resisted mightily. The "letter of intent" has been a principal mechanism of control. Issued after the fact and having been discussed and agreed on in conference, it directs agencies in the spending of appropriated funds. In 1986 one question that arose was whether the letter of intent could be used to erode the governor's line-item veto power. Governor Graham the year before had vetoed several projects in the Public Education Capital Outlay (PECO) bill. The house challenged the vetoes in the Florida Supreme Court, arguing that the Florida Constitution limited the governor to using the line-item veto only for "general appropriations bills." The court held that, for purposes of the line-item veto power, the PECO bill was a general appropriations bill. In an attempt to circumvent the court's decision, the legislature in 1986 included funds for a large number of projects in one line item of the appropriations bill and then used the letter of intent to specify on which projects the money should be spent.[26]

Governor Graham felt that the legislature had gone too far. He objected to its putting in the PECO bill projects on school construction and specifying by letter of intent what should be done. According to Graham, the legislature should make general policy and allow management—in this case, the Board of Regents—to determine specifics such as construction projects.

After the session, Graham reviewed lump-sum appropriations that included a number of projects inserted by the legislature to benefit their districts. The governor was firm as a matter of principle. "If we capitulate," he declared at a meeting with his staff, "we saddle the next governor with an erosion of constitutional authority." But with a lump-sum appropriation, specified only in the letter of intent, the governor found the item veto too blunt an instrument to use. He would have to veto every project, rather than being able to pick and choose. "For policy reasons," he announced, "the veto of the whole thing is the thing to do." Staff argued that some of the projects were good and a number would be difficult to challenge without political costs. The tension between the governor's belief in his constitutional authority on the one hand and the exigencies of politics on the other created a dilemma. As the meeting concluded, Graham indicated he would explore a number of options to protect the constitutional power of the governor by challenging the legislature's letter of intent. But it was late in the game; Graham would be leaving office in six months and was already engaged in a campaign to unseat a Republican incumbent in the U.S. Senate. He could not afford to offend too many groups or constituents by vetoing a host of projects.

It was up to Graham's successor to take up the cause of the executive. For several reasons, including the hostility of a Democratic legislature after the services tax debacle and his need to show strength, Republican governor Bob Martinez took a firm position on the issue. In 1988, after the session had concluded, the legislature sent the governor a letter of intent and "working papers," which spelled out in much greater detail than the appropriations act how the money should be spent. Martinez used his line-item veto to strike specific items from the letters, memoranda, and records of deliberations that together showed legislative intent. Legislative leaders brought a lawsuit challenging him; a lower court ruled in the legislature's favor, and the governor then appealed to the state supreme court.

Just before the legislature convened in April 1989, the court rendered its ruling in the case.[27] It held that items in a letter of intent are not subject to veto, thus invalidating five gubernatorial vetoes of nearly $800,000 in projects. More important, however, the court ruled that legislative working papers lacked the force of law and were not legally binding on the executive branch. Because the letter of intent was not passed as a law, it was not part of the appropriations bill and was unenforceable. The court found that these documents were "a manifestation of how the legislature thinks—in its considered opinion as a representative of the people—appropriations should be spent." But they were not law.

The governor's authority was formally upheld, yet the legislature's influence was not diminished. As the chair of the house appropriations committee, T. K. Wetherell, pointed out with regard to such legislative directives: "The agencies don't have to take them. . . . If they don't, we'll deal with them next year." The remedy for agencies ignoring the nonbinding directives of the legislature is a political one. Since they must go to the legislature for appropriations annually, they are apt to heed the wishes of those who feed them. And lest legislators forget what they directed the agencies to do, the appropriations committee staff will be there to remind them.

LEGISLATIVE REVIEW OF REGULATIONS

Just as legislatures have had to entrust appropriated funds to the executive branch for spending, they have also had to entrust policies they enacted to the executive for implementation. Just as legislatures could not spell out everything in an appropriations bill, so they could not dot every *i* and cross every *t* in a bill pertaining to policy. They are not able to anticipate or to agree on each and every detail. Thus, they appreciate that the most prudent course requires some degree of flexibility.

Whatever the motivations behind a particular bill, the fact is that much legislation is cast in terms of broad ends, with the means left to the devices of departments and agencies of the executive branch. Legislatures necessarily have delegated to the executive the power to fill in the details, a process that is accomplished largely through the bureaucratic development of rules and regulations. But such delegation leaves legislatures uneasy, because they do not trust bureaucracies in their rule making always to conform to what the legislature may have intended. Moreover, as has been mentioned, legislatures try to safeguard their own power and to limit that of the executive. So they attach strings to what they delegate.

One way in which they have been able to delegate power with one hand and cling to it with the other is by reviewing proposed agency regulations. Currently four-fifths of the nation's legislatures have some formal means of reviewing such regulations for conformity to enabling legislation before they go into effect. In over half the states, moreover, legislatures have had the power in one way or another to prevent regulations from going into effect.[28] In practically every case, legislative committees have considerable influence over what the legislature decides and what action an agency ultimately takes.

The Legislative Veto

Processes vary greatly from one state to another. In Wisconsin, after the Legislative Council Rules Clearinghouse engages in an examination of the proposed rules, appropriate standing committees of the senate and assembly undertake a review. These committees can approve the regulations, object to them, or request modifications. When an agency refuses to comply, a committee takes its objection to the legislature's joint committee for review of administrative regulations. If the joint committee upholds the objection, legislation to that effect is introduced and enacted, and is subject to a gubernatorial veto. The joint committee has agreed with about 40 percent of standing committee objections, while overturning 60 percent and permitting the agency's rule to stand. In Michigan, after the rules are formally proposed, they are sent to the legislature's joint committee on administrative rules. If the committee disapproves, the rule cannot go into effect until legislation is passed to reverse the committee's action. In Tennessee the house and senate operations committees, meeting jointly, can vote to suspend agency rules.[29]

In states such as in Michigan and Tennessee, where objections by a committee have the effect of nullifying a rule or regulation, a "legislative veto" exists. Such a provision requires the executive to gain assent from the legislature before implementing a law. Legislatures adopted the legislative veto because of what they believed to be the law making that took place during the formulation of rules and regulations by administrative agencies. "Expanding use of the legislative veto," wrote one student of the subject, "is the most far-reaching step taken by legislatures to redress their loss of control over executive branch rule-making." [30]

Governors naturally object to the practice, either vetoing legislation providing for a legislative veto or challenging it in the courts as a violation of the separation-of-powers clause of the state constitution. New Jersey's Governor Byrne had considerable success in contesting the legislature on this issue. In 1981 the legislature passed the Legislative Oversight Act, which required executive agencies to submit their proposed rules to the legislature for approval. According to the act, the legislature might, within sixty days, adopt a concurrent resolution disapproving of a rule or barring it for an additional sixty days. Byrne vetoed the act; but both houses of the legislature overrode Byrne's veto by unanimous votes—a unique occurrence in New Jersey, or anywhere else for that matter. The legislature brought suit, and in a 1982 decision, *General Assembly v. Brendan T. Byrne*, the New Jersey Supreme Court declared the Legislative Oversight Act in violation of the separation-of-powers clause and therefore unconstitutional. The court reasoned that: (a) allowing the legislature to control agency rule making frustrated the executive's mandate to execute the law; (b) the use of the concurrent resolution was tantamount to passage of a new law, but without the approval of the governor, and thus violated the presentment clause of the state constitution; and (c) other opportunities existed for legislative input with respect to rules and regulations.

The nation's governors have made headway in challenging the legislative veto in court. Focusing on the separation of powers, state courts have enunciated as a basic principle that an agency performs an executive function when exercising power delegated by the legislature. Once the power has been delegated, the legislature then must pass a new law in order to make whatever changes it desires. As in the 1983 case of *Immigration and Naturalization Service v. Chadha*, where the U.S. Supreme Court invalidated a one-house veto, courts in a number of states have invalidated legislative vetoes in recent years. The states' highest courts have done so in Alaska (1980), New Hampshire (1981), West Virginia (1981), New Jersey (1982), Kentucky (1984), and Kansas (1984), and trial courts have acted similarly in Connecticut (1981) and Montana (1982). After negative rulings by the courts, or in order to overcome a governor's veto, several legislatures have put constitutional amendments on the ballot to authorize the legislative veto, if both houses acted. Such amendments were approved in Connecticut (1982) and Iowa (1984), but rejected in Alaska (1980 and 1984), Florida (1976), Michigan (1984), Missouri (1976 and 1982), and Texas (1979). The legislative veto is in decline, with only nine states still making use of it by the end of 1985.[31]

ALTERNATIVE METHODS

Some legislators believe that if the legislature does not have the veto power, it will not be able to affect rule making within the administration. They want to have the ability to exert control outright, and not through persuasion or indirection. Yet if legislatures are concerned strictly with the reasonableness of proposed rules and with their conformity to statute, the legislative veto is not necessary. Other methods have been devised to oversee administrative rule making. One is to make the governor responsible for supervising the agencies. In Hawaii, Indiana, Nebraska, and Wyoming the governor's signature is required on all regulations before they go into effect. In Iowa, Louisiana, Missouri, and Nevada the governor can veto regulations after they have gone into effect. North Carolina has an administrative review commission within the Department of Justice.[32] One of the most effective systems is California's. Here the legislature in 1980 established an Office of Administrative Law, which is headed by a gubernatorial appointee. It reviews administrative rules for clarity, consistency, authority, and necessity. Finally, in some states proposed rules and regulations must be reviewed by the legislature or its committees or both, but legislative objections are advisory only.

Kentucky has made a strong effort to revise its rule-making structure. After the state supreme court overruled a 1982 statute that permitted the Legislative Research Commission to suspend administrative regulations, the general assembly in frustration passed a law in 1986 requiring state agencies to submit all regulations as potential statutes. It further stipulated that any regulation not enacted into law by

1988 would expire. Governor Martha Layne Collins vetoed the act, in the belief that agencies needed to be able to change regulations in order "to react to changing situations." But the legislature overrode her veto. The result was a flood of paper work, which overwhelmed the legislature. At its 1988 session the general assembly repealed the law.[33] The Kentucky legislature would have to employ more conventional means of oversight.

EFFECTS OF LEGISLATIVE REVIEW

It is interesting to speculate on the effects of legislative review of rules and regulations, whether done by command or by suggestion.

One effect is that legislators have a way of sidestepping difficult political conflicts over regulatory policy. They can leave the law vague, hand over the problems to the bureaucrats who are insulated from political heat, and later on they can still veto, or have changed, whatever proves to be unpopular.[34] They can avoid responsibility by delegating authority to others, but they can still blame the agencies for failing to fulfill legislative intent.

Another effect, even if the legislature lacks the power to veto, is that agencies became more responsive to legislative criticisms and suggestions. Practically speaking, the agencies have little choice. Minnesota's Legislative Commission for Review of Administrative Rules demonstrates how accommodation takes place. The commission is reluctant to suspend rules, but the very threat, made by the five senators and five representatives who deal with legislation and appropriations affecting the agency, "seems to be enough to induce the agency to satisfy the Commission's objectives." Analysis of the process in Kentucky also shows that legislative review has made bureaucracies marginally more responsive and less independent of the legislature.[35]

A third effect is agency discipline. Agencies become more careful when drafting rules, because they know the legislature is "looking over their shoulder." Moreover, the quality of the rules is said to have improved. In Pennsylvania, for example, the Independent Regulatory Review Commission reported that in the two years before its establishment regulations had been issued at the average rate of twenty-eight per month. Since the commission began overseeing the process, the rate has dropped to twelve per month. Evidently, agencies have become more restrained as a result of the legislature's involvement.[36]

A fourth effect is learning, both by agencies and legislators. Agencies gain a better idea of legislative intent, while legislators learn of the agencies' problems in drafting rules. "It is a two-way street," stated a legislative staff director in Idaho, "with a good deal of communication going back and forth." In addition, the process of reviewing rules and regulations, as legislators do in Pennsylvania, appears to stimulate greater legislative concern with oversight generally.[37]

Finally, the farthest-reaching effect of legislative review is that a new avenue for influence has become available and the nature of agency regulations has been affected. One comparative study found that states with rule review by a legislative committee had less strict and less complex regulations than states without such authority. Another study, focusing on rule review by the Michigan, Tennessee, and Wisconsin legislatures, supported the idea that a stronger legislative role reduces regulatory stringency, but also suggested that review by the legislature "most often favors regulated and client groups." Data from Kentucky support these findings, suggesting that both business and governmental interest groups are particularly successful in obtaining less stringent regulations after legislative review. Such oversight processes, therefore, "may simply create a new access point for interests already successful in obtaining influence." [38]

One scholar has referred to the process as one that benefits special interests, and especially business, at the expense of broad, diffuse interests.[39] Representatives of business overwhelmingly approve of legislative review of agency regulations. They feel that they have better access to legislators than to the bureaucrats and technicians who will regulate business. In any case, if they are dissatisfied with the agency's formulation they can always appeal to the legislature for redress. They have virtually nothing to lose and much to gain.

THE CONDUCT OF LEGISLATIVE OVERSIGHT

As an outgrowth of the development of their capacity and independence, legislatures have taken on the previously neglected function of "legislative oversight." Governor Reubin Askew of Florida described what has happened, from an executive perspective:

> You wind up staffing the legislative branch in order to give it some independence. Then the staff has to have something to do. So they wind up really usurping the authority of the executive branch under the guise of oversight.[40]

Whatever the causes, legislatures today are engaged in a variety of activities that commonly go by the name of oversight. Two of them— legislative review of the expenditure of funds and legislative review of the making of rules by the executive—have already been discussed.

One major purpose of the oversight enterprise is for the legislature to find out, after a law has been passed, how it is working. As a consequence of such review, scrutiny, watchfulness, or evaluation, the law can be modified or a new law enacted. But the policy purpose of oversight is by no means the only one; in addition, legislatures have become involved in matters of administration and management, assessing the performance of state agencies and exercising control over their operations.

VARIETIES OF OVERSIGHT

Oversight practices vary greatly. They range from casework by members and their staffs to committee hearings, investigations, sunset reviews, performance audits, and evaluation studies. The form of oversight that has become ubiquitous is that of legislators intervening with an administrative agency on behalf of a constituent or a group in their district. Some illustrations are offered in a recent book about Arkansas. When the Livestock and Poultry Commission filed suit against a barn that held livestock sales, alleging failure to comply with state brucellosis regulations, the senator from that district attached an amendment to the commission's appropriations bill to weaken the regulations. This prompted the commission director to resign. When the speaker at a conference sponsored by the governor's Commission on the Status of Women offended the sensibilities of a woman in the audience, she complained to her representative, who tried to have the commission abolished. In Arkansas oversight is "episodic and punitive," prompted more by parochial pressures than by general public policy concerns.[41] It is that way in many places.

This form of oversight, focusing on specific cases involving individuals and groups who are usually located in the legislator's district, is not without effect on the conduct of administration. Most commonly in making constituency related requests, legislators want either to know why an agency took a particular action or to speed up agency action. Sometimes an individual case has broader ramifications, serving as a red flag to alert administrators to a problem and leading to a change in agency practice. But "narrow gauge" oversight prompted by casework is inimical to bureaucratic values, such as equity and neutral competence. "Casework is also not the best or most efficient way that an agency can gain feedback on its operations," according to one study of the subject.[42]

Much of the oversight conducted by legislatures is neither systematic nor comprehensive. It is piecemeal and inadvertent, and may arise in the course of committee hearings or investigations as well as through constituents' and groups' complaints. Take education policy, for instance.[43] After a spate of educational reforms was enacted by state legislatures across the country in the mid-1980s, attempts were made to monitor and assess their effectiveness. Legislatures would not delegate monitoring and assessment to state departments of education, in part because of their lack of trust in them. In Arizona's legislature, for example, a joint legislative committee was created to implement as well as monitor the career ladder program for teachers, because the legislature was dissatisfied with the department's management of earlier reforms. Florida's legislature, which also had poor relations with the state education department, established the Quality Instructional Incentive Council, with legislators as members. Although mechanisms such as these to oversee the educational reforms either were newly established or already existed, legislatures in most places (South Carolina being a notable exception) made relatively little use of them. Oversight took place when "fire alarms" sounded, that is when complaints from local districts or interest groups drew the attention of legislators. In Pennsylvania, for example, when groups appealed, the education committees tried to remedy problems informally. Legislative staff met with departmental staff to suggest how rules might be changed. The department assented in one case, but refused in another, whereupon the legislature repealed the rule by legislation. Similar processes occurred elsewhere.

PERFORMANCE AUDITS AND PROGRAM EVALUATIONS

Another form of legislative oversight, one that is more systematic and coherent, reviews ongoing policies and programs by means of performance audits or program evaluations. Generally, this oversight is conducted by legislative auditors or special legislative evaluation staffs, usually under the supervision of bicameral and bipartisan legislative committees. Today legislatures in about forty states engage in oversight of this nature.

The development of performance auditing began in the 1960s when legislatures took over the postaudit function from the executive, where it had normally resided.[44] Governors, of course, resisted the legislative grab, and conflict ensued as veto and override occurred. The experience in Florida is interesting in this regard. Until 1967 Florida's state auditor (now the auditor general) reported to the governor and cabinet. But with the election of Claude Kirk as the first modern-day Republican governor, the Democratic legislature "had its attention drawn to the fact that perhaps there was a need to understand better the importance of the true separation of powers between the executive and the legislature." As a result, the legislature passed a bill creating the office of legislative auditor. It is said that the governor thought the bill meant that the legislature itself was going to be audited by the auditor general, so he did not veto the measure and there was no necessity for the legislature to override. As soon as the act took effect, the state auditor resigned his executive branch office to assume duties as legislative auditor, and he thereafter brought over to the legislature most of the staff, records, and information.[45]

The transformation from executive to legislative auditor took place in a short span of time, and now the audit function is a legislative responsibility in four out of five states. Legislative auditors soon began the job of performance auditing, creating special divisions that operated alongside units that were engaged in conventional fiscal and management audits, the bread and butter of the audit trade. By now performance auditing has become a significant part of the operation in states such as California, Colorado, Hawaii, Kansas, Minnesota, and Wisconsin.

At about the same time that auditors' offices were expanding in many states, special agencies were being established to conduct performance auditing or program evaluation in other states. Connecticut's Program Review and Investigations Committee, Mississippi's Joint Legislative Committee on Performance Evaluation and Expenditure Review, New York's Legislative Commission on Expenditure Review, Kentucky's Program Review and Investigations Committee, and Virginia's Joint Legislative Audit and Review Commission are examples.

The production of written performance audits and program evaluations by these agencies has grown markedly in the 1970s and 1980s. Nationwide, during the first three years of the enterprise only fifty reports were completed; by 1975 about a hundred were being turned out each year; and in the early 1980s there were about two hundred reports issued annually. Use of these reports, however, varies greatly. In some places—Virginia is probably the most notable example—both legislators and administrative officials are extremely responsive to the studies conducted by audit and evaluation staffs. In others, the results are sporadic, depending largely on timing and the interest of one or several members of the legislature. In a few places, auditors and evaluators are far removed from the legislative process, and their studies have little effect whatsoever.

Several conditions account for the overall effectiveness of performance audits and program evaluations in the states. First, the shape of the political environment counts, especially the balance of power between the executive and legislative. A strong, independent legislature, such as Colorado's, makes for a more potent enterprise. Partisan control of state government also matters. There is more incentive, particularly in competitive party states, for the legislature to be critical of the executive branch when control of government is divided. Second, the commitment to oversight by the legislature's leaders is practically a requirement for success. Leaders can express such commitment by encouraging able legislators to serve on the oversight committee or commission, and then by appointing the best people and not only the ones who are left over when the major committee slots have been filled. Leaders can also encourage the enterprise not only by serving on the committee or commission themselves, but by seriously participating in the work that goes on. This commitment is relatively rare, but it has existed since the establishment of Virginia's Joint Legislative Audit and Review Commission (JLARC). Third, and related to the previous factor, the composition of the committee or commission probably means the most as far as effectiveness is concerned. The ability and reputation of members and their continuity of service, with the collective memory that develops, are quite important here. Finally, the quality of professional staff and staff leadership cannot be overlooked. They account to some extent for the impact of the work of performance-auditing and program evaluation agencies. Generally speaking, these staffs have been of the highest quality.

EFFECTS OF OVERSIGHT

What, then, are the effects of this form of legislative oversight, and particularly the effects on administration? One is the redirecting and restructuring of programs. Some of this has come about because of sunset legislation, which was first enacted in Colorado in 1976 and then adopted in about three-quarters of the states. Under sunset laws, and depending on the particular state, each year (on a six- or seven-year cycle) from five to fifteen agencies automatically terminate unless reauthorized by legislation. A study is conducted, the focus of which takes into account questions regarding an agency's function, its very existence, and its structure. Usually, instead of terminating an agency, the legislature reorganizes it or consolidates it with another similar enterprise. Occasionally, sunset laws have cast a broader net, including major units and critical services of state government. The trend, albeit a gradual one, has been to shift legislative scrutiny from regulatory agencies alone to other programs and to larger agencies.

Most of the restructuring and redirection of policies and programs have come about not as a result of sunset legislation, but because of performance audits or program evaluations themselves. A few programs have been abolished, and more have been kept from growing. Budget allocations have been changed, and economies have been achieved. But, it should be noted, some legislative oversight studies have justified increased rather than reduced resources being devoted to a program.

That is because the legislature usually has greater expectations and less funds for many of the programs it enacts; thus, an evaluation is likely to lead to recommendations for additional funding if the program is to work as the legislature intended. From the perspective of an executive agency with underfunded programs, scrutiny by legislative staff is not always threatening. It may, in fact, provide an opportunity for the agency to promote its interests and increase its appropriations.

Many of the findings and recommendations of audits and evaluations are not directed toward policies or budgets and do not require specific legislative action. Rather they are directed toward administration and management, including the administrative process and agency structure, and they are meant for top administrators in the executive branch. These studies point out problems and deficiencies, identifying areas in need of administrative attention. In many cases administrators receive from the legislature consultative assistance with ideas that help them improve the performance of their agencies. In other cases administrators receive reinforcement for their own views from recommendations that they might have implemented anyway. This way they can justify their action in terms of the legislative report. In any event, the process of review signals to the executive branch the legislature's concern about an agency or its programs.

Consider the Joint Legislative Audit and Review Commission in Virginia, which since its establishment has had considerable influence on management practices in the executive branch. It has examined the organization, staffing, and management structure of departments and agencies. In only a case or two, where an agency was distrustful of the legislature and its staff, was there clear resistance to JLARC recommendations. Otherwise, as the commission's biennial monitoring (required by statute) revealed, compliance with its recommendations was overwhelming. In one recent project, for example, the Department of Planning and Budget set aside $250,000 for JLARC to conduct a technical cost study as part of its overall examination of the Department of Information Technology. The executive branch was funding part of the legislature's inquiry. The recommendations that resulted were highly administrative in nature, including proposals for a new billing structure, a customer service center, and a council on information management.

Performance auditing and program evaluation, as practiced in the states, have helped legislatures in their policy-making and budget review roles. But this type of oversight, in addition to other types discussed earlier, also affords the legislature a say in administration, an area that traditionally has been the responsibility of the executive branch. An argument can be made that the legislature must probe administration and management, if it is to perform adequately its role on policy and budget. Furthermore, if the legislature, through a staff agency, does not exercise oversight here, no one else will be able to do it as well. An executive unit in a department of administration has less stature and less clout. Administrators are unlikely to pay as serious attention to its recommendations. A legislative agency, by contrast, is more credible and more threatening too. Its reports are public documents, and the legislature will usually stand behind them. If an executive agency refuses to take action or stonewalls, the legislature can always hold a piece of its budget hostage.

Such intrusion into the executive function can raise the hackles of administrators, when their agencies are the subjects of inquiry, and of governors, when their attention is drawn to the subject. Some years ago, Governor Dan Walker of Illinois noted that many legislatures were moving into the oversight role, which he regarded as interference with the executive branch. He pointed out two baneful results: first, that "the legislature gets mixed up in this whole business of running the executive branch of the government," and second, that "the bureaucrats out there start looking to the legislature for guidance more than they do to their line bosses, so it obscures the lines of responsibility and makes it much more difficult to control the bureaus." [46] The process has now gone much further than it had in 1979 when Walker commented, and the issues today are even more serious from the chief executive's viewpoint.

Despite the reservations of governors, legislative oversight—by means of performance auditing or program evaluation, casework by individual members, review of administrative rules and regulations, and control of expenditures—is here to stay. If not yet institutionalized in all respects, the various forms of oversight have still proven a valuable tool for legislatures in their competition with the executive branch. Legislatures now tell the executive branch specifically how to spend appropriated monies. They tell agencies whether proposed rules and regulations are reasonable or conform to legislative intent. They assess how agencies are functioning and programs working out. And they diagnose administrative and management deficiencies and recommend specific procedural remedies.

Because of the decentralized nature of legislatures, executive departments and agencies naturally will receive mixed signals. Audit or evaluation staff or both and committees may take issue with one point, standing committees with another, appropriations committees with still another, and individual members with practically anything that might arise. To whom does the executive branch respond? Who speaks for the legislature when it comes to the administration of government? It is not easy to know.

Problems in executive-legislative relations are more likely because legislatures are now probing into administration. If the legislature is to make policies and appropriate monies most effectively, it has to perform oversight and consider how, and how well, executive departments and agencies are working. But it goes further, much further. The legislature today may not actually be running state government, but it is trying to direct the administrators and the bureaucrats who are charged with doing so. And it is making its weight felt more than ever before.

NOTES

1. *Washington Post*, August 9, 1988.
2. William T. Gormley, Jr., *Taming the Bureaucracy* (Princeton, N.J.: Princeton University Press, 1989), 194-223.
3. Peter J. Haas and Deil S. Wright, "The Changing Profile of State Administrators," *Journal of State Government* 60 (November/December 1987): 275; Jeffrey L. Brudney and F. Ted Hebert, "State Agencies and Their Environments: Examining the Influence of Important External Actors," *Journal of Politics* 49 (February 1987): 191-193.
4. Richard Elling, "Federal Dollars and Federal Clout in State Administration: A Test of 'Regulatory' and 'Picket Fence' Models of Intergovernmental Relations" (Paper presented at the annual meeting of the Midwest Political Science Association, Chicago, April 17-20, 1985); Glenn Abney and Thomas P. Lauth, "Legislative Influence in the Appropriations Process: A Comparative Analysis" (Paper presented at the annual meeting of the American Political Science Association, Chicago, September 1-4, 1983), 41; and Phillip M. Gonet and James D. Nowlan, "The Legislature," in *Inside State Government: A Primer for Illinois Managers*, ed. James D. Nowlan (Urbana, Ill.: Institute of Government and Public Affairs, University of Illinois, 1982), 86-87.
5. H. Edward Flentje, "The Political Nature of the Governor as Manager," in *Being Governor: The View from the Office*, ed. Thad L. Beyle and Lynn R. Muchmore (Durham, N.C.: Duke Press Policy Studies, 1983), 85.
6. National Governors' Association, *Reflections on Being Governor* (Washington, D.C.: Center for Policy Research, NGA, February 1981), 104, 128, 184, 143, 266.
7. Martha Wagner Weinberg, *Managing the State* (Cambridge: MIT Press, 1977), 209.
8. Alan Rosenthal, ed., *The Governor and the Legislature* (New Brunswick, N.J.: Eagleton Institute of Politics, Rutgers University, 1988), 8.
9. See David Adamany, "Wisconsin Gov. Lucey: Successful Hands-Off Management," *Journal of State Government* 62 (July/August 1989): 140-146; and Chase Riveland, "Gubernatorial Styles: Is There a Right One?" *Journal of State Government* 62 (July/August 1989): 136-139.
10. Thad L. Beyle and Robert Dalton, "Appointment Power: Does It Belong to the Governor?" in *Being Governor*, 108-110.
11. Charles G. Bell and Charles M. Price, *California Government Today*, 2d ed.

(Homewood, Ill.: Dorsey Press, 1984), 225.

12. Rosenthal, *The Governor and the Legislature*, 27.
13. Abney and Lauth, "Legislative Influence in the Appropriations Process," 48.
14. As recounted by Thornburgh in Rosenthal, *The Governor and the Legislature*, 24-26.
15. This section is based on three seminars with cabinet officials and gubernatorial office staff of the Kean, Byrne, Cahill, and Hughes administrations, held at the Eagleton Institute of Politics, Rutgers University, in February, March, and April 1989.
16. Gormley, *Taming the Bureaucracy*, 221.
17. Ibid., 197.
18. Eric Lane, "Legislative Oversight of an Executive Budget Process: Impoundments in New York," *Pace Law Review* 5 (Winter 1985): 226-228.
19. House Committee on Rules, "Item Veto: State Experience and its Application to the Federal Situation," 99th Cong., 2d sess., 36-37; Lane, "Legislative Oversight of an Executive Budget Process," 228-229.
20. Lucinda S. Simon, "Legislatures and Governors: The Wrestling Match," *Journal of State Government* 59 (Spring 1986): 3; Tony Hutchison and Kathy James, *Legislative Budget Procedures in the 50 States: A Guide to Appropriations and Budget Processes* (Denver: National Conference of State Legislatures, September 1988), 96-101.
21. Richard G. Sheridan, *State Budgeting in Ohio*, 2d ed. (Columbus: Ohio Legislative Budget Office, 1983), 269-271.
22. Marlin Schneider, in an address to the annual meeting of the National Conference of State Legislatures in Reno, July 26, 1988.
23. Sheridan, *State Budgeting in Ohio*, 322-323.
24. Lane, "Legislative Oversight of an Executive Budget Process," 212-213; Gerald Benjamin, "Budget Battles Between the Governor and Legislature: A Perennial New York Conflict," *Comparative State Politics Newsletter* 7 (August 1986): 16.
25. Lane, "Legislative Oversight of an Executive Budget Process," 225.
26. Alan Rosenthal, "The State of the Florida Legislature," *Florida State University Law Review* 14 (Fall 1986): 420.
27. This account is based on Randolph Pendleton, "Both Sides See Victory in Vetoes Ruling," *Florida Times Union*, March 24, 1989, and Editorial, "Veto on the Line," *Miami Herald*, March 27, 1989.
28. Rich Jones, "Legislative Review of Regulations: How Well Is It Working?" *State Legislatures*, September 1982, 8; Advisory Commission on Intergovernmental Relations, *The Question of State Government Capability* (Washington, D.C.: ACIR, January 1985), 116.
29. Marcus Ethridge, "Consequences of Legislative Review of Agency Regulations in Three U.S. States," *Legislative Studies Quarterly* 9 (February 1984): 163-164.
30. Stephen F. Johnson, "The Legislative Veto in the States," *State Government* 56 (1983): 99.
31. L. Harold Levinson, "The Decline of the Legislative Veto: Federal/State Comparisons and Interactions," *Publius* 17 (Winter 1987): 121-124.
32. Ibid., 129.
33. Malcolm E. Jewell and Penny M. Miller, *The Kentucky Legislature: Two Decades of Change* (Lexington: University Press of Kentucky, 1988), 169-170.
34. Marcus Ethridge, "Legislative-Administrative Interaction as 'Intrusive Ac-

cess': An Empirical Analysis," *Journal of Politics* 43 (May 1981): 491.

35. Philip P. Frickey, "The Constitionality of the Legislative Veto in Minnesota" (St. Paul: Hubert Humphrey Institute of Public Affairs, University of Minnesota, September 1985), 12; Jewell and Miller, *The Kentucky Legislature*, 176-177.

36. Jones, "Legislative Review of Regulations," 8; Sidney Wise, *The Legislative Process in Pennsylvania*, 2d ed. (Harrisburg: Bipartisan Management Committee, House of Representatives, 1984), 98.

37. Jones, "Legislative Review of Regulations," 8; Wise, *The Legislative Process in Pennsylvania*, 98.

38. Ethridge, "Legislative-Administrative Interaction as 'Intrusive Access'," 473-492; Jewell and Miller, *The Kentucky Legislature*, 176-177; Ethridge, "Consequences of Legislative Review of Agency Regulations in Three U.S. States," 174.

39. Gormley, *Taming the Bureaucracy*, 211.

40. National Governors' Association, *Reflections on Being Governor*, 33.

41. Diane D. Blair, *Arkansas Politics and Government* (Lincoln: University of Nebraska Press, 1988), 182.

42. Richard C. Elling, "The Utility of State Legislative Casework as a Means of Oversight," *Legislative Studies Quarterly* 4 (August 1979): 353-379.

43. This paragraph is based on Priscilla Wohlstetter, "Assessing Legislative Control of Bureaucracy: The Implementation Contract" (Paper presented at the annual meeting of the Association for Public Policy Analysis and Management, Bethesda, Md., October 29-31, 1987).

44. In those states where the function was performed by an official who was elected statewide, legislatures were less likely to gain control.

45. Herbert F. Morgan, "Need for Legislative Oversight and Legislator Expectations of Evaluation Staff," in *Proceedings of the Conference on Legislative Oversight*, Joint Legislative Audit and Review Commission of Virginia General Assembly (October 13-15, 1985), 17-18.

46. National Governors' Association, *Reflections on Being Governor*, 232.

8

Conflict and Cooperation

By taking a long-term overview of relationships between the governor and the legislature, it is possible to see which branch has had the edge in the exercise of power. The balance of power, which is rooted in a state's political culture, has a persistent quality. Yet over time it changes.

THE BALANCE OF POWER

In some states the governor has tended to dominate. New York has traditionally had a strong governorship, with the likes of Franklin Roosevelt, Herbert Lehman, Thomas Dewey, and Nelson Rockefeller. Governors in Georgia, Hawaii, Illinois, Maryland, and New Jersey have also dominated state politics during their tenures. In a few states, by contrast, the legislature has traditionally been the dominant branch of government. Arizona, Mississippi, and South Carolina are strong legislative states. So is Colorado, where Governor Richard Lamm lamented that "the governor of Colorado has the responsibility but not the authority to run state government." [1] The primary reason for legislative ascendancy is the weakness of the office of governor, and not necessarily the strength of the legislature.

In most states today, although the governor may have an advantage, the two branches are in rough balance. Virginia is one of these places. The governor here is institutionally strong,[2] in part because Virginia's political culture is a deferential one, with considerable respect accorded to the chief executive. Yet Virginia's political elites have a keen sense of institutional boundaries, so the legislature can reign in its domain while the governor reigns in the executive domain. For the most part, the lines are not crossed, and power is wielded subtly and shared amicably between the executive and the legislature. Other states where the balance is generally equal—but not for the same reasons—are Iowa, Maine, Minnesota, Ohio, and Wisconsin.

Executive-legislative power is not a zero-sum game, however. The fact that a governor is powerful does not mean that a legislature need be weak, or vice versa. Both can have substantial capacity, ability, and will to govern. The balance of power may seesaw, giving first the governor and then the legislature a temporary advantage, but overall the two institutions can be strong and relatively equally matched. Today, California and New York would fit that pattern.

Nor is the executive-legislative power balance static. It has been changing over the last twenty years. Overall, it has been tending toward greater equilibrium. In the few places where the office of governor tended to be weak, the office has become stronger, as a result of institutional change or the effect of individual leadership. In the many places where the legislature lacked the capacity and will to share in governing, a more dramatic shift has occurred as legislatures have assumed a coequal role. Kentucky surely exemplifies this category of states.

By examining more closely the subject of governors and legislatures, the elements that make up the balance of power can be more clearly discerned. The matter of focus is extremely important.

Focusing on the governor, as was done at the beginning of this exploration, we found that the executive has imposing powers and appears to have considerable advantage in any contest with the legislature. The governor is one, the legislature many. The governor commands the attention of the media, the legislature is more likely to suffer its disdain. The governor, as long as he or she is not victim of a deteriorating economy or an untoward event, can build and maintain personal popularity. The legislature, at best, can grab hold of the governor's coattails and share popularity. The governor can give and the governor can withhold: to legislators in need, such power is formidable.

This array of gubernatorial powers can be converted into influence in the legislature. When governors have widespread support outside, as well as the tools to deal within, diehard resistance to their policies is likely to diminish. The ability of governors to persuade is ordinarily impressive. Of course, how governors exercise the power at their disposal—dependent upon their orientation toward the legislature and style of interaction with the legislature—also counts in the equation. There are more and less effective ways for governors to relate, if they hope to achieve their policy purposes.

Focusing on the legislature, as was done next, we found that legislatures have one principal weapon vis-à-vis governors in competing for power. They can make governors' lives difficult, deny policies and programs that they want, and tarnish their record of achievement. Legislatures can press governors on a number of fronts, as long as they have the capability and the will to do so. And the legislatures today have the capability and the will to compete seriously with the executive. Nearly everywhere, as a consequence of the legislative modernization movement of the late 1960s and 1970s, legislatures acquired the where-withal to do the job. Capacity then fed their development of a strong sense of independence and a spirit of assertiveness. Legislatures cer-tainly have made institutional progress but, on the basis of cataloguing and comparing powers, it still would be difficult to consider them a match for the executive.

As we explored further and focused on the arenas in which governors and legislatures do everything from rub elbows to wage combat, we found that the legislative role assumed much larger propor-tions.

True, governors' priorities are visible in the press and high on the legislature's agenda. If governors limit their legislative objectives, as most do nowadays, they are likely to achieve success. Their habit of going outside—priming the press, preparing the public, and employing blue-ribbon commissions—normally produces dividends. And even when governors fail, as they do on some issues—and particularly taxes—if they persist and persevere, they are likely after a while to obtain much of what they want.

But a governor's policy-making role is very limited and by no means unilateral. While most governors focus on relatively few initia-tives, the rest are left to the leaders, committees, and individual members of the legislature. Even the few items that governors claim as their own are usually shared with the legislature. They anticipate what leaders and members would like, they consult and negotiate, they compromise their positions, and they trim their proposals. Meanwhile, legislatures are on the front lines responding to lobbyists, constituents, and executive agencies—to the major and minor matters in which governors play a less direct role.

The control over state expenditures by governors, which derives from the fact that in most places the budget is put together in the executive branch, is thought to be their principal power. Gubernatorial power in the budgetary domain is significant, but not unchecked. The legislature's role here has grown significantly, due mainly to the legislative development of fiscal staffing, revenue projections, and fiscal information systems. No longer do legislators accept what the executive branch offers. Today they take the governor's budget apart and put it back together again, after their own fashion and with their own spending preferences. The process has been transformed, and policies emerge differently as a result. In the domain of budgeting a perpetual tug of war is taking place.

The least obvious, but probably the most controversial, change in the legislature's role vis-à-vis the governor has occurred in the domain of administration itself. Although governors are responsible for the administration of government, legislatures have become far more concerned, and more meddlesome, than they used to be. Their efforts— through statutory or nonstatutory language accompanying the budget, the review of administrative rules and regulations, constituency service and case work, sunset reviews, and performance auditing and program evaluation—weigh heavily upon the executive branch. And governors express grave concern over this. In this last area, more than any other, the two branches engage in conflict that is not resolved through political negotiations. Settlements often require decisions by the state courts or sometimes by the public in referendum. The legislature shows no signs of retreat here, and governors insist upon their constitutional prerogatives.

All in all, there can be little doubt that the contemporary legislature exercises influence over the executive branch, not only in making policy and in determining budgets but also in running state government. Thus, the nation's states have progressed—or regressed, some might say— from gubernatorial dominance to substantial legislative participation and a condition of true coequality between the two branches of government. One of the byproducts of legislative resurgence and the shifting balance has been increased conflict between the governor and the legislature. The stakes today are higher and the motivation to contend for power runs deeper.

THE WAR BETWEEN THE BRANCHES

Conflict is not new to America's system of separation of powers and checks and balances. Built into state constitutions centuries ago, it is by no means an invention of the resurgent legislature or the modern-day governor. Just as the president and Congress are compelled to quarrel, except in periods of national crisis,[3] so governors and legislatures also come into contention with one another.

Executive-legislative conflict in the states is deeply rooted in the nature and history of the institutions, in the political personalities of the people involved, and in the partisan struggle for control.

ROOTS OF CONFLICT

Constitutions of forty states provide specifically for state government to be divided into three branches; thirty-five of them refer to checks and balances whereby the executive checks the legislature and vice versa. Although five constitutions contain no references to checks and balances and ten have no provision for a separation of powers, these principles have become ingrained in the practices of governing nonetheless. Checking and balancing as an enterprise must engender conflict.

It is not at all easy for separate institutions to share power. It becomes even more difficult when these institutions do not have similar bases of representation or perspectives toward their jobs and responsibilities. The legislature is composed of two houses, each with a distinct culture and interests and in most instances one hundred or more members who represent people in particular districts. The governor is a single individual who represents the entire state. Legislators, moreover, have to share responsibility for their collective product, while governors have it all to themselves—whether they like it or not. There are other important differences, but the point is that such differences cast the two leading actors in the governance of a state in very different roles.

What is new about the institutional bases of conflict is the sense of independence and the assertiveness of legislatures nowadays, and the defensive posture assumed by governors. Legislatures are breaching the invisible boundary between the two branches; governors are doing their utmost to draw the constitutional line and repel such incursions. At issue is power. The National Governors' Association notes that its members have been expressing strong concern about the intrusion of the legislature into executive activities. "Constitutional relations between the branches are delicate," the association advises, "but the governor must be ready to move forcefully and to circumvent any erosion of executive power and authorities." [4]

The field in the states is more crowded than before. With some devolution of federal power and some deregulation of economic life, the states have been left with considerably more on their plates. New issues are in contest, and their outcomes matter to one or several groups or to a large number of individuals. Many more interests are competing, each with its constituencies, associations, and lobbyists. The resources of interest groups are greater, and the techniques of influence that are brought to bear range from grass-roots mobilization to political action committees. Legislatures, and also governors, cannot stay out of the conflict engendered by the group struggle.

Add to all this the habit of the media, and particularly the press, of focusing on conflict. A battle between the governor and the legislature has appeal, and the capitol press corps will report and elaborate on executive-legislative rivalry and disputes with far greater enthusiasm than on executive-legislative cooperation. For the press, the former is news, the latter is not. The preferences of the press exaggerate the contest between the governor and the legislature; they may also tend to exacerbate conflict. The stories of correspondents, read closely by insiders if not by the public generally, tend to feed jealousies and resentments rather than to assuage them.

Political personalities—individual egos and ambitions—also play an important part in the competition between the governor and the legislature. Some governors feel the need to assert themselves toward the legislature. But for the most part it is legislators who challenge the governor, while the governor tries to sidestep personal, political issues. More than a few legislators are envious of the status that governors enjoy. They aspire to gubernatorial office; some have in mind succeeding or challenging the incumbent. A few will jockey for position, making use of policy to advance their political ambitions. Nearly all have as their first concern reelection to their current offices, or to higher office if the opportunity presents itself. They have their own goals, their own programs, and their own constituencies, which must take precedence over the governor's, even if the governor is of their own political party. Few legislators today will walk the plank in order to advance the executive's agenda, and few legislative leaders or even governors expect them to do so.

Contemporary legislators, whose calculus of electoral support affects much of their behavior, are inclined to acquiesce to constituents and groups who want them to enact legislation on their behalf. Given reciprocity within legislative bodies, many bills are enacted that governors—from their perspectives and given their values—are inclined to veto. Having a bill vetoed by the governor is no inducement for cooperation. But, on their parts, governors feel that they must take a stand in opposition to legislators who are inclined to let too much go through. In response to the unbridled entrepreneurship of legislators, governors have to show their strength.

Finally, partisanship promotes conflict, especially—although not exclusively—when power is divided between the branches. Competition for the office of governor between the Democratic and Republican parties is as close today as it has been in a long time. In just about any state, a candidate of either party can be elected governor. Although Democrats still control two-thirds of the ninety-nine legislative houses, Republican strength has grown in a number of key places. In more states than previously, either party can win control of one or both houses. An emerging pattern is that of divided government, with the governorship in the hands of one party and the legislature, or at least one house, in the hands of the other party.

The fires of partisanship are fueled by close competition. Where one party controls or has overwhelming numbers in the legislature, the minority plays ball with the majority. There is little prospect for a reversal of roles, so not much incentive exists for partisanship. To go along is to get along. But as the minority increases in strength, or if one of its own takes gubernatorial office, motivations change. The minority will organize in the legislature in order to promote its cause electorally and make further gains. It may strive to obtain enough members to prevent the majority from suspending the rules or overriding the governor's veto, or it may have a realistic hope of becoming the majority party in the house, senate, or both bodies. It is likely to be assisted by partisan staff, which encourages more partisan behavior.

In any case, legislative parties are becoming preoccupied with impending elections and the possibilities of maintaining their majority, winning a majority, or making significant gains. In two-party states, much rides on being in the majority, and partisans are often willing to set aside individual differences and pull together. Increasingly, parties use whatever they can to maneuver for electoral advantage. This may include policies up for deliberation in the legislature, and a governor's initiatives, too. A governor's programs can easily become pawns in the partisan game of electoral politics. When control of the legislature is a factor, the effects are pervasive, and executive-legislative conflict is heightened.

CONSEQUENCES OF CONFLICT

The lack of harmony between executives and legislatures in the United States is a serious problem, according to Governor Richard Snelling of Vermont. He notes that "there is so little that binds together the chief executive, the governor or the president, and the state general assembly or the Congress of the United States." It is impossible to plan very far ahead, laments Snelling, when the two branches are at odds, as they so frequently are.

> The fear that I have for governors in the states and presidents of the United States is for our ability to act upon long-term goals in a successful way, before they become thoroughly understood and shared by the general populace, and before the problems we seek to avoid become crisis.[5]

Endemic conflict not only makes planning for the long run virtually impossible, it also makes stalemate in the short run a greater likelihood.

Stalemate is one of the troublesome consequences of conflict. At the national level divided government, with Republicans controlling the presidency and Democrats commanding in Congress, is the contemporary pattern. In a fragmented-power system like ours, partisan division of government is one of the heaviest burdens that policy has to bear. The durable coalitions that are needed to resolve the nation's demanding problems, as Hedrick Smith writes, are few and far between. The result at the national level is politicians "wallowing in deadlock," "inconclusive quarrels," "endless ventilation of the same spent themes," and "repeated stalemate." [6]

Fragmentation and the lack of cohesion are not as grave a problem in the states as in Washington, although in many places the situation appears to be moving in that direction. Divided government and the overriding partisan goal of winning power have made it more difficult—but not impossible—to resolve disagreements over controversial policy. The political stakes are too high for either the governor or the legislature to risk going out on a limb. Instead each party and each contender maneuvers for advantage, disagreeing over the substance of the policy itself but even more intent on dramatizing one side's virtue and the opposition's villainy.[7] It used to be that officeholders only had to worry about elections in one year out of every two. Nowadays, every year is election year as far as they are concerned.

Even when government in a state is divided, governors and legislatures settle many more issues than they deadlock on. But when the two branches are at loggerheads over matters like the budget or taxes, state government can be brought practically to a halt. Fights over the budget that ran well into the fiscal year have had this effect in Massachusetts, New York, and Pennsylvania. Occasional stalemate is no stranger to America's states; in some places—such as California, where Republican governor Deukmejian confronts a Democratic legislature— stalemate appears to be the case more often than cooperation. In light of the fierce rivalry between the institutions, the incidence of divided government, and the increase in partisanship, what might loom ahead is more deadlock and less policy.

A second consequence of conflict is the invitation to the state judiciary to serve as referee between the executive and legislative branches. The courts are thus involved, along with governors and legislatures, in making policy.[8] And now, when governors and legislatures cannot resolve differences over their respective authority, they are turning to the courts to decide for them. In about one-third of the states, the courts have issued rulings on the question of legislative involvement in the appropriation of federal funds. In some, the courts have decided the constitutionality of the legislative veto under the separation-of-powers clause. And in even a larger number, the courts have rendered decisions on the item veto. The period from 1970 to 1984, in fact, marked an extraordinary upsurge in the number of court cases on the item veto, as approximately fifty decisions were delivered.[9]

Judicial intervention in the pushing and pulling that is natural to the relationship between the executive and legislature is not inevitable. In Illinois, for instance, the governor and legislature have clashed over the executive's use of the amendatory veto. But the issue has been kept out of the courts during the years of the Thompson administration. Speaker Michael Madigan, in an effort to curb the governor's use of this device, in the 1987 session refused to call up a number of bills that Thompson had vetoed with amendments and in effect killed them. Since these were bills that Thompson wanted, he got the speaker's message and began to temper his use of the amendatory veto. Neither side in Illinois was anxious to rush into court.

There are good reasons for governors and legislatures to show restraint in calling upon the judiciary for its judgment. As David Frohnmayer, Oregon's attorney general and a former legislator, points out, the courts may not have the competence needed for deciding in this arena. The judicial branch is poorly positioned to gather political intelligence about the two other branches when they are in conflict. Moreover, judicial decisions on the allocation of powers usually do not lend themselves to compromise. Therefore, there is a tendency—an unfortunate one in Frohnmayer's view—for the court to decide more than the victor in a single skirmish. "It may be deciding who won the war, if its decision on the allocation of power leads to a permanent diminution of the authority of another branch."[10] From the standpoint of legislatures, in particular, who lose more decisions than they win, it is better to try to work out institutional differences than to resort to the courts.

A third consequence of conflict is a loss of public confidence. Conflict between political institutions, as reported by the media, does capture the public's interest. Still, people do not approve of the squabbling that they read about or see capsulated on television. They do not appreciate the differing institutional perspectives, partisan positions, and policy preferences of governors and legislators. If disagreement has to exist, they expect it to be resolved smoothly. And they see no reason why the policies they value should not be enacted. Nourished by mass media that promote cynicism rather than an understanding of democratic character and representative government, public tolerance for the ambiguity and disorder of democratic politics is rather low.

State government overall is the loser, although legislatures are more culpable in the eyes of the public than are governors. When there is a dispute, people are more likely to ask why the legislature will not cooperate with the governor than to ask why the governor will not cooperate with the legislature. Because governors have the power of unity, the ability to communicate broadly through the media, and the potential to build popularity, the public is more likely to side with them in a confrontation between the branches. Most important, people can identify personally with an individual governor, as they cannot with a multimember institution like the legislature.

The legislative process is not an appealing one. It is messy and often chaotic—necessarily so, since the resolution of conflict in a relatively open forum is one of the legislature's principal functions. Yet too much conflict, and particularly conflict between major political institutions, taxes the public beyond its limits of tolerance. The result is lower approval ratings for the job performance of legislatures and a lessening of the diffuse support that exists for representative government.

A final consequence of institutional conflict, and of the deadlock it engenders, is greater resort to the initiative and referendum in the states. Through these constitutionally mandated processes, the legislatures are bypassed; indeed, citizens can be the legislature—correcting, ratifying, and actually doing their representatives' work. Direct democracy substitutes for representative democracy, at least on particular issues. The initiative, which exists in twenty-three states, is the more potent force. It bypasses the legislature altogether, whereas the referendum does not. In the past two decades, the initiative has been used more and more, and with especially telling effect in California.[11] Automobile insurance, environmental regulation, and civil rights issues, among others, have all been put on state ballots by petition. Individual advocates, such as Howard Jarvis of Proposition 13 fame, interest groups, and even elected officeholders in the legislative and executive branches all take advantage of this method to circumvent the legislative process, accomplish their objectives, and build their reputations.

The legislature itself has been a prime target of the initiative. Proposals to reduce legislative pay, limit the terms of members, provide a method of reapportioning, reduce the size of the legislature, provide for a unicameral body, and curtail the powers of the majority party and majority party caucus have made it to the ballot. Although only a few such measures have passed, the threat persists. The assault on the legislature in California tells much about the erosion of support for representative government. Since 1970 about 15 percent of all initiatives filed here have been by officeholder proponents. Increased partisanship and bitterness in the legislature have prompted the Republican minority to resort rather frequently to the initiative, in order to "tweak Democratic noses." In the last decade Republican incumbents have proposed twice as many initiatives as have Democrats, although some Democrats have filed petitions to overcome a veto or threat of a veto by Governor Deukmejian. Mavericks and politicians who want to generate publicity in anticipation of running for higher office also try to cash in on this system.[12]

The initiative process has had considerable impact on state legislatures, helping to set their agendas and often determining the outcomes of difficult issues. As two political scientists summarize the situation in California: "In reality, the problems such as heightened partisanship, special-interest influence, political opportunism, public distrust and friction between the governor and the legislature have contributed to a shift to initiative lawmaking and away from legislative lawmaking." [13]

Both governors and legislatures will be affected if the initiative surge continues. On the one hand, they will be forced to surrender control of the policy agenda and of the power mutually to shape the settlements that are worked out. On the other hand, they will be able to avoid responsibility by delaying action and leaving it to a ballot proposition to take care of the matter. As far as state government is concerned, however, there is a fundamental question of whether good and workable policy can be crafted by a yes/no vote of the electorate. Is such a decision-making process preferable to the one of deliberation, negotiation, and compromise that takes place in the legislative arena, where governors, legislators, and interest groups all are major actors?

BURYING THE HATCHET

Conflict between the executive and legislative branches is unavoidable, but it need not undermine the successful conduct of government. Consensus cannot be expected, at least not on certain issues, but there is still reason for optimism. As Governor Richard Thornburgh of Pennsylvania stated:

> Out of this furor that occurs from time to time, the seeming animosities that ... develop, sometimes very heated, sometimes real, comes the closest we can get to consensus in a society that has built-in structural tension—the separation of powers and the two-party system.

The scars of battle do heal, and the combatants go on to the next issue and another contest.[14]

The debilitating effects of conflict are not inevitable, although contemporary forces appear to be pushing executives and legislatures in that direction. It is possible for them to bury the hatchet, not entirely or permanently, but long enough to move the business of the state forward.

POSSIBILITIES OF COOPERATION

The possibilities, of course, are somewhat greater where the executive and legislative branches are in the hands of the same party and where the legislature is under one party's firm control. In places like Georgia, Louisiana, and Mississippi, partisanship and majority-party status are not salient issues. Maryland, too, has one dominant party and consequently little partisan strife. Even in Vermont, which now has two-party competitive politics, a spirit of nonpartisanship hangs over from the past. It may be in some jeopardy today; nonetheless, it still exists. Members serving in multimember districts and not running directly against one another, the lack of party registration, and Republicans helping to elect a minority Democratic speaker of the House in Vermont all temper the conflict that normally accompanies partisanship. In sharp contrast is Florida, now a fiercely competitive state, where the growth in the power of the Republican party in the senate and house and the recent election of a Republican governor have occasioned bitter strife. It will take time for Florida to make the adjustment to two-party, competitive politics.

Government dominated by one party, without any real prospect of the outs displacing the ins, may not rank high in the professional esteem of political scientists and other scholars and commentators. It does, however, serve to reduce strife between the branches and within the legislature. Visionary proposals for cabinet government and a more responsible party system are advanced periodically to cure the ills of division. Such proposals, it is argued, would alleviate some of the contentiousness of our present system by giving one party control and responsibility. The likelihood of constitutional change is remote, and chances are that the structures of government will remain essentially as they are, with party competition and partisanship vigorous in more and more places.

PATTERNS OF COOPERATION

In any case, if conflict and its consequences are the problems, restructuring is not the practical answer. What is required—and what has been forthcoming in various places and in many instances—is skillful leadership by the governor and from within the legislature. It is up to both institutions to cooperate, and particularly on the difficult issues.

What promotes cooperation, as much as anything else, is governors' and legislative leaders' recognition that each will benefit thereby. The governor can easily make the legislature look bad, and the legislature can certainly keep the governor from looking good. A sense of responsibility acts as a restraining force, however. Each branch of government is intent on solving problems and wants to be perceived by the press and public as doing so. Although they may disagree over the specifics, the tendency, and even the direction of some policies, they share the same agendas and they agree on the needs that exist. Because of their realization that it takes both branches to get something done, most disputes tend to be settled—if not immediately, then in time.

The governor and the legislature are also restrained by an appreciation that if conflict gets out of hand, they both will suffer. Not only will they accomplish little or nothing, but in addition they risk retaliation at the polls by voters who do not distinguish which branch of government deserves the blame. Instead, voters may blame everyone in office! In Missouri, for instance, Republican governor John Ashcroft and the Democratic legislature agree that "when there's partisan fighting in Jeff City, everyone loses." Conflict occurs in Missouri, but ultimately the governor and the legislature manage to agree on the difficult issues. Even in California, with a Democratic legislature confronting Republican governors Ronald Reagan and George Deukmejian, agreements could be reached. During his second term in office, Reagan and Bob Moretti, speaker of the assembly, succeeded in compromising their differences. The relationship between Deukmejian and Democratic leaders, after partisan warfare in 1983-1984, improved markedly, although it was still "more in the nature of a mutual nonaggression pact than an example of bipartisan collaboration in the making of public policy." [15]

Only when the governor and the legislature are able to settle their differences can consensus for policy be built. And most of today's governors believe in the consensus-building approach, rather than in confrontation. They have basic respect for the legislative role, although they may feel that their own legislature in some instances goes too far. The purest consensus builders will not jump into litigation in order to resist legislative incursion on executive authority. They will negotiate with the legislature to get the result they want, rather than attempt through the courts to deny the legislature certain power.

Contemporary governors are skillful practitioners of communication, conciliation, compromise, and cooperation. They inform legislative leaders of their intentions, welcome their counsel on strategy, tactics, and substance, and exercise personal and political restraint. Southern Republican governors have tried to downplay partisanship in order to get along with their Democratic legislatures. Despite the fact that he had served earlier as state party chairman, James Holshouser (1973-1977) of North Carolina resisted being labeled as "too much a partisan," in part because he had established good personal relationships and personal credibility with most of the legislature's leadership.[16]

Other governors have shown restraint in campaigning. Democratic governor George Sinner of North Dakota, for instance, is not a partisan and not overly fond of the political parts of his job. He cannot put his heart into campaigning against legislative incumbents. Thus, he never becomes so involved in the partisan struggle that the Republicans become riled up and ready to oppose his programs. Because he operates in a bipartisan manner and avoids legislative races, Sinner has managed to bring the two parties together in steering a program through the legislature. When the opposition controls the legislature, governors have a better chance with their priorities if the issues are not used in a campaign for partisan purposes. That threatens legislators where they live, imperiling their seats and their majorities. If governors refrain from exploiting issues for electoral purposes, their chances of achieving results in a legislature controlled by the opposition party improve.

Not only do today's governors moderate their partisan inclinations, they also keep political conflicts from affecting personal relationships. If governors take criticism and opposition personally, they will not be as effective playing the inside legislative game—a game in which personal relationships count heavily. Democrat Scott Matheson had more than his share of confrontations with Republican legislators in Utah, but few involved personal feelings that lasted for very long. "That is because ultimately," he declared, "you really do have to forget that side of the process and move on to the job of governing." [17] If governors can establish and maintain friendly personal relations—as do James Thompson in Illinois, John Waihee III in Hawaii, and Thomas Kean in New Jersey—their legislative agendas will benefit. Collegiality and friendship increase the possibilities of executive-legislative cooperation.

Finally, and perhaps most important, modern-day governors accept the legislature as coequal in policy making, entitled to share both leadership in and credit for what is accomplished. They allow the legislature a real role throughout the process, consulting in the formulation of a program and negotiating the details of enactment. When governors are successful, their office will naturally take credit, and in any case the media will ordinarily heap credit upon them. Although the legislature may have done most of the heavy lifting, it normally receives less approbation (just as it usually shoulders less blame for an unpopular tax increase). But governors who employ an inside strategy will cheerfully extend credit to the legislature, recognizing that there is enough for both branches. Credit claiming is not a zero-sum game.

Governors, through their words and actions, have to extend the olive branch to their legislatures. Given their singular position, principal responsibility lies with them. But legislatures, through the agency of legislative leadership, also have to perceive the need for cooperation and take a conciliatory approach. For the most part, they do. Leaders may talk tough and behave assertively. They might like to criticize the governor now and then, but most of them will avoid attacks that might jeopardize relations. However, they too appreciate that it may not be in their own interest to engage in needless or prolonged conflict with the governor. When push comes to shove, contemporary legislative leadership is ready to deal.

John Martin, the Democratic speaker of the Maine house, is one of the nation's most powerful and effective legislative leaders. He operates from a position of considerable strength, but so does the Republican governor. Taking the budget as an issue, Martin acknowledges the power of each branch. The governor has the authority to line-item veto and his party has enough votes to sustain his action. "So what's the sense of fighting over it," says the speaker. "We might as well get to an accommodation as quickly as we can and get on with business." [18]

PROSPECTS FOR LEADERSHIP

It is remarkable that despite the tradition of separated powers, the incidence of divided government, and the rise in partisanship governors and legislatures today manage to work together much of the time. Mainly because of the common interests of the individual governors and legislative leaders involved, they see the advantages of cooperation and pursue cooperative paths. They meet together, communicate their concerns to one another, consult broadly, and share in the governmental enterprises. In order to do so, political and personal skill on the parts of both governor and legislative leaders is required. Cooperation depends in large part on leadership that has the institutional strength and personal self-confidence to negotiate and compromise. Such leadership is not uncommon today, yet it cannot be taken for granted. There are dangers ahead.

One danger lies on the gubernatorial side. Governors may be distracted from their legislative relationships by their new roles as entrepreneurs and media personalities. A formidable power of governors at present and into the future is that of publicity. It is likely that the advance of technology will expand that power. Even now, the outside strategy in the making of policy or the determination of budgets has great appeal, and that appeal may grow in the future. It is, and will continue to be, tempting for governors to choose the long pass through the media to the public over the grunting line play with the legislature between the forty-yard stripes. But line play is a vital part of the game, and publicity and popularity outside cannot substitute for the inside politics that governors have to play.

Working with the legislature may be the most difficult part of a governor's job,[19] and it is understandable that governors might choose to devote their energies to more pleasant—and what they might deem to be more productive—tasks. To ignore the nitty-gritty of executive-legislative relationships, however, would be tantamount to abdicating influence over policy. Only through continuing, face-to-face relationships with legislators can governors help give specific shape to outcomes. Only by engaging in such relationships with the governor can the legislature play its proper role. Together, the two sets of perspectives offer the best prospect for responsible policy in the state.

Another danger, and one that is clear and present, lies on the legislative side. In order to present a strong and coherent front, a legislature must rely on its leadership. Fifty, one hundred, or two hundred individuals cannot represent the house and senate in dealing with the governor. James Sundquist makes a relevant argument in support of executive leadership at the national level. According to him, a body made up of individuals looking out for themselves cannot act responsibly. Lacking discipline and a measure of individual subordination to the group, Congress is irresponsible. It follows, then, that the executive branch, which is accountable and has the will to govern, must lead.[20]

Sundquist has a point. But a collectivity can act responsibly, if it has the benefit of strong leadership. Legislative leadership is required to mediate among members, bring disparate views together, arrive at the best consensus possible, and negotiate with the governor. Furthermore, leaders, far more than most members, can take the heat for action on controversial or unpopular issues. Without leadership the legislature functions as an assemblage of individual entrepreneurs, each representing a particular constituency and array of interests. Leadership brings all these together, to the extent that is possible. Speaker Leo McCarthy of California made the case for strong leadership: "The more cohesive legislative leadership is, the more able the legislature to make its own judgments." A legislature, in McCarthy's view, is very different from a governor. It is a forum for public differences that is not supposed to speak with a single voice. Once it has deliberated and hammered out legislation, it must act as a group.[21]

An absence of legislative leadership not only undermines the legislative institution, it also fails to serve the purposes of the governor. A governor is better off negotiating with strong leaders, even though they may drive a hard bargain, than negotiating with many individual members. The product that emerges is more likely to represent what the state needs and even the preferences of the membership. And with strong leadership, responsibility is more clearly established.

The danger that faces the states is the weakening of legislative leadership.[22] Legislatures have been democratized as a result of modernization. Power and resources are distributed more broadly among members, with the gap between leaders and rank and file narrowed. Increasingly, members who once were expected to follow their leaders do not do so.

Not only have the pressures on leadership increased, but also leaders today are under threat from members themselves. There are more instances of leaders being overthrown by their own caucuses and more cases of leaders being ousted by bipartisan coalitions. There are specific reasons for each challenge to leadership. It may be a leader's personality, politics, or approach. But underlying all of this is the growing individualism and ambition of legislators themselves. Many contemporary legislators do not want to be constrained for the sake of the party, the house, or the legislature. Nor do they look favorably on being subject to another legislator's power. Furthermore, they no longer rotate in and out of office. They are in public life for the long haul, as professionals and not citizen politicians. They are anxious to advance. If few opportunities for higher office outside the legislature present themselves, they must seek advancement within. Leaders feel the pressure of ambitious members and respond by establishing additional committees and task forces, more positions of leadership. Still, members eye the top rungs of the ladder, impatient with those who stay on them too long.

With all of this, leadership in state legislatures remains far stronger than that in Congress. Will it continue that way? If the current trend toward an erosion of leadership persists, the impact on executive-legislative relations will be substantial. The legislature will lose some of its power, while the governor will not necessarily gain. Cooperation will be more difficult to achieve.

The prospects identified here—governors who resort more and more to outside strategies and legislatures that deny themselves leadership—are by no means inevitable. Governors and legislators can choose. They have done so with remarkable judgment in the recent past. And they can continue to do so now and in the future. However they decide, the two branches will continue contending for power, engaging in conflict, cooperating on major and minor issues of public policy, and serving the American states.

NOTES

1. Thomas H. Simmons, "Colorado," in *The Political Life of the American States,* ed. Alan Rosenthal and Maureen Moakley (New York: Praeger, 1984), 77.
2. National Governors' Association, Office of State Services, *The Institutional Powers of the Governorship: 1965-1985* (Washington, D.C.: NGA, June 1987, rev. 1989), 1-17.
3. James L. Sundquist, "The Crisis of Competence in Our National Government," *Political Science Quarterly* 95 (Summer 1980): 192.
4. National Governors' Association, Office of State Services, *Transition and the New Governor* (Washington, D.C.: NGA, November 1982), 97.
5. Alan Rosenthal, ed., *The Governor and the Legislature* (New Brunswick, N.J.: Eagleton Institute of Politics, Rutgers University, 1988), 21-22.
6. Hedrick Smith, *The Power Game: How Washington Works* (New York: Random House, 1988), 652, 711.
7. Smith refers to this as the "blame-game politics" of divided government, in *The Power Game,* 656-657.
8. Lawrence Baum and David Frohnmayer, eds., *The Courts: Sharing and Separating Powers* (New Brunswick, N.J.: Eagleton Institute of Politics, Rutgers University, 1989), 5-47; also Louis Fisher "How the States Shape Constitutional Law," *State Legislatures,* August 1989, 37-39.
9. House Committee on Rules, "Item Veto: State Experience and its Application to the Federal Situation," 99th Cong., 2d sess., 1986, 37.
10. David Frohnmayer, "The Courts as Referee," in Baum and Frohnmayer, *The Courts,* 51-63.
11. David B. Magleby, "Legislatures and the Initiative: The Politics of Direct Democracy," *Journal of State Government* 59 (Spring 1986): 32-33.
12. Charles G. Bell and Charles M. Price, *California Government Today,* 2d ed. (Homewood, Ill.: Dorsey Press, 1984), 382-383.
13. Ibid., 384.
14. Rosenthal, *The Governor and the Legislature,* 40.
15. Bell and Price, *California Government Today,* 237; John C. Syer, "Olive Branch Politics," *Comparative State Politics Newsletter* 6 (August 1985): 2.
16. National Governors' Association, *Reflections on Being Governor* (Washington, D.C.: NGA, February 1981), 134.
17. Rosenthal, *The Governor and the Legislature,* 40.
18. Ibid., 55.
19. Thad L. Beyle, "Governors' Views on Being Governor," in *Being Governor: The View from the Office,* ed. Thad L. Beyle and Lynn R. Muchmore (Durham, N.C.: Duke Press Policy Studies, 1983), 25.
20. James L. Sundquist, *The Decline and Resurgence of Congress* (Washington, D.C.: Brookings Institution, 1981), 456.
21. William K. Muir, Jr., *Legislature: California's School for Politics* (Chicago: University of Chicago Press, 1982), 173-174.
22. Alan Rosenthal, "Challenges to Legislative Leadership," *Journal of State Politics* 60 (November/December 1987): 265-269, and "A Vanishing Breed," *State Legislatures,* November/December 1989, 30-34.

Index